The Catholic Biblical Quarterly
Monograph Series
26

Creation Accounts
in the
Ancient Near East
and in the Bible

BY

Richard J. Clifford

The Catholic Biblical Quarterly
Monograph Series
26

To My Brothers
Jere, Bill, Peter, Paul, Bob, and David
and the Memory of My Sister Connie

© 1994 The Catholic Biblical Association of America
Washington, DC 20064

Produced in the United States

Library of Congress Cataloging-in-Publication Data

Clifford, Richard J.
    Creation accounts in the ancient Near East and the Bible / by
Richard J. Clifford.
        p.   cm. — (The Catholic Biblical quarterly. Monograph
series ; 26)
    Includes bibliographical references and index.
    ISBN 0-915170-25-6
    1. Creation—Comparative studies.   2. Bible. O.T.—Criticism,
interpretation, etc.   3. Middle East—Religion.   I. Title.
II. Series.
BL325.C7C55   1994
233'.11—dc20   94-26565
                                                              CIP

Contents

Preface

How the world began is a question that fascinated biblical authors and their neighbors no less than modern peoples. To know the origin of something is somehow to know its essence. Modern and ancient quests differ, of course, in their assumptions and precise questions, but both seek meaning from stories about beginnings. This book is about stories of creation in the literatures of Mesopotamia, Egypt, Canaan, and the Bible.

Scholars have long recognized that some ancient cosmogonies played an important role in rituals connecting people to basic forces in the world, and that other cosmogonies, not tied to operations, functioned as the equivalent of our philosophy and theology, exploring important social issues. A new interest in the old creation accounts or cosmogonies is discernible today among historians, biblical students, and theologians. Archeological excavations over the past decades have turned up new cosmogonies, and the interpretation and translation of both new and long-known texts has become more precise. Heightened modern sensitivity to nature, "creation," and our interdependence with it has fueled interest in ancient accounts. In biblical studies, the theme of creation, once a poor cousin to the theme of "history," has come into its own. The study of biblical wisdom literature (Proverbs, Qoheleth, Job, Sirach, Wisdom of Solomon), which deals with the created world and how it works, is enjoying a renaissance. Finally, scientific cosmology is raising fresh questions about the origin of the universe, provoking interest in cosmogonies both ancient and modern. The time is ripe for looking again at creation in the ancient world.

This book seeks to clarify the meaning of creation in the ancient Near East and in the Bible, and thereby to establish a broad context in which individual themes can be compared. I have not attempted to make an exhaustive study of all biblical creation accounts but to provide a perspective that others can develop.

This book differs from other studies of ancient creation in four ways. First, it limits the topic of creation by confining itself to cosmogonies, accounts of creation, rather than by studying every reference to creation. Creation is so frequent in ancient texts that investigating each mention is far beyond one author and one book. Cosmogonies are rarer, and their study is within reach.

Second, the book puts biblical cosmogonies in their ancient contexts. The introductory chapter reviews some recent scholarship and describes the characteristics of ancient creation accounts. Part One looks at the literatures of Mesopotamia, Egypt, Canaan, and Phoenicia, both for their own value and to lay a foundation for later comparison with the Bible. The two chapters on Mesopotamia are by necessity lengthy because the material is exceptionally diverse and rich and at a new stage of organization. The book attends to genres of literature where that is possible, for comparing genres is more productive than comparing isolated motifs. It resists attempts to make the Bible always superior to other literatures; the beauty and profundity of nonbiblical cosmogonies does not diminish the biblical stories.

Third, in Part Two (on the Bible), the book ranges beyond Genesis 1–11 to less familiar cosmogonies—those in the Psalms, Isaiah 40–55, and the Wisdom Literature (Proverbs and Job). Genesis sometimes so dominates discussion of creation that one forgets there are other creation accounts in the Bible. For the biblical texts I do not attempt a complete discussion, writing instead an essay on each work, showing how each cosmogony functions within its genre and relates to other traditions. Essays differ from text to text, depending on my satisfaction with the scholarly consensus and the complexity of the cosmogonic concepts in each. Comprehensive coverage of all relevant biblical texts would have unduly lengthened the book and hindered its comprehensive aim. Better to sketch the whole and leave to others the task of detailed exegesis! I limit myself to the Hebrew Bible, leaving to others to develop the ideas in this book in the literature of early Judaism and the New Testament.

Fourth, the book is by design the work of a single author, thus differing from recent volumes by specialists in Sumerian, Akkadian, Ugaritic, and Egyptian literature. Teams of specialists produced the valuable *La naissance du monde* (Source orientales 1; Paris: Seuil, 1959) and *La création dans l'Orient Ancien* (LD 127; Paris: Cerf, 1987). Another team is reported to be working on the theme of ancient Near Eastern creation under the direction of Professor Karel van der Toorn at Leiden. A team approach is not, however, the method of this book. Specialists offer mastery of a field but usually limit themselves to that field. A team can easily operate with differing assumptions and definitions, leaving the poor reader to make the comparisons and draw the conclusions. A single author, though limited, at least can keep to a single method throughout and maintain a view of the whole. As the sole author of this book, I have tried to be an accurate reporter of what I do not know firsthand (Sumerian and Egyptian) or am far from current in (Akkadian). For these fields, I have followed recognized schools and scholars, e.g., Jan van Dijk for Sumerian literature, and Erik Hornung and James Allen for Egyptian, well aware that material so distant from our own culture can be interpreted differently by other scholars. Elsewhere I remain in conversation with other scholars but do not hesitate to strike out on my own.

The book does not deal with the burgeoning scientific field of cosmology despite the fact that the latter supplies us with images that influence our reading of the Bible. There are well written and brief scientific accounts in English: James S. Trefil, *The Moment of Creation* (New York: Macmillan, 1983); Steven Weinberg, *The First Three Minutes* (New York: Basic Books, 1988); and Alan Lightman, *Ancient Light* (Cambridge, MA: Harvard University, 1992).

Parts of this book have appeared elsewhere. Some of the introductory material on ancient concepts of creation and on Canaanite cosmogonies originally appeared in *Or* 53 (1984) 183–201. A version of creation in the Psalms appeared in *Creation in the Biblical Traditions* (ed. R. J. Clifford and J. J. Collins; CBQMS 24; Washington, D.C.: Catholic Biblical Association, 1992). Some of the material in the chapter on Isaiah 40–55 appeared in the *CBQ* 55.1 (1993) 1–17. Except where noted, all translations are my own.

So wide ranging a book as this one could not have been written without much encouragement and expert advice from others. James Swetnam, S.J., Professor of Greek at the Pontifical Biblical Institute encouraged me to develop a lecture delivered to the Catholic Biblical Association in 1985 into a book. During my sabbatical semester in 1987 spent at the Pontifical Biblical Institute and a second semester there as Visiting Professor in 1991, Silvano Votto, S.J., and Chris Sturtewagen shared with me their ideas on creation in Mesopotamia and Egypt. The Librarian of the Pontifical Biblical Institute, Henry Bertels, eased my way into the Institute's excellent library. Professor Jan van Dijk, professor emeritus at the Biblical Institute, kindly read parts of the manuscript, offering expert advice and in one case translating a difficult text especially for this book. I am indebted also to Professor William L. Moran, professor emeritus at Harvard University, whose lectures on Mesopotamian religion suggested stimulating new approaches and questions. I have learned much from Professors Jon D. Levenson, Mark S. Smith, and my colleague at Weston, John S. Kselman, S.S. Colleagues in the Hebrew Scriptures/Old Testament Colloquium of the Boston Theological Institute have listened to these ideas, probably more often than they would have liked, and provided me with valuable responses. None of these scholars, needless to say, can be taxed with the shortcomings of this book; responsibility for all opinions is my own. I am also grateful to faculty colleagues at Weston and elsewhere whose interest and questions encouraged me to bring the work to completion when shorter projects beckoned. Last but by no means least, Liza Burr has been an exemplary editor, insuring consistency in style and offering perceptive suggestions on the argument. A grant from the Lilly Endowment made possible the Roman sabbatical.

Richard J. Clifford, S.J.
Weston School of Theology
Cambridge, MA 02138

Abbreviations

Abbreviations used throughout this work are those found in the "Instructions for Contributors," *CBQ* 46 (1984) 393–408, with the following additions:

AbhLeipzig   Abhandlungen der Sächsischen Akademie der Wissenschaften zu Leipzig: Philologisch-historische Klasse 65/4 (Berlin: Akademie, 1976)

AEPHE   Annuaire de l'École practiques des hautes études. Sec. IV. 1978–79. Paris: Klincksieck, 1982

Albertz,   *Weltschöpfung und Menschenschöpfung unter-*
Weltschöpfung   *sucht bei Deuterojesaja, Hiob und in den Psalmen* (Calwer Theologische Monographien A/3; Stuttgart: Calwer Verlag, 1974)

Allen,   James P. Allen, *Genesis in Egypt: The Philosophy*
Genesis   *of Ancient Egyptian Creation Accounts* (Yale Egyptological Studies 2; New Haven, CT: Yale University Press, 1988)

AS   *Acta Sumerologica*

Bottéro, LD   J. Bottéro and S. N. Kramer, *Lorsque les dieux faisaient l'homme: mythologie mésopotamienne* (Bibliothèque des histoires; Paris: Gallimard, 1989)

BWL	W. G. Lambert, *Babylonian Wisdom Literature* (Oxford: Clarendon, 1960)
La création	*La création dans d'Orient Ancien* (Lectio divina 27, Congrès de l'ACFEB, Lille [1985], ed. F. Blanquart; Paris: Cerf, 1987)
Cross, CMHE	F. M. Cross, *Canaanite Myth and Hebrew Epic* (Cambridge, Mass.: Harvard University Press, 1973)
CT	*Cuneiform Texts from Babylonian Tablets in the British Museum* (London: Department of Western Asiatic Antiquities, 1896–)
Dalley, MFM	S. Dalley, *Myths from Mesopotamia: Creation, the Flood, Gilgamesh and Others* (Oxford: Oxford University Press, 1989)
Jacobsen, Harps	T. Jacobsen, *The Harps that once . . . : Sumerian Poetry in Translation* (New Haven, Conn: Yale University Press, 1987)
KAR	Keilschrifttexte aus Assur religiösen Inhalts, Wissenschaftliche Veröffentlichungen der deutschen Orientgesellschaft XXVIII, XXXIV (Leipzig, 1919, 1923)
Kindlers	*Kindlers Literatur Lexikon* (Zurich: Kindler, 1970–74). 12 volumes
Lambert-Millard, Atrahasis	W. G. Lambert and A. R. Millard, *Atra-ḫasis: The Babylonian Story of the Flood* (Oxford: Clarendon Press, 1969)
LÄ	*Lexikon der Ägyptologie* (ed. W. Helck and E. Otto; Wiesbaden: Harrassowitz, 1972–86). 6 volumes
Lichtheim, AEL	M. Lichtheim, *Ancient Egyptian Literature* (Berkeley: University of California Press, 1975–80). 3 vols.
MSL	*Materialien zum sumerischen Lexikon* (Rome)
Pettinato, Menschenbild	G. Pettinato, *Das altorientalische Menschenbild und die sumerischen und akkadischen Schöpfungsmythen* (Heidelberg: Winter, 1971)
RLA	*Reallexikon der Assyriologie*
SANE	Sources and Monographs from the Ancient Near East

SLT	E. Chiera, *Sumerian Lexical Texts from the Temple School of Nippur* (Oriental Institute Publications 11; Chicago: University of Chicago Press, 1929)
TCL	*Textes cunéiformes* (Musée du Louvre)
TD	T. Jacobsen, *The Treasures of Darkness: A History of Mesopotamian Religion* (New Haven, Conn.: Yale University Press, 1976)
TIT	T. Jacobsen, *Toward the Image of Tammuz and Other Essays on Mesopotamian History and Culture* (ed. W. L. Moran; Cambridge, Mass.: Harvard University Press, 1970)
WM	*Wörterbuch der Mythologie I* (ed. H. W. Haussig; Stuttgart: Klett, 1965)
ZÄS	*Zeitschrift für Ägyptische Sprache und Altertumskunde*

CHAPTER 1

The Concept of Creation

I. Creation and Myth

That the gods created the world was simply taken for granted throughout the ancient Near East. The belief appears in all kinds of writings—hymns, laments, fables, imprecations, epics, instructions for young people, titles given to gods. In view of this omnipresent assumption and the multiple ways in which the idea of creation functioned in ancient literature, our first task is to set forth clearly how creation will be understood in the present study.

Definitions of creation such as the god's or gods' bringing something into being are too general and must be made more precise. The historian of religion C. H. Long, for example, distinguishes six basic types according to structure: creation from nothing, creation from chaos, creation from a cosmic egg, world-parent myths (e.g., separation of heaven and earth in Sumerian mythology), emergence myths (e.g., earth as mother, gestation or birth with little attention to the father), and earth-diver myths (e.g., someone dives into the deep for a piece of earth).[1] The biblicist Claus Westermann distinguishes four types according to the type of action: creation by birth or succession of births, creation as the result of struggle or victory, creation by an action or activity (e.g., separation, formation of human beings), and creation through a word.[2] Such specifications of

---

[1] "Cosmology," in *The Encyclopedia of Religion* (ed. M. Eliade; New York: Macmillan, 1987) 4.494–96.

[2] C. Westermann, *Genesis 1–11: A Commentary* (Minneapolis: Augsburg, 1984) 26–41.

the broad concept are valid and helpful, but the understanding of creation in this book is narrower still.

I am interested in cosmogonies rather than in every allusion to creation. Creation is too general a topic for a book that aims to be both brief and comprehensive. Hence I will discuss only cosmogonies — accounts of creation — which occur much less frequently in ancient literature than do statements about creation. The word cosmogony is derived from the Greek words *kosmos* ("order, ornament, the universe") and *genesis* ("origin, generation"); it means the origin of the (ordered) world. According to Long's definition, cosmogony "has to do with myths, stories, or theories regarding the birth or the creation of the universe as an order or the description of the original order of the universe," and cosmogonic myth "is one type of narrative portraying meanings and descriptions of the creation of the universe."[3] To take a biblical example, Proverbs contains many allusions to God the creator (14:31; 16:4; 17:5; 20:12; 22:2; 29:13) but only two cosmogonies (3:19–20; 8:22–31). Only the two cosmogonies will be discussed. The focus on cosmogonies cannot be maintained with perfect consistency, however. In Job, for example, creation is very important but tends to be treated obliquely, in hymns to the creator and in the divine speech of chapters 38–41.

Although the cosmogonies examined in this book are often classed as cosmogonic *myths* I will only make a few preliminary remarks about myth rather than attempt a definition. The word has so many definitions and nuances that adequate discussion of would add length but not necessarily greater clarity to this study.[4] First, myths cannot be regarded solely as intellectual explorations of the great problems of the human race: death, the purpose of life, chance, evil. For the most part ancient Near Eastern cosmogonies functioned within rituals designed to put the worshiper in touch with primordial power. Neither is a purely operational view excluding the exploratory aim of cosmogonies justified. In Mesopotamia most cosmogonies were tied to an operation or a ritual, but others such as *Atrahasis* were incorporated into a narrative explor-

---

[3] "Cosmology" 4. 94.

[4] The reader is referred to competent studies such as G. S. Kirk, *Myth: Its Meaning in Ancient and Other Cultures* (Sather Classical Lectures 40; Berkeley: University of California, 1970). See also *Myths, Rites, Symbols: A Mircea Eliade Reader* (ed. W. C. Beane and W. G. Doty; New York: Harper, 1976) 2–39, *Encyclopedia of Religion,* and *Mythologies* (ed. Y. Bonnefoy and W. Doniger; Chicago: University of Chicago, 1991).

ing "philosophical" problems. In the Bible, cosmogonies are "exploratory" in Genesis 1–11 and, to a certain extent, "operational" in hymns and communal laments. Second, "myth" and "history" should not be opposed in a dichotomous manner. History writing in ancient oriental texts was not religiously neutral but sought to depict divine activity in human action. In the Bible the perspective in historical books is usually "earthly" but occasionally "heavenly" as when God and angels appear to human beings. By intent and sometimes by technique, mythic and historical narrative have much in common.

II. Previous Scholarship on Cosmogonies: Brandon and Westermann

Most of the scholarship on ancient creation will be discussed under individual topics but two books deserve brief discussion at this point. Nearly thirty years ago, S. G. F. Brandon wrote the first comprehensive work on ancient Near Eastern creation[5] and Claus Westermann's work on creation in the Bible[6] has influenced a whole generation of biblical scholars.

Creation Legends of the Ancient Near East by Brandon, professor of comparative religion at the University of Manchester, presented "the first comprehensive study of the ancient Near Eastern cosmogonies" (p. vi). The book opens with a brief chapter on the origin of the concepts of creativity and beginnings in time. This is followed by lengthy chapters (averaging forty-five pages) on Egypt, Mesopotamia, Israel, and Greece. The book concludes with a short survey of Iran and a four-page epilogue.

The data available for Mesopotamia in 1963 were barely sufficient for a synthesis. S. N. Kramer's pioneering treatment of Sumerian mythology had been drastically revised by Thorkild Jacobsen, but Jacobsen's important revisions did not find their way into Brandon's chapter on Mesopotamia. Since the mid 1960s much Akkadian material has come to light; *Atrahasis* was properly published only in 1969, *Enūma elish* is much better understood today, and many "minor" cosmogonies have been carefully studied. For Egypt, Brandon was able to use Serge Sauneron's important

[5] S. G. F. Brandon, *Creation Legends of the Ancient Near East* (London: Hodder and Stoughton, 1963).

[6] *Genesis 1–11, Genesis 12–36, Genesis 37–50* (3 vols.; Minneapolis: Augsburg, 1984–86).

synthesis, yet much more systematic work has been done over the past two decades. The situation in Canaan has not changed substantially since Brandon though refinements have been made and the nature of creation continues to be discussed.

Brandon was content to describe various cosmogonies without imposing any massive theses. His brief introduction and epilogue, however, make some speculations about the origin of the concept of creation and the Bible's transformation of creation into a philosophy of history. One of Brandon's leading ideas — religion is a human response to the inexorable passage of time — accounts for his constant search for the origin of the concept of creation within human experience. Since the world gives an impression of permanence rather than of instability that might suggest a beginning in time, the idea of a beginning must have arisen from the human observation of birth and artistic creativity. Because Brandon finds the source for the ancient concept of creativity in the experience of biological birth and artistic creativity rather than in the experience of impermanence in the world, he is ultimately led to distinguish creation of man from creation of the universe. The distinction is questionable, however. How can one reconstruct ancient modes of thinking where no texts exist? Brandon himself concedes that his speculations are not borne out by textual evidence: "It is surprising, therefore, that the earliest recorded cosmogonies seem more concerned with accounting for the origin of the world than for that of mankind or of the animals" (p. 14).

To Brandon, Egyptian and Mesopotamian creation accounts fare poorly in comparison with the Bible. The nonbiblical accounts "were not generally motivated by a desire to speculate about the beginning of things; instead they were designed to promote the interests of some sanctuary or city. . . . the pursuit of such purpose was crudely managed, taking the form of a brief exposition of the priority of some deity in certain basic acts of creation." In contrast, the Hebrew accounts of the human race and its destiny were "an integral part of a veritable philosophy of history designed to trace out the purpose of Israel's god, Yahweh, from the very creation to the settlement of his chosen people in the land of Canaan" (pp. 120–21). On the contrary, as will be shown in later chapters, both Egyptian and Mesopotamian cosmogonies display a genius for pursuing important "philosophical" and "theological" problems concretely, shrewdly, and sometimes poignantly. Finally, in discussing the Bible, Brandon limits himself to Genesis 1–3; Psalms, Isaiah, Proverbs, and Job are outside his purview.

The three-volume commentary on Genesis by Claus Westermann, professor of Old Testament at Heidelberg, is comprehensive and written from a Christian theological perspective. It is generally regarded as a landmark for its broad coverage and sober judgment. In method Westermann is predominantly a form critic; from that perspective he has published extensively on the Psalms, Job, and Isaiah 40–66. He has written a popular book on creation[7] and more than a third of the introduction to his commentary on Genesis is devoted to the general topic. His ideas on creation, particularly his distinction between creation of the whole and creation of the one, have been extremely influential. Rainer Albertz has used that distinction in his study of Second Isaiah, Job, and Psalms,[8] and Peter Doll has applied it to biblical Wisdom Literature.[9] Some remarks on his views on creation are therefore necessary.

Westermann's contribution to the understanding of Genesis 1–11 is considerable; he rightly connects chapters 2–3 to chapters 4–9, emphasizes their concern with "culture," and shows how the stories of the creation and flood complement those of the rebellion against God and one's fellow human beings in chapters 3–4. Two of Westermann's ideas on creation are especially important for the theses of this book: his insistence on comparing the traditions of Genesis 1–11 with folklore from *all* nations (not just ancient Near Eastern traditions), and his distinction between creation of the whole and creation of the one.

Westermann's bringing undifferentiated world mythologies to bear on Genesis 1–11 is problematic. Myths from outside the ancient Near East are not part of the world of ideas of Genesis; they did not contribute to Genesis as did *Atrahasis* nor do they illustrate Near Eastern ideas as do *Enūma elish* and Philo of Byblos. Westermann gives no explanation as to why he uses indiscriminately world mythologies and ancient Near Eastern mythologies for comparison. Is his practice perhaps a corollary of his theory of the Pentateuch? For Westermann, the core of the Pentateuch is contained in Exodus 1–18, and Genesis 1–11 extends the significance of the exodus core to world events (p. 2). "World" for him refers not simply to neighboring cultures but to the entire world.[10] If he is

---

[7] *Creation* (Philadelphia: Fortress, 1974). See also R. E. Clements, "Claus Westermann on Creation in Genesis," *Southwestern Journal of Theology* 32 (1990) 18–24.

[8] Albertz, *Weltschöpfung.*

[9] P. Doll, *Menschenschöpfung und Weltschöpfung in der alttestamentlichen Weisheit* (SBS 117; Stuttgart: Katholisches Bibelwerk, 1985).

[10] Westermann, to be sure, compares the Akkadian *Atrahasis* epic to the biblical flood

using world mythology for comparison because Genesis 1–11 refers to the whole world, a theological judgment is determining his handling of comparative evidence.

A second idea, the sharp distinction between creation of the whole and of the individual, has significance for the entire Bible, not just Genesis:

> As we survey the creation stories through the world we can draw some clear lines of distinction between the creation of the one and the creation of the whole. There are many more stories of the creation of the one, *so that we can say in general that the creation of the one is an earlier type,* and that the creation of the whole belongs to a later stage (p. 23, italics mine).

This statement is not borne out by the ancient Near Eastern evidence. The argument that the sheer number of extant exemplars demonstrates temporal priority is invalid, since "time and chance" often determine what texts survive. Moreover, Westermann's observation is factually wrong for the ancient Near East, for more cosmogonies are extant than "anthropogonies." His most important ancient Near Eastern argument is that individual Sumerian myths have been incorporated into compendious Babylonian epics like *Gilgamesh* and *Enūma elish,* thus showing that creation of the individual preceded creation of the whole. The argument does not stand up. Anu's creation of the individual Enkidu in the Old Babylonian version of *Gilgamesh* I.i was the contribution of the Akkadian composer; it was not in the Sumerian source. Tablet XI of *Gilgamesh* borrows the story of the flood from the Sumerian Flood Story which told originally of creation of the whole. Westermann's argument from African mythology would be valid for the ancient Near East if he were able to prove borrowing between African mythology and the Bible, but he does not attempt to do so. His distinction between creation of the whole and the individual informs his work on Second Isaiah and the work of his students on other biblical texts. The results are unconvincing because most cosmogonies are systems and individual entities, including human beings, are created within the system.[11]

---

story, but he puts it on the same level as Apollodorus and Ovid and flood stories of early civilizations. See *Genesis 1–11,* 399–405.

[11] J. C. de Moor is also dissatisfied with the distinction: "C. Westermann argues that the traditions about the creation of the world have to be kept apart from the accounts of man. The book of his pupil R. Albertz . . . is the best illustration of the difficulties

III. Differences between Ancient
and Modern Concepts of Creation

To understand ancient Near Eastern cosmogonies one must reckon with the differences between ancient and modern concepts. There are four significant areas of divergence between the ancient Semitic and modern views of creation: the process, the product or emergent, the manner of reporting, and the criteria of truth.

The process: Ancient Near Eastern people frequently imagined cosmogony on the model of human activity or natural processes. Often it involved wills in conflict, with one party winning victory over another. Moderns, on the other hand, see creation as the impersonal interaction of physical forces extending over aeons; they reject any psychologizing of the process. Ancient Near Eastern texts did not make the modern dichotomous distinction between "nature" and humankind, and sometimes offered psychic and social explanations for nonhuman phenomena.

The product: In the ancient Near East, what results from the process is human society organized for the service of the gods. To modern people, on the other hand, creation issues in the physical world, typically the planet fixed in the solar and stellar system. Community and culture do not come into consideration. If life is discussed in connection with creation, it is usually life in its most primitive biological sense. This important point needs illustration.

The Akkadian epic *Enūma elish* from the late-second millennium B.C., often held up as "the standard cosmogony,"[12] reaches its climax when Marduk, after his conquest of Tiamat, is enthroned as king over the world of gods and human beings. Paralleling the exaltation of Marduk among the gods in Tablets IV and VI is the organization of Babylonian society. Men and women are created to serve the gods (VI.5–8, 29–37, 106–20), chiefly Marduk himself in his temple at Babylon. The fifty names, bestowed by the grateful gods upon Marduk in Tablets VI and VII, glorify

---

one runs into if one accepts such a theory as dogma." "El the Creator," in *The Bible World: Essays in Honor of Cyrus H. Gordon* (ed. G. H. Rendsburg et al.; New York: Ktav, 1980) 186, n. 75.

[12] It is so described by L. Fisher in "Creation at Ugarit and in the Old Testament," 15 (1965) 320–21; E. A. Speiser in *ANET* 60; A. Kapelrud in "Creation in the Ras Shamra Texts," *ST* 34 (1980); and B. Margalit in "The Ugaritic Creation Myth: Factor or Fiction," 13 (1981) passim.

the divine sustainer of order and life on earth and in heaven. The victory of Marduk established the institutions of divine and human governance (Babylonian kingship and related institutions) that a people required in order to exist.

The Bible, too, contains similar cosmogonies narrating the establishment of a society in a particular place. Psalm 77, a communal lament, recalls "the wonders of old" that brought Israel into existence:

> [17]The waters saw you, O God,
>   The waters saw you, they were convulsed.
>   Yea, the deep quaked.
> [18]The clouds poured forth waters,
>   the clouds thundered forth.
>   Yea, the lightning bolts shot to and fro.
> [19]The crash of your thunder was in the whirlwind,
>   your lightning lit up the world.
>   The earth quaked and trembled.
> [20]In the sea was your way,
>   your path through the mighty waters,
>   your tracks could not be seen.
> [21]You led your people like a flock
>   by the hand of Moses and Aaron.

Yahweh creates a way through his enemy, Sea, destroying with his storm Sea's power to keep the people from his land. What emerges from the conflict and victory is a people led by Yahweh to a secure land. Moses and Aaron are appointed as leaders of the people.

In language less suprahistoric, poems like Exod 15:1–18 and sections of poems like Ps 78:41–55 portray the same event: movement from a state of social disorganization, because of unrestrained forces, to structure and security in Yahweh's land.[13] Ancient cosmogonies were primarily interested in the emergence of a particular society, organized by means of patron

---

[13] "In Mesopotamia, Ugarit, and Israel the *Chaoskampf* appears not only in cosmological contexts but just as frequently—and this was fundamentally true right from the first—in political contexts. The repulsion and the destruction of the enemy, and thereby the maintenance of political order, always constitute one of the major dimensions of the battle against chaos. The enemies are not other than a manifestation of chaos which must be driven back." H. H. Schmid, "Creation, Righteousness and Salvation: 'Creation Theology' as the Broad Horizon of Biblical Theology," in *Creation in the Old Testament* (ed. B. W. Anderson; Philadelphia: Fortress, 1984) 104.

gods and worship systems, a divinely appointed king (or some other kind of leader), and kinship systems. The something new which was not there before is not the mere physical universe but rather the "world" of human beings organized to serve the gods.

Manner of reporting: The third area of divergence is the manner of reporting the process: drama versus scientific report. This difference is a consequence of two essentially different conceptualizings of the process. Modern conceptualizing tends to be evolutionary and impersonal, proceeding according to scientific laws. As A. R. Peacocke, a physical biochemist and theologian, pointed out in the Bampton Lectures of 1978:

> In religious cosmologies the primary focus is "on describing the cosmos from the point of view of what assumptions are necessary if human beings are to live optimally in the world" and so include a value judgment about what "living optimally" is. However the physical and biological scientific enterprise is principally directed to describing and making models of or hypotheses about nature, and so empirical reference and feedback are its main aim; it does not place human concerns at the centre of its attention and intention.[14]

The ancients saw things differently: process often meant wills in conflict, hence drama; the result was a story with a plot. The mode of reporting corresponds in each case to the underlying conceptions of the process.

Each approach handles new data and problems in a different fashion. Scientists offer new hypotheses as new data have to be explained. Ancients devised new stories, or wove variations into existing ones, when they wished to explain new elements of their world. It is not always easy for modern people, who typically regard a story as either entertainment or illustration, to take the story itself as a carrier of serious meaning. Yet for the ancients who saw creation as involving wills, story was the natural way of reporting the act. Nuances and perspective were conveyed by the selection and omission of narrative detail and by development of the plot. The ancients' tolerance for several versions of a single basic plot is traceable to this understanding. Further, drama favors verbs and concrete

---

[14] A. R. Peacocke, *Creation and the World of Science* (Oxford: Clarendon Press, 1979) 32–33. The quotation within the quotation is from P. Hefner, "Basic Christian Assumptions about the Cosmos," in *Cosmology, History and Theology* (ed. W. Yourgrau and A. D. Breck; New York: Plenum, 1977) 350.

& comprehensive

nouns. The gods thunder forth their kingship, and their palaces expresses their sovereignty.

Criterion of truth: Moderns expect a creation theory with its empirical reference to explain all the data, to be compatible with other verified theories and data. Failure to do so makes the hypothesis suspect. There is a tendency to demand a complete explanation. The criterion of truth for ancient Near Eastern cosmogonies, on the other hand, was dramatic and revolved around the plausibility of the story. In one sense, it was no less empirical than the scientific account, but its verisimilitude was measured differently. Drama selects, omits, concentrates; it need not render a complete account. The story can be about a single aspect and leave others out of consideration. *Enūma elish* is interested in the divine establishment of Babylonian society; *Atrahasis,* in the balance of elemental forces necessary for human beings to live safely. Cosmogony in Psalm 89 includes the installation of the Davidic king. Genesis 1 focusses on the place of human within the universe.

PART ONE

Creation Accounts in the Ancient Near East

CHAPTER 2

Creation Accounts in Mesopotamia
Sumerian Texts

Among the vast quantities of clay tablets excavated in Mesopotamia are a number of cosmogonies written in the Sumerian and Akkadian languages. The texts range in date from the middle of the third to the end of the first millennium B.C. Most belong to the so-called "stream of tradition": texts controlled, maintained, and kept alive by generations of professional scribes. As part of their elaborate training, scribes had to copy out a prescribed body of texts, which were preserved in both private collections and temple archives. The same work can thus be found on tablets of diverse areas and dates.[1] The cosmogonies preserved by the stream of tradition, therefore, were not idiosyncratic works but widely known and distributed—in other words, "canonical."

The stream of tradition extended far beyond Mesopotamia. Standard texts have been found at Boghazköy (ancient Hattuša) in the Hittite Empire, at Ugarit, and even at Megiddo in Palestine (a fragment of *Gilgamesh*). Recent excavations have turned up an impressive library at Meskene (ancient Emar) in eastern Syria, an ancient crossroads between Mesopotamia and the Levant. The library belonged to a twelfth-century B.C. priest and contained several canonical texts. The find is exceptionally

---

[1] A. L. Oppenheim, *Ancient Mesopotamia: Portrait of a Dead Civilization* (rev. by E. Reiner; Chicago: University of Chicago, 1977) 13–24; W. G. Lambert, "Ancestors, Authors, and Canonicity," *JCS* 11 (1957) 1–14; and F. Rochberg-Halton, "Canonicity in Cuneiform Texts," *JCS* 36 (1984) 127–44. Oppenheim estimates that "fifteen hundred would represent, at a maximum, the entire corpus of cuneiform literature that embodied, at any time or place, what we call the stream of tradition" (*Ancient Mesopotamia*, 17).

important in that it illustrates the movement of "canonical" texts from east to west.[2] Mesopotamian texts were understood by Levantine scribes, since Akkadian was a diplomatic language in the late second and early first millennia. We can reasonably assume that at least some scribes employed in Canaanite and Israelite temples and palaces were trained in the traditional manner—by copying standard texts. Given east-west commercial and diplomatic activity, it is not surprising to find Mesopotamian influence on Canaanite and biblical literature, e.g., the genre of the creation-flood story at Ugarit and in the Bible.

The extant Mesopotamian cosmogonies differ in language, genre, purpose, and date, making classification somewhat artificial. The following division is based on chronology and genre:[3]

I) third- and early-second millennium cosmogonies ("Sumerian"):
   A) god lists;
   B) narrative texts of the Nippur tradition or "cosmic motif";
   C) narrative texts of the Eridu tradition or "chthonic motif";
   D) KAR: a unique text [cf. p. 49];
II) mid-second and first millennium cosmogonies ("Akkadian"):
   A) minor cosmogonies;
   B) the anthological cosmogonies *Atrahasis* and *Enūma elish;*
   C) the *Dunnu Theogony.*

Because of the number and complexity of Sumerian and Akkadian cosmogonies, they are discussed in separate chapters.

Sumerian was a living language in the third millennium B.C., surviving into the second and first millennium as a language of learning and culture. Most Sumerian texts are from the third- and early second-millennia. After the Old Babylonian period, scribes ceased copying certain genres of Sumerian texts, e.g., royal hymns, dialogues, and many epic texts. Some scholars today no longer sharply distinguish Sumerian and Akkadian culture, preferring to speak of a single Mesopotamian civiliza-

[2] D. Arnaud, "La bibliothèque d'un devin syrien à Myskéné-Emar (Syrie)," *CRAIBL* (Paris: Klincksieck, 1980) 375–87, especially 383–84, and W. G. Lambert, "The Interchange of Ideas Between Southern Mesopotamia and Syria-Palestine as Seen in Literature," *Mesopotamien und seine Nachbarn* (ed. H. J. Nissen and J. Renger; Berlin: Reimer, 1982) 311–16. Lambert concludes that "the Babylonian material transformed and embedded in Genesis 1–11 reached Syria-Palestine in the Amarna period [fourteenth century B.C.], became local oral tradition in this area, and in this form eventually reached the Israelites" (p. 315).

[3] Bottéro's headings "theogonies," "cosmogonies," and "anthropogonies" in *AEPHE* and *LD* imply a (false) dichotomy between the creation of man and of the world.

tion known from both Sumerian and Akkadian texts.[4] But because the three senior scholars who have given the most sustained attention to early cosmogonies—Thorkild Jacobsen, Samuel Noah Kramer, and Jan van Dijk—term the material "Sumerian," this chapter uses the term also, though without denying the unity of Mesopotamian culture.

No *ex professo* Sumerian treatise on how the world began has yet been found.[5] Descriptions and allusions to creation are found in god lists, introductions to rituals and prayers, and myths. Altogether, the texts do not yield a standard cosmogony. Ancient Near Easterners apparently did not expect a single coherent account, tolerating instead different versions of the beginning of the world.

The Sumerologist most interested in systematizing Sumerian cosmogonic thought is Jan van Dijk. In an important article of 1964 he classified the extant texts under two ideal "motifs" or systems—cosmic and chthonic—thereby bringing some order to a confusing set of texts. The cosmic motif is based on the perception that heaven and earth are not separate entities but interdependent; one does not customarily speak of distinct celestial, astral, and chthonic phenomena but of heaven and earth as a cosmic reality. The interdependence was explained by a cosmogony: the universe arose through a cosmic marriage in which Heaven (An) fertilized Earth (Ki), and from their union arose gods, human, and vegetation.[6]

Van Dijk's cosmic motif has a scenario: a precreation period (or embryonic world), a day of creation that includes creation of human beings through *emersio* (=emergence of man, plantlike, from the earth loosened

---

[4] Such scholars point out that Akkadian names are attested almost as frequently as Sumerian ones in the third-millennium cities of Sumer; that pottery types from Sumerian cities are found at northern sites of the same period; and that Akkadian and Assyrian scribes copied Sumerian texts for two millennia. So M.-J. Seux, "La création du monde et de l'homme dans la littérature suméro-akkadienne," in *La création,* 43; J. S. Cooper, "Sumerian and Akkadian in Sumer and Akkad," *Or* 42 (1973) 239–46 and *JAOS* 93 (1978) 581–85; and G. S. Kirk, *Myth: Its Meaning and Function in Ancient and Other Cultures* (Berkeley: University of California, 1970) 85–86.

[5] J. van Dijk, "Existe-t-il un 'Poème de la création' Sumérien?" *Kramer Anniversary Volume: Cuneiform Studies in Honor of Samuel Noah Kramer* (ed. B. L. Eichler et al.; Neukirchen-Vluyn: Butzon & Bercker, 1976) 127; S. N. Kramer, *From the Poetry of Sumer: Creation, Glorification, Adoration* (Berkeley: University of California, 1979) 20.

[6] Van Dijk, "Le motif cosmique dans la pensée sumérienne," *Acta Orientalia* 28/1–2 (1964) 1–59. Cosmic is "what pertains to the universe considered as an interdependent totality" (p. 5).

by a pickax), and the spread of civilization. The motif arose among a predominantly pastoral population for whom rain sufficed for life. Its center of diffusion was Nippur, the city of Enlil's main temple, Ekur; in historical times Ekur was the leading sanctuary of Sumer. Enlil is prominent in the cosmogony because as firstborn he separated heaven from earth (see *Praise of the Pickax* below). Enlil then united with the mother goddess (see the disputation *Summer and Winter* below), a union that set the stage for the organization of the universe.

In van Dijk's chthonic motif Ea brings the earth to life by inundating (or inseminating) it with the underground waters via rivers and canals. Human beings are created by *formatio:* Ea forms the clay supplied by earth. This motif originated among agricultural folk for whom canals rather than rain were essential for life. Its center of diffusion was Eridu, an early rival of Nippur and the site of a sanctuary to the god Enki, who was associated with water. Van Dijk devotes a long article to the cosmic motif but provides much less detail regarding his chthonic motif.[7] This chapter adopts van Dijk's classification, though in place of "cosmic" and "chthonic" it adopts the categories Nippur and Eridu traditions.

Some evidence for both systems is found in god lists (*A* below). The narratives are, however, the best sources by far for the Nippur (*B* below) and Eridu traditions (*C* below).

A. The God Lists

Among the many sign and word lists compiled by Mesopotamian scribes are lists of divine names. Van Dijk is one of the few specialists who find traces of cosmogonies in a few lists. Other scholars are reluctant to use the lists as sources for cosmogonies on the grounds that their organizing principles are unknown or that they reflect exotic priestly speculation rather than popular piety.[8] For van Dijk, however, the lists (especially

---

[7] He discusses the chthonic motif in "Sumerische Religion," in *Handbuch der Religionsgeschichte* (ed. J. P. Asmussen et al.; Göttingen: Vandenhoeck & Ruprecht, 1971) 1.450, 466–70.

[8] Degrees of caution are expressed by D. O. Edzard, "Göttergenerationen" and "Götterlisten" in *WM*, 74–75; and W. G. Lambert, "Göttergenealogie" and "Götterlisten" in *RLA* 3.469–79 and in "The Historical Development of the Mesopotamian Pantheon: A Study in Sophisticated Polytheism," *Unity and Diversity: Essays in the History, Literature, and Religion of the Ancient Near East* (ed. H. Goedicke and J. J. M. Roberts; Baltimore: Johns

their initial sequence of names) reflect genuine cosmogonies.[9] Three lists are especially important.

The first extant god list with cosmogonic speculation is from Nippur (SLT 122–24); it is extant only in Old Babylonian unilinguals.[10] The text is in a single column.

an	^{d}nin-ḫur-sag-g-á	^{d}ma-ma
an-tum	^{d}nin-dingir-re-e-ne	^{d}*be-li-it-i-lí*
^{d}uraš	^{d}nin-maḫ	^{d}nanna
^{d}en-líl	^{d}nin-tu	^{d}su'en
^{d}nu-nam-nir	^{d}nin-men-na	^{d}en-ki
^{d}nin-líl	^{d}a-ru-ru	[plus 191 more names
^{d}šul-pa-è	^{d}maḫ	in no. 124, and 60 more
		in nos. 122, 123.]

In this list van Dijk distinguishes two types of genealogies: "vertical" descent of father through son, and "horizontal" descent in which different spouses enter the system by way of syncretism. He illustrates the two genealogies for this genealogy in the chart below (p. 16).

An marries Antum (=Uraš). Enlil (=Nunamnir) marries Ninlil. The goddesses from Ninḫursaga to *Bēlet-ilī* were originally local mother goddesses. Syncretism accounts for Uraš (another name for Ki, "earth") being

---

Hopkins University, 1975) 94–97. According to Lambert, "God lists should be considered primary documents of ancient Mesopotamian religion, but their full value cannot be obtained until their organization is understood, and studies along these lines have hardly begun" (*RLA* 3.478–79). A. L. Oppenheim is more severe: god lists are learned speculations rather than reflections of popular religion and do not reflect *Ordnungswille* (*Ancient Mesopotamia,* 180, 248).

[9] Van Dijk distinguishes cosmogonies from etiologies, which also can introduce prayers and didactic compositions. Etiologies explain only an aspect of the world of gods or humans and begin from the day of creation or after it, whereas authentic cosmogonies include the period before creation as well as the act of creation ("Existe-t-il un 'Poème de la Création' Sumérien?" 128).

[10] Van Dijk, "Le motif cosmique," foldout between pp. 6–7. All the god lists noted here are taken from van Dijk's transcriptions in the foldout. In these lists, italics indicate Akkadian names. His discussion is found on pp. 6–16. There are two fragments in addition to SLT 122–124, as noted in W. G. Lambert, "Götterlisten," *RLS* 3.374. According to convention, Sumerian is transliterated into modern languages without italics or underlining whereas Akkadian (and other semitic languages) are transliterated with italics or underlining.

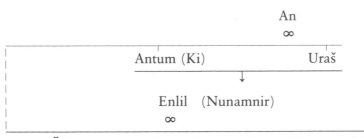

named with Antum (=Ki), and for the mother goddesses being equated with Ninḫursaga. In the list (not in van Dijk's chart above), Nanna (Sumerian) and Su'en (Semitic) are moon gods. Enki, the lord of the earth, is Enlil's brother. The main intent of the god list seems clear, despite intrusions from local systems: the pantheon originates from the marital union of heaven and earth. An (Heaven) marries Ki (Earth), from which union issues Enlil, lord of the earth, and the other gods. Before the marriage there was an "embryonic" or pre-creation period.

Two later god lists (TCL XV 10=de Genouillac list, and An=*Anum*) combine both Eridu and Nippur motifs. TCL XV 10 is an Old Baby-lonian unilingual known exclusively from a virtually complete single copy with 473 names.[12] It provided the basis for the canonical Babylonian god list An=*Anum*. TCL XV 10 opens with father-mother gods,[13] then has sections on An, Enlil, and Enki (here distinct from the parent god Enki of the opening pair).

den-ki	dnin-ki
den-mul	dnin-mul
den-ul	dnin-ul
den-nun	dnin-nun

[11] Šulpa'è is the spouse of Ninḫursaga at Adab, and that tradition is strong enough to force the intercalation here.

[12] The list was first published in H. de Genouillac, "Grande Liste de noms divins sumériens," *RA* 20 (1923) 89–106, and "Liste alphabétique des dieux sumériens," *RA* 25 (1928) 137–39, with corrections to the earlier article.

[13] Each god's name begins with the masculine en- [lord] or the feminine nin- [lady] element.

ᵈen-kur	ᵈnin-kur
ᵈen-kin-gal	ᵈnin-kin-gal
ᵈen-šár	ᵈnin-šár
ᵈen-ḪAL	ᵈnin-ḪAL
ᵈen-bùlug	ᵈnin-bùlug
ᵈen-giriš	ᵈnin-giriš
ᵈen-da-šurim-ma	ᵈnin-amaš[14]
ᵈen-du₆-kù-ga	ᵈnin-du₆-kù-ga
ᵈen-an-na	ᵈnin-an-na
ᵈen-u₄-ti-la	ᵈnin-u₄-ti-la
ᵈen-me-šár-ra	ᵈnin-me-šár-ra

ᵈnammu (= ᵈama-tu-an-ki)[15]
ᵈuraš (=nin-ì-li)
ᵈen-uru-ul-la
an-šár-gal
an
ᵈen-líl
[the entourage of Enlil]
ᵈen-ki
[the entourage of Enki]
[the mother goddesses]

The parent gods at the beginning of the list (and in An=*Anum*) do not, in van Dijk's view, constitute a genealogy but are the inhabitants of the primeval city before the act of creation.[16] The best evidence for a primeval city of gods prior to the act of creation are the parent gods'

[14] Van Dijk supplies here ᵈnin-da-šurim-ma and ᵈen-amaš to match the pairs ("Le motif cosmique," foldout between pp. 6–7).

[15] The actual text reads: an an-šár-gal ᵈen-uru-ul-la ᵈuraš ᵈnin-ì-li ᵈnammu ᵈama-tu-an-ki, but many scholars reverse the sequence because of the appearance at the end of the list of the primeval god (to judge by her name), and make ᵈama-tu-an-ki ("Mother-who-gave-birth-to-Heaven-and-Earth") head the list. Nammu, to whom the title apparently belongs by right, should therefore head the list. See further W. G. Lambert, "The Cosmology of Sumer and Babylon," *Ancient Cosmologies* (ed. C. Blacker and M. Loewe; London: Allen and Unwin, 1975); and T. Jacobsen, "Sumerian Mythology: A Review Article," *JNES* 5 (1946) [*TIT* 115–16]. Van Dijk ("Le motif cosmique," 12) regards Enurulla and Anšargal as epithets of An here.

[16] "Primeval city" is van Dijk's term for the "embryonic period" prior to the marriage of Earth and Heaven.

names. Their etymologies signify cosmic forces: Enki and Ninki are "the earth lord/lady"; Enkur and Ninkur are "the lord/lady mountain"; Enul and Ninul are "the lord/lady long ago"; Enurulla and Ninurulla are "the lord/lady of the primeval city."[17] According to some texts, the parent gods inhabited the primordial hill, Sumerian ḫursag.[18]

Van Dijk finds in TCL XV 10 two genealogies: a vertical one of the embryonic universe culminating in the generation of An, and a subsequent horizontal one leading to the generation of Enlil and Enki.

Enki ∞ Ninki
↓
[thirteen divine pairs]
Enmešarra ∞ Ninmešarra
↓
An (=Anšárgal, Enurulla)
∞

↓			↓
dUraš	dnin-ì-li		dNammu
↓			↓
Enlil			Enki

The theogony of the earlier list, SLT 122–124, has been expanded by a series of divine pairs living in the embryonic universe that precedes An. The cosmic marriage of An with Earth (called Uraš here) takes place

---

[17] The identifications of the inhabitants of the primeval city are taken from van Dijk, "Sumerische Religion," 1.451. Other lists include among the primeval gods Duri and Dari, "the Lord/Lady Time," and Enmešarra and Ninmešarra, "the Lord/Lady Cultural Institutions." The names are asyndetic, i.e., "Lord Earth" or "Lady Earth," not "Lord of earth."

[18] *Ewe and Wheat* begins, "Upon the Hill of Heaven and Earth / When An had spawned the divine Godlings." On the basis of these and similar texts, some early Assyriologists concluded that the holy hill was a *Weltberg*, i.e., the cosmos was a mountain with earth as its lower slope and heaven as its upper one. The term is not much used today. Jacobsen explains the Sumerian word ḫursag as the rocky mountainous area in the east that surfaces in the west as the vast, gravelly desert. It contrasts dramatically with the alluvial soil of Sumer proper. Viewed from the plain, the lofty mountains indeed seem to belong to both heaven and earth (*Weltberg*). The ḫursag is thus the area on which the people of Mesopotamia lived as on a rocky surface or subsurface, but it was not a mountain. See T. Jacobsen, "Sumerian Mythology: A Review Article," in *TIT*, 118; and R. J. Clifford, *The Cosmic Mountain in Canaan and the Old Testament* (Cambridge, MA: Harvard University, 1972) 9–25.

after the period of the primeval city. An rules the city with the title Enurulla, "lord of the primeval city."

Largely on the basis of this text, van Dijk proposes a scenario for his cosmic motif: (1) a preexisting embryonic universe where the gods of inchoate culture live; (2) it is conceived as a "primeval city" (uru-ul-la); (3) there arises An, Heaven, who becomes "lord of the primeval city (en-uru-ul-la)"; (4) heaven unites with earth in a cosmic marriage, and (5) at a definite moment heaven separates from earth; (6) from their union the great gods arise through *emersio*.[19]

The last relevant list is the An=*Anum* god list of the late Old Babylonian period. Much expanded and revised, it is the most systematic of the lists. It names the gods who existed before the separation of heaven and earth. The parallel column gives the Akkadian equivalent or other information about the god mentioned in the first column.

an	^{d}*a-nu-um*
an	^{d}*an-tum*
an-ki	^{d}*a-nu-um u an-tum*
[eight more divine pairs]	
^{d}en-uru-ul-la	^{d}nin-uru-ul-la

21 en ama-a-a-an-na-ke$_4$-ne, "the parents of An"

^{d}nin-ì-li	=dam-an-na-ke$_4$
^{d}nin-úr-sal-la	=dam bàn-da-an-na-ke$_4$
^{d}nammu	=ama-^{d}en-ki-ga-ke$_4$
	=mí-agrig-zi-é-kur-ra
^{d}ama-ù-tu-an-ki	= ^{d}nammu
^{d}nin-bára	= ^{d}*an-tum* = ^{d}*iš-tar*
^{d}nin-ì-li	= ^{d}šem-bi-zi = ^{d}*iš-tar*

[the gods of the court of An, twenty pairs]
[the gods of the court of Enlil]

This theogony changes the traditions of TCL XV 10. Heaven and earth are androgynous and originate themselves, as the name An-ki (Heaven-Earth) in third place suggests. Enlil is not subordinate to An but on the same level, as is implied by their parallel genealogies. Enlil is not descended from the "mothers and fathers of An" as in TCL XV 10. Further changes are the transfer of ^{d}Uraš to the ancestors of An, the creation of

---

[19] Van Dijk, "Le motif cosmique," 13.

dNin-uru-ul-la to match dEn-uru-ul-la (thereby eliminating the concept of the primeval city), and the introduction of Ishtar. Thus, concludes van Dijk, the god lists reflect cosmogonic traditions solid enough to be subject to syncretism and elaboration.[20]

Van Dijk's use of the god lists is not accepted by all specialists, as noted above.[21] Kramer posits an entirely different series of primordial acts: a primeval sea begot the cosmic mountain of heaven and earth united, from which the air god Enlil was begotten.[22] He does not, however, present much evidence for his thesis.

How convincing is van Dijk's use of god lists to reconstruct a precreation embryonic city? Does the placement of the gods at the head of the lists express simply their general prominence in the pantheon or their cosmogonic roles as well? Van Dijk successfully demonstrates that the lists reflect theological speculation. The mother and father gods of TCL XV 10, with their en- and nin- prefixes and names evoking cosmic forces, imply a precreation period. The title en-uru-ul-la, "lord of the city," suggests a city. Van Dijk's basic conclusions are plausible but difficult to prove out because of the elliptical nature of the material. Of the narrative texts only one develops the concept of the primeval city.

B. Narrative Texts of the Nippur Tradition

The extant texts of the Nippur tradition all narrate the same cosmogonic act—the marital union of heaven and earth—while differing widely in their function. The cosmogonies are told not to provide factual information about the past, but to ground or explain some aspect of present reality. The six texts examined below represent diverse literary genres, each with its own purpose in depicting the origin of the world. Hence context is extremely important. For all Sumerian mythological texts, a disclaimer to the reader is necessary. The Sumerian language is not completely understood. Formidable linguistic problems render interpretations tentative; even specialists differ radically.[23]

[20] Ibid., 14–16; and Lambert, "Götterlisten," *RLA* 3.476.

[21] In n. 6. Only Jacobsen agrees that a primeval city preexisted the cosmic marriage. See n. 27.

[22] S. N. Kramer, *The Sumerians: Their History, Culture, and Character* (Chicago: University of Chicago, 1963) 292.

[23] The distinguished Sumerologist Thorkild Jacobsen, reviewing Kramer's *Sumerian*

One of the most instructive Nippur texts is the cosmological introduction to the ca. 300-line poem, *Gilgamesh, Enkidu and the Underworld*. It has four main sections: (1) the prologue (lines 1–26); (2) the huluppu-tree episode (lines 27–148); (3) the pukku-mekku incident (lines 149–254); and (4) the description of the underworld (lines 254-end). The Sumerian word u_4-ri-a, literally "in that day," begins this and several other cosmogonies.

> [1]In[24] primeval days, in distant primeval days,
> In primeval nights, in far-off primeval nights,
> In primeval years, in distant primeval years —
> In ancient days when everything vital had been brought into existence,
> [5]In ancient days when everything vital had been nurtured,
> When bread had been tasted in the shrines of the land [Sumer],
> When bread had been baked in the ovens of the land —
> When heaven had been moved away from the earth,
> When earth had been separated from heaven,
> [10]When the name of man had been fixed —
> When An had carried off heaven,
> When Enlil had carried off earth,
> When Ereshkigal had been carried off into the *kur* as its prize —

Mythology (Memoirs of the American Philosophical Society 21; Philadelphia: American Philosophical Society, 1944), retranslated and reinterpreted much of the book, in *JNES* 5 (1946) 128–52 [*TIT* 104–31]. Kramer's considerable differences with Jacobsen were later aired in his review of *TIT* in *CBQ* 33 (1971) 266–68.

[24] Translation by S. N. Kramer, *From the Poetry of Sumer: Creation, Glorification, Adoration* (Berkeley: University of California, 1979) 23–24. Tablet XII of the standard version of Gilgamesh is a literal Akkadian translation of the second part of the Sumerian text. For the Sumerian text, see A. Shaffer, "Sumerian Sources of Tablet XII of the Epic of Gilgameš" (unpublished Ph.D. dissertation, University of Pennsylvania, 1963) 48–50, lines 1–27. Other translations are by van Dijk, in "Le motif cosmique," 17–21 (with important comments on u_4-ri-a); Jacobsen, "Sumerian Mythology," *TIT* 114–18; and S. N. Kramer, in *Sumerian Mythology*, 37–39, and *The Sumerians*, 197–205. See also A. Falkenstein, *RLA* 3.361–63 and C. Wilcke, "Kollationen zu der sumerischen literarischen Texten aus Nippur in der Hilprecht-Sammlung Jena," AbhLeipzig 65/4 (1976) 19. Van Dijk in a private communication comments on the translation: lines 4–5, "in ancient days," can also be rendered, "when the day of yore"; "everything vital" is perhaps better rendered as "primeval culture," reading níg-ul-e, with ul as the substantive "luxuriance" instead of níg-du$_7$-e; in lines 15–25 Enki sets sail for the underworld and has to face small and large stones hurled at him both by human hands ("stones of the hand") and by ballistas (preferable to Kramer's "Make reeds dance"); in line 16, "the little ones" are stones; in line 26, "the lone tree" is, more accurately, "the unique tree" (i.e., the world tree).

When he had set sail, when he had set sail,
15When the father had set sail for the *kur,*
Against the king it hurled the little ones,
Against Enki it hurled the big ones,
Its little ones being "stones of the hand."
20Its big ones being stones that "make reeds dance."
They overwhelm the keel of Enki's boat like onrushing turtles
Against the king, the waters at the bow of the boat
25Strike dead like a lion—
In those days, a lone tree, a lone huluppu-tree, a lone tree
Planted on the bank of the holy Euphrates . . .

The following lines tell how the huluppu-tree was uprooted and floated down the Euphrates. The goddess Inanna had a pukku and mekku (probably drum and drumstick) made from it, which she presented to Gilgamesh. Somehow the items fell into the underworld, and Gilgamesh's servant Enkidu went to retrieve them. Disregarding his master's advice to observe the mourning rites appropriate to the land of the dead,[25] he was detained. Only Enkidu's ghost was allowed to come back and tell his master what he had seen. The cosmogony explains the underworld as primordially violent and chaotic, a place that seizes Ereshkigal and fights Enki. Gilgamesh was traditionally linked to the underworld and this cosmogony explains the link.

Creation in the myth, though complex, is a single act: the union of heaven and earth with life and organization flowing from it. The Sumerian literary device of repeating key words (day, night, year, flowers, divine plan, land of Sumer, heaven, earth, took charge, embarked) unifies the diverse actions. A chiasm highlights the centrality of the marriage act in *b:*

a "everything vital" and bread (line 4)
   b the marriage act (chiastic couplet, lines 8–9)
a' creation of man and division of the chief gods' authority
   (lines 10–13)

In the lines preceding the marriage act, fecundity is implanted within the earth ("everything vital" and bread), and in the lines following it, the human race and the social order (expressed as the great gods' division of authority) are instituted. The sections *a* and *a'* together express the

---

[25] A. Koefoed, "Gilgameš, Enkidu and the Netherworld," *AS* 5 (1983) 17–23.

fullness of creation: both "everything vital" and vegetative life (grain for bread) and civilization, social order. The question why creation took place is not answered.

Another text associates a great storm with the first day.

> That[26] day, it was
> because of that day;
> that night, it was
> because of that night;
> that year, it was
> because of that year:
> the storm raged,
> lightning flashed.
> (Over) the shrine of Nippur
> the storm raged,
> lightning flashed:
> (it was) heaven (An) who spoke
> with earth (Ki);
> (it was) earth (Ki) who spoke with heaven (An). . .

The marriage of Heaven and Earth occurs amid a fierce storm, presumably bringing fertilizing rains. The text possibly interprets the thunder as speech. Elements known from other cosmogonies appear: the phrase "that day," a storm, the proleptic mention of a temple city, which will be built after the marriage. After a break in the text, the mother goddess Ninhursag and Enlil appear in the next column. Presumably they were born after the union of heaven and earth.

A third cosmogony appears in the genre of debate—*Tree and Reed*. In this widely attested genre, two beings, animate or inanimate, debate which is the more noble and useful, each trumpeting his or her virtues. Most disputations begin with a cosmogony, which mention the origin of the debaters is the origin of the universe. When the debate concludes, the winner is declared, often a god announcing the decision. Such disputations were learned and witty and were intended, most probably, for the entertainment of the king and his court; in the case of *Tree and Reed*, the king was Shulgi (2046–1998 B.C.). Vanstiphout lists ten extant Sumerian disputations: *Hoe and Plow, Summer and Winter, Tree and*

---

[26] My rendering of van Dijk's translation in "Le motif cosmique," 37. Other texts associating storm and cosmic marriage are on pp. 35–39 in his article.

Reed, Heron and Tortoise, Goose (or *Crane?*) and *Raven, Ewe and Wheat, Bird and Fish, Herdsman and Farmer, Upper and Lower Millstone,* and *Copper and Silver.* Most have a cosmogonic introduction. The genre is found also in Akkadian literature (See II.7*ab* below).[27]

> [1]The[28] Great Foundation (ki-ùr-gal-e) made herself resplendent, her
> body flowered joyously.
> Vast Earth adorned her body with precious metal and lapis-lazuli.
> She adorned herself with diorite, chalcedony, carnelian (and) elmeshu.
> [Heaven] clothed the plants in beauty, stood by their majesty.
> [5]Pure [Ea]rth made herself verdant in a clean place for pure An.
> An, high Heaven, consummated marriage with vast Earth,
> He implanted the seed of the heroes Tree and Reed in (her womb).
> Earth, the good cow, received the good seed of An.
> Earth gave herself to the happy birth of the plants of life.
> [10]Earth joyously produced abundance; she exuded wine and honey.
> Having given birth to Tree and to Reed, she heaped up grapes and honey
> in the storehouses.
> When Reed became as verdant as Tree, they were in full harmony:
> Tree and Reed together, with their splendid stalks, sang their own praises.

This cosmogony describes first the origin of the two debaters Tree and Reed and then their growth. Because the plants are rooted in the earth and live off its fertility, the cosmogony emphasizes the sexual beauty of Ki and her receptivity to the seed of An. Earth bursts into bloom *before* the marriage act, a sign of associative rather than sequential logic. In line 1, the noun ki-ùr ("leveled earth," "foundation," "building place") may be a proleptic reference to the temple precincts. Temple building is associated with creation; a part of the temple of Nippur was called ki-ùr and bore the epithet "the great land."

---

[27] See B. Alster, "Sumerian Literary Dialogues and Debates and their Place in Ancient Near Eastern Literature," *Living Waters: Scandinavian Orientalistic Studies Presented to Professor Dr. Frede Lokkegaard* (ed. E. Keck et al.; Copenhagen: Museum Tusculanum, 1990) 1–16; Alster, *Dispute Poems and Dialogues in the Ancient and Mediaeval Near East: Forms and Types of Literary Debates in Semitic and Related Literatures* (ed. G. J. Reinink and H. L. J. Vanstiphout; Louvain: Peeters, 1991); H. J. L. Vanstiphout, "Mesopotamian Debate Poems: A General Presentation (Part I)," *AS* 12 (1990) 271–318; Bottéro, *LD* 479–81, and D. O. Edzard, *RLA* 7.43–44.

[28] My rendering of van Dijk's translation in "Le motif cosmique," 46–47. Van Dijk has recently suggested, in a private communication, that ki-ùr-gal-e ("Great Foundation") may have the meaning "building place."

The cosmogonic introductions take up to a third of such compositions, as in *Ewe and Grain* and *Summer and Winter*. Vanstiphout, in contrast to van Dijk, believes that the cosmogonies are specifically tailored to the aim of each disputation; they are not general: "The conclusion seems to be that the introductions are indeed used more for presenting the contenders and their qualities, to give the framework and terms of the debate, and thus to lead to or even contain the *occasio litigandi*. The mythological aspect is artificial, relatively unimportant, and possibly secondary."[29] J. Bottéro points out, rightly in my view, that the cosmogony links the disputants to their origin, to the time when their "destiny"[30] was assigned. The characters, he points out, are not *a* tree and *a* reed but *the* tree and *the* reed, "prototypes" in his terminology. The conflict between the two disputants is original because their constitutive features were fixed by the creator gods in the beginning. For a people "encore démunis de tout accès à l'abstraction conceptuelle," the first occurrence replaces the generic abstract name. The disputation is a way of understanding things through analyzing, defining, opposing, so that their true character emerges.[31] Whether the disputations are so philosophical or not, they surely presuppose a destiny given on the first day.

An important feature of the Nippur creation scenario is the precreation period and a recently published text (NBC 11108) gives intriguing detail. The precreation period, "the city of yore," has already been mentioned in the god lists TCL XV 10 and *An–Anum*. Van Dijk takes the precreation or embryonic world as inchoate: "Life and vegetation began to exist *after* and in an embryonic universe where everything existed 'in

---

[29] "The Mesopotamian Debate Poems," 291, less completely, in "Lore, Learning and Levity in the Sumerian Disputations: A Matter of Form or Substance?" in *Dispute Poems and Dialogues*, 23, n. 2. Van Dijk believes they are not properly creation accounts but are meant to "encase" the dispute in a cosmic context, which is known by the hearers, in *La sagesse suméro-accadienne* (Leiden: Brill, 1953) 39.

[30] For Mesopotamian ideas of destiny and how they differ from English "fate" and "destiny," see A. L. Oppenheim, *Ancient Mesopotamia*, 202–6; W. G. Lambert, "Destiny and Divine Interpretation in Babylon and Israel," *The Witness of Tradition* (OTS 17 [1970] 65–72); F. Rochberg-Halton, "Fate and Divination in Mesopotamia," *AfO* Beiheft 19 (1982) 36–71; and A. George, "Sennacherib and the Tablet of Destinies," *Iraq* 48 (1986) 133–46. Oppenheim defines *šīmtu* as "a disposition originating from an agency endowed with power to act and to dispose, such as the deity, the king, or any individual may do, acting under specific conditions and for specific purposes" (p. 202).

[31] "La 'tension' de la réflexion sur les choses en Mésopotamie," *Dispute Poems and Dialogues*, 7–22, especially 20–22.

ratione seminali.' They owed their existence to the marital union of heaven and earth."[32]

> [1]An,[33] (being) Bel (an en-né), made heaven resplend[ent],
> earth was in darkness, the lower world was [invi]sible;
> the waters did not flow through the opening (in the earth),
> nothing was produced, on the vast earth the furrow had not been made.
> The high priest of Enlil did not exist, the rites of
> purification were not carried out,
> the h[ierodul]e(?) of heaven was not adorned, she did not
> proclaim [the praises?].
> [5][Heaven (and) Ea]rth were joined to each other (forming) a unity,
> they were not [married].
> The moon did not sh[ine,] darkness spread;
> Heaven showed its shining face in Dagan [=heavenly dwelling],
> as it coursed, it could not reach the fields.
> The rule of Enlil over the land had not yet come about,
> the p[ure Lad]y? of E'anna had not yet [receiv]ed [offerings]?
> The gr[eat gods], the Anunna, were not yet active,
> the gods of heaven, the gods of ea[rth] were not yet there.

The text depicts the period before creation. Heaven and earth were undifferentiated; they had not yet separated so that they could come back together in marriage. Only heaven enjoyed light (lines 1, 9); the underground waters did not yet flow up to earth through an opening to fertilize the fields through rivers and canals (line 2).

According to line 1, An was lord (Bel) of the primeval city, as in the god list TCL XV 10. An's lordship poses a problem, however. In Sumerian theology Enlil, not An, was lord of Sumer and Akkad (later to be succeeded by Marduk). Van Dijk's solution to this problem is to compare the Hittite myth Kingship in Heaven, which tells of the succession of ruling gods. Alalu was driven from the throne by Anu and takes refuge

[32] Van Dijk, "Le motif cosmique," 20 (italics his). See further his "Sumerische Religion," 449–52. The realities do not actually come into existence until after the marriage. Jacobsen's conception differs slightly: in that period, death "was and ruled before life and all that is came into being—that is, all life originated in (or emanated from) death, lifelessness" ("Sumerian Mythology," in *TIT*, 115).

[33] Van Dijk, "Existe-t-il un 'Poème de la Création' Sumérien?" 125–33. The translation is my rendering of van Dijk.

in the underworld; Kumarbi, Alalu's son, drives Anu from the throne. The fall of An, god of heaven and lord of the primeval city (En-uru-ul-la) to the underworld can be inferred, van Dijk argues, from the Curse of Agade: "Their tears, the tears of the mothers and fathers of Enlil."[34] The primeval gods are attested as gatekeepers of the seven underworld gates.

In addition to the narratives, several epithets assigned to An imply cosmic marriage: numun-è a-a-nì-nam-šár-ra ("he who makes the seed grow, father of the whole universe"); an-lugal en numun-i-i un ki-gar-ra ("An, the king, the lord who made the seed grow, made people dwell on earth"); sag-íla diri nínda numun-i-i ("who lifts his head high, the bull who makes the seed grow").[35]

Though the creation of the human race is part and parcel of the cosmic marriage (particularly in *Gilgamesh, Enkidu, and the Underworld,* and in the epithets above),[36] several texts directly concern the human beings that sprouted on "that day." *Emersio* is van Dijk's term for the human sprouting.

The opening lines of the *Hymn to E'engura* (the Enki temple in Eridu) link cosmic marriage and *emersio.*

> [1]When[37] the destinies had been fixed for all that had been engendered (by An),
> when An had engendered the year of abundance,

[34] *ANET,* 650, line 206. The primeval gods received no cultic veneration, but are mentioned in oaths and figure in the cult drama of the dying god. In Babylon the body of the primeval god Enmešarra was carried in procession on New Year's Day. In the Eridu tradition these representatives of inchoate culture are replaced by the seven wise men, who arose from the sea. See van Dijk, "Sumerische Religion," 452; and D. O. Edzard, "Enmešarra," *WM,* 62. Van Dijk calls this text "le mythologème de la succession."

[35] Van Dijk, "Le motif cosmique," 34. For the sign that he read as ùku in the second epithet in the 1964 article, van Dijk now reads un (private communication).

[36] "Mais l'homme n'aurait pas pu naître de la terre si cette dernière n'avait pas été fécondée par le ciel" (M.-J. Seux in "La création du monde et de l'homme dans la littérature Suméro-Akkadienne," in *La création,* 60).

[37] Lines 1–3 are my rendering of van Dijk's translation in "Le motif cosmique," 23. Lines 4–6 are my rendering of the translation of A. Falkenstein and W. von Soden, *Sumerische und Akkadische Hymnen und Gebete* (Die Bibliothek der Alten Welt; Zurich: Artemis, 1953) 133. For the Sumerian text, see A. Al-Fouadi, "Enki's Journey to Nippur. The Journeys of the Gods" (unpublished Ph.D. dissertation, University of Pennsylvania, 1969) 69, lines 1–6. See also A. Falkenstein, *Sumer* 7 (1951) 119–25; and C. Wilcke, *Kindlers* 6.2130.

> when humans broke through earth's surface like plants,
> then built the Lord of Abzu, King Enki,
> ⁵Enki, the Lord who decides destinies,
> his house of silver and lapis lazuli.

The creative actions described in the lines are in parallel: the fixing of destinies, the engendering of the year of abundance, human beings emerging from the earth's surface, and the building of the temple. As one expects in a temple hymn, Enki builds his house on the very day of creation.

Phrases from two other texts, which will be discussed in detail below, also show human beings sprouting from the seed implanted by heaven: *KAR 4,* 54, "they sprout from the ground like barley"; and *The Rulers of Lagash,* 5, "As the black headed people had risen in their clay."[38]

The most important Nippur text on the creation of man is the 108-line poem, *Praise of the Pickax.* Its manuscripts seem not to predate the Old Babylonian period, but the poem may date from the Early Dynastic period (ca. 2500 B.C.). Interpretation is made difficult by textual variants and abnormal spellings, word and sign plays, and perhaps deliberate obscurantism for a learned audience. The first part is mythological, containing a cosmogony in lines 1–34, followed by a description of the relationship of the pickax to various gods in lines 35–77. The second part consists of word plays on the word "pickax," and the third part is on the use of the pickax. A doxology concludes the poem. Claus Wilcke has analyzed the very obscure cosmogony: separation of heaven and earth by Enlil with the pickax (1–11); description of the pickax (12–17); creation of humans by Enlil with the help of the pickax and brick mold (18–21); request of the Anunna gods for human workers (22–25); birth of humans by the agency of Ninmenna, Enlil's giving of their names, the allotment of humans to the gods, and the bestowal of the pickax upon them (26–34). Lines 1–24 are relevant.[39]

---

[38] For *KAR 4,* see below, pp. 43–47, and for *Rulers of Lagash,* pp. 41–42. The Sumerian text of the *Chaldean Cosmogony* (II.6) 20–21 reads, "[Marduk] created humankind, Aruru [mother goddess] together with the gods made the seed of humankind grow." The text, however, dates to the Seleucid period; its wooden Sumerian seems to have been translated from the Akkadian.

[39] The translation has been made by J. van Dijk especially for this book, to whom I most grateful. For background, see Wilcke, "Hacke," *RLA* 4.37–38 and *Kindlers* 10.9106. Other translations are in Bottéro, *LD,* 509; G. Pettinato, *Menschenbild,* 83–84; van Dijk,

1The lord brought into being the beginnings splendidly,

The lord, whose decisions cannot be changed,

Enlil, to make the seed of the kalam (=Sumer) sprout from the earth/the netherworld,

To separate heaven from earth he hastened,

5To separate earth from heaven he hastened.

To make light shine in Uzumúa,[40]

He bound the pillar[41] (of Heaven and Earth) in Duranki.[42]

He worked *with* the pickax; the light of the sun came out.

He fixed (its) task: the work of hoeing.

10He fixed the pickax and the basket (to be carried) in the arms.

Then Enlil sang the praise of the pickax; his pickax is (of) gold, (its) teeth are lapis lazuli,

His pure pickax is of fine silver (and) gold.

His pickax, its blades (lit. "wings") are of . . . lapis lazuli.

Its teeth are a battering ram against a fortress wall.

15The Lord *chose* the pickax and fixed its destiny,

Crowned it with a floral crown (?), a pure crown.

In order to create the first man in Uzumúa with the pickax,

He put the first of mankind in the mold.

Before Enlil, (the people) of the *kalam* (=Sumer) broke through (the surface of) the earth.

20He looked with favor on his black-headed people.

The Anunna (gods) came rushing to him,

In reverence brought their hands to their mouth,

Soothed (the heart of) Enlil with their prayer,

(And) distributed the pickax to the black-headed people.

"Le motif cosmique," 23–24; S. N. Kramer, *Sumerian Mythology*, 51–53; and T. Jacobsen, "Sumerian Mythology," *JNES* 5 (1946) 128–52 [*TIT* 111–14].

[40] Lit., "the place where flesh sprouts." For this interpretation of sag. . . .mú mú s.v. *nabātu* in *CAD*, and see *MSL XVII*, 207, no. 230.

[41] The Sumerian sign is bulug: 1. chisel; 2. needle, pin, splinter; 3. latch; 4. axis (metaphorical use); 5 border (?). *The Sumerian Dictionary of the University Museum of the University of Pennsylvania B* (ed. A. W. Sjöberg; Philadelphia: Babylonian Section of the University Museum, 1984–) 173–76. For the last usage, *The Sumerian Dictionary* renders bulug-an-ki-(ka) as "axis (between) heaven and earth" (epithet of Isin) and translates line 7, "At Duranki he set up the axis" (p. 175). *AHW*, s.v. *pulukku:* "the cosmic needle," "the pillar (sustaining heaven)." Jacobsen read the sign as "wound, cleft," in "Sumerian Mythology," *TIT*, 113, a meaning which is not found in *The Sumerian Dictionary*.

[42] Lit., "bond of Heaven and Earth."

"Lord" Enlil (lines 1–2), as the firstborn of the cosmic union, separates his parents. His purpose is to make the seed of Sumer sprout (line 3). He joins the now-separated heaven and earth with a pillar, which is either the navel, i.e., umbilicus, of the world ("axis") or a mooring for the floating earth.[43] Duranki, a kenning for Nippur, is the place where Heaven implanted his seed; included in the seed were human beings ready to emerge when the hard soil would be loosened by the pickax. Enlil uses the pickax to complete the work of creation and then assigns to the pickax its destiny (namtar) — to be the instrument of human labor (lines 9–10). Lines 17–18 seem to presuppose that man was in a mold before his birth from the earth; the lines appear to blend *formatio* and *emersio* traditions.[44] The pickax is given to the human race so that with this new technology human beings might better serve the gods. The gift resembles the grain and animals given to human beings in the *Ewe and Grain* (see below).

To summarize the Nippur tradition, creation takes place through the marriage of Heaven and Earth. The act is comprehensive, including the fertilizing of earth to produce vegetal, animal, and human and social life from Heaven's seeds. The act occurs within a scenario — the primeval city with its "parent gods," the marriage, the resultant universe.

C. Narrative Texts of the Eridu Tradition

In the five extant major cosmogonies of the Eridu tradition, Enki the spring water fertilizes earth by means of rivers and canals, causing life (including human life and cities) to rise along their banks. Under this tradition is included the distinct tradition of Enki's creating individual human beings out of clay.

To understand how Enki creates one must review the Sumerian experience of the divine. Central to the Sumerian perception of reality was the concept of me,[45] variously translated as "to be" or "being." Dynamic rather than static, me made up the essence of things. The Sumerian word

---

[43] In the first conception, Nippur would be the navel of the universe. In the second, the mooring would be at the edge of the world, like the pillars of Hercules (van Dijk, private communication).

[44] Van Dijk, private communication.

[45] Me is a Sumerian word. As pointed out in n. 10, Sumerian words are transliterated into English without italics or underlining.

for power in the divine sphere was me-lam (lit., "shining being," hence "divine majesty"), the indwelling power (me) and its brilliant manifestation (lam).[46] Three examples illustrate me-lam. In *Gilgamesh*, Gilgamesh, intent on killing the monster Huwawa, persuades him to lay aside his sevenfold me-lam by pretending to give his sister in marriage to him. Without his me-lam, Huwawa is defenseless and easily slain by Gilgamesh. In *Gilgamesh and Agga*, Gilgamesh appears on the walls as his men are losing the battle. One glance is enough to make his enemies fall dead (line 85). In *The Descent of Inanna*, Inanna, wishing to be queen of the underworld as well as heaven, clothes herself for the descent. Each piece of her clothing contains me. Ereshkigal, her sister and queen of the underworld, has Inanna stripped of one item of clothing at each of the seven gates of the underworld until she arrives before Ereshkigal, naked and utterly powerless. The me, "the divine," is thus something more than the god: "For the Sumerian, god is the personified divine."[47] It is not god but is possessed by the god.

In the Eridu tradition, the principle of life is not cosmic but chthonic; water from under the earth makes the earth fertile. Water plays a large role in Enki's myths and cult: "Everything that lives in water arises from water; in other words it owes its existence to the god of water. Water endows the being with form; it gives the form its beauty and makes the created beings into useful beings. This wisdom is immanent in the water and hence also in the god. . . ."[48] Enki's connection with the world of settled folk made it natural for him to become the god of artisans, wisdom, and the arts.

The five myths with Enki as creator are: *Enki and the World Order, Enki and Ninhursag* (The *Dilmun Myth*), the introduction to the disputation *Bird and Fish, Enki and Ninmah,* and the *Sumerian Flood Story.* Unlike the single-act cosmic marriage of the Nippur tradition, the Eridu cosmogonic traditions are included within extended narratives in which Enki's actual creating comprises only one part. The versatile and inventive Enki required many lengthy stories for his varied adventures. In *Enki and the World Order* Enki creates in several stages—by bringing water

---

[46] The most recent extended treatment of the difficult concept of me is G. Farber-Fluge, *"Inanna and Enki" unter besonderer Berücksichtigung der List der m e* (Studia Pohl 10; Rome: Biblical Institute, 1973).

[47] Van Dijk, "Sumerische Religion," 446 and 439–49.

[48] Van Dijk, "Sumerische Religion," 467.

up to the world and designating the gods of culture. *Enki and Ninhursag* opens with a remarkable tableau of the society not yet created by Enki before going on to the act of creation. The disputation *Bird and Fish* explicitly attributes the existence of towns on the banks of canals to Enki. The satirical *Enki and Ninmah* describes Enki's forming man from clay. The fourth myth, *Enki and Ninmah,* invites special attention to the *formatio* of man, which is prominent in this text. The fifth myth, the *Sumerian Flood Story,* divides the establishment of the human race into two stages. After the flood story, we examine other texts of creation in two stages.

Enki and the World Order is known from Old Babylonian copies and dated by Wilcke to the Isin period (1953–1730 B.C.). It consists of a hymnic section and two narrative sections. In his first self-praise, Enki says, "From[49] the Ekur, the house of Enlil, / I brought craftsmanship to my Abzu of Eridu [Enki's temple]. / I am the fecund seed, engendered by the great wild ox, I am the first born son of An, / I am the 'great storm' who goes forth out of the 'great below,' I am the lord of the Land. . . ."

In the first narrative section, Enki travels to several places and blesses them — Nippur, Ur, Meluhha, Dilmun. He then imparts fertility to the fields by inseminating the Tigris and Euphrates with water from beneath the earth; the rivers will bring that water to the fields. Enki is spring water and so creates through the life-giving rivers.

> 250After[50] he cast his eyes from that spot,
> After father Enki had lifted it over the Euphrates
> He stood up proudly like a rampant bull,

[49] Kramer in *The Sumerians,* 174–83, gives a nearly complete translation; the quoted passage is on p. 175. For the Sumerian text, see C. A. Benito, "'Enki and Ninmah' and 'Enki and the World Order'" (unpublished Ph.D. dissertation, University of Pennsylvania, 1969) 89, lines 66–69. See also A. Falkenstein, *ZA* 22 (1964) 44–113; van Dijk, "Sumerische Religion," 467–468; Wilcke, *Kindlers* 10.9106, and "Kollationen zu der literarischen Texten," 9. Van Dijk, in a personal communication, suggests that "the great storm" may refer to Enki as the storm personified as a lion; *AHW,* 1420, s.v. *ūmu* c.

[50] Translation of Kramer, *The Sumerians,* 179. For the Sumerian text, see C. A. Benito, "Enki and Ninmah," 99–100, lines 250–62. Van Dijk, in a private communication, suggests emendations to the translation: line 251, "had lifted (his eyes) upon"; line 256, "in the *fenced/hedged* pen" (reading gir-tab=*se-er-tab*); line 257, "[The Tigr]is he took in/with his arm/horn, like a rampart bull" (reading á-na. . . dab$_5$); line 258, "[stood ready (reading the verb tím)] to give birth"; line 259, "The water rose: sparkling water, its 'wine' tastes sweet."

He lifts the penis, ejaculates,
Filled the Tigris with sparkling water.
The wild cow mooing for its young in the pastures, the scorpion
    (-infested) stall,
[The Tigr]is surre[ndered] to him, as (to) a rampant bull.
He lifted the penis, brought the bridal gift,
Brought joy to the Tigris, like a big wild bull [rejoiced(?)]
    in its giving birth.
The water he brought is sparkling water, its "wine" tastes sweet,
²⁶⁰The grain he brought, its checkered grain, the people eat it,
He fi[lled] the Ekur, the house of Enlil, with possessions,
With Enki, Enlil rejoices, Nippur [is delighted].

Creation is through providing water essential for life. In the temporal perspective of the text, all forms of life (including human life) are in existence before the insemination. Nonetheless, the text may intend to attribute all life to Enki's intervention despite the temporal "inconsistency."

In the second narrative section of *Enki and the World Order,* Enki assigns the gods responsibility for the culture of Sumer. Three gods are made responsible for the water supply of Sumer, another god for fishing in fresh water and still another for fishing in salt water; there will be a goddess for grain, two gods for architecture, one each for wild and domestic animals, one for judicial administration, and a goddess for spinning and weaving. This list is not complete but it shows that Enki's creation includes organizing the world of human society.[51]

The second myth of Enki the creator is *Enki and Ninhursag,* known also as the *Dilmun Myth,* which is preserved on three tablets totaling 278 lines and was copied in the Old Babylonian period.[52] The locale of

---

[51] Wilcke, *Kindlers* 10.9106.

[52] My interpretation follows Pascal Attinger, "Enki et Ninhursaǧa," *ZA* 74 (1984) 1–52. See further D. O. Edzard in *Kindlers* 10.9110; and B. Alster, *Berliner Beiträge* 2 (1983) 52–73. S. N. Kramer's translation appeared in *ANET,* 37–40, and his recent interpretations are given in "Sumerian Mythology Reviewed and Revised," in *Biblical Archaeology Today: Proceedings of the International Congress on Biblical Archaeology, Jerusalem, April 1984* (Jerusalem: Israel Exploration Society, 1985) 290–92, and in S. N. Kramer and J. Meier, *The Myths of Enki, The Crafty God* (New York: Oxford University Press, 1989), chap. 1. Jacobsen, *The Harps that once. . . .* 181–204, offers a discussion and full translation. Kramer's and Edzard's interpretation of the primal time as paradisiacal misunderstands the negative phrase "when there was not" as is pointed out by van Dijk, in "Sumerische Religion," 468, M.-J. Seux, "La création du monde et de l'homme," in *La création,* 62–64; and Attinger, "Enki et Ninhursaga."

the myth is Dilmun (modern Bahrain in the Persian Gulf), an important trading center in the early historical period. Not far offshore are freshwater wells; these are the wells of Enki. Enki in this myth is not the old and wise counselor of the gods; he is young and sexually insatiable.

The story opens with a remarkable tableau of Sumer and Dilmun before creation. Enki is with his daughter and wife Ninsikila (variously called in the story Nintu, Damgalnuna, and Ninhursaga).

> At[53] Dilmun, no crow cries "ka'gu,"
> no francolin [type of partridge] goes "dardar,"
> 15no lion kills,
> no wolf takes a lamb.
> Unknown is the dog herding the goats,
> unknown is the pig, eater of grain.
> The widow does not spread malt on the roof,
> 20no bird in the sky forages for it.
> No dove goes with head held high.
> No one with eye disease says, "I have an eye disease,"
> no one with a head disease says, "I have a head disease."
> No old woman says, "I am an old woman,
> 25no old man says, "I am an old man."
> No young woman, not yet bathed, makes her ablutions in the city.
> No man crossing the river cries, "*Mine*" [a work song?].
> No herald tours the frontiers in his charge.
> No singer utters an "*elulam*,"
> 30utters an "*ilu*," at the edge of the city.

Like other cosmogonies, this text describes the precreation state concretely as the absence of particular elements of society rather than abstractly as unspecified nothingness.[54] Society is conceived as a system; there are significant distinctions between animals in contact with human beings and those not (the shepherd dog at line 17 marks the transition between the two), between "natural man" (old age considered to be illness, shown by the parallel lines 22–23 and 24–25) and "civilized man" (old people as wise and custodians of culture). Song, the last item

[53] My rendering of Attinger, "Enki et Ninhursaga," 7–9.

[54] Biblical examples are Gen 2:5 ("when no plant of the field was yet in the earth and no herb of the field had yet sprung up") and Prov 8:23–26, which describes the creation of Woman Wisdom when there were no depths and springs, mountains and hills, earth and soil.

mentioned, is the highest art. Generally life is portrayed as action and nonlife as nonaction.[55]

		13–14 (2) birds
	13–16 (4) wild animals	15–16 (2) quadrupeds
13–21 (9) animal life		17–18 (2) quadrupeds
	17–21 (5) domestic animals	19–21 (3) birds
	22–25 (4) "nature"	22–23 (2) sicknesses
22–30 (9) human life		24–25 (2) old people
	26–30 (5) "culture"	26–28 (3) bodily care trades
		29–30 (2) song

It is significant that immediately after the precreation tableau Ninsikila prays to her father Enki for water for the city that he has given her (I.31–64). Enki responds by creating.

> [65]He,[56] the wise, before Nintu, the mother of the country,
> Enki, the wise, before Nintu, the mother of the country,
> with his penis cuts a trench for the water,
> with his penis bathes the reeds in the water,
> with his penis makes gush a great . . . clothing
> [70]He cries out, "I allow no one to pass through the marsh."
> Enki cries, "I allow no one to pass through the marsh."
> He swears by heaven.
> "Lie down in the marsh, lie down in the marsh, that (will be) splendid!"
> Enki besprinkles Damgalnuna with his seed (?).
> [75]He pours out seed into her womb, the seed of Enki.
> The first day was for her the first month.

[55] These remarks owe much to P. Attinger, "Enki et Ninhursağa," 33–34; the outline of the tableau is his.

[56] My rendering of Attinger, "Enki et Ninhursağa," 15.

Ninmu is born after nine days, each day equaling a month. Enki then impregnates Ninmu. After nine days she bears Ninkurra. He impregnates Ninkurra, and she gives birth to Uttu (the spider goddess, goddess of weaving). Enki turns his amorous attentions toward Uttu, but she, on instructions from Ninhursaga, steals his seed and sows it on the steppe. From it various plants grow, which Enki eats and so becomes pregnant. As a male, he cannot bring them to term and falls ill. Ninhursaga cures him by giving birth to the eight deities, each from a different part of Enki's body. The story ends with Ninhursaga assigning roles to the newborn gods. The last of them, Ensag, Enki destines to be lord of Dilmun.

What is the interpretation of this enigmatic myth? The city of Dilmun is society *in nuce*. As long as Dilmun is without water, neither animal nor human life can exist. Enki brings Dilmun to life by digging a hole with his penis through the earth to the underground waters, the same act he performs in *Enki and the World Order* and in *Bird and Fish*. The life brought by Enki is not only vegetative or animate; it is also the urban civilization of the cities along the river banks. Less clear are the second and third sections of the epic, which detail Enki's incestuous relations with his daughter and wife Ninsikil, then with his daughters Nin.SAR, Ninkurra, Ninimma, Uttu, and finally the eight plants from his seed that Enki eats, the last of whom turns out to be Ensag, lord of Dilmun. S. N. Kramer, citing the principle that the end of a Sumerian work rather than its beginning is the most significant part, emphasizes the importance of the last-named god, Ensag. On Ensag Enki bestows the lordship of Dilmun in gratitude for the healing of his body. The myth, therefore, probably explains how the relatively obscure Ensag became lord of Dilmun. Possibly too, as Attinger suggests, Enki's persistent incest symbolizes the period before exogamy, which is a characteristic of civilized life.[57]

The third myth about Enki the creator is the cosmogonic introduction to the disputation *Bird and Fish,* from the Ur III period (2064–1955 B.C.).

1After,[58] in primeval days, a kindly fate had been decreed,
and of the cosmos, An and Enlil had established its rule,

[57] Ibid., 4–5.
[58] The translation is that of S. N. Kramer, *From the Poetry of Sumer*, 46–47. See also Bottéro, *LD*, 517–20.

Nudimmud, the noble prince, the lord of wide understanding,
Enki, the fate-decreeing king, being their third,
5Collected all the waters, established their dwelling-places,
Let flow at his side the life-giving waters that begat the fecund seed,
Suspended at his side the Tigris and Euphrates, brought into them the
    waters of land,
Cleansed the small canals, made furrow-ditches alongside them.
Father Enki spread wide the stalls, provided them with shepherd
    and herdsmen,
10Founded cities and towns, multiplied the black-haired people,
Provided the king for shepherdship over them, exalted him for princeship
    over them,
Made the king rise over the lands as a steadfast light.
The lord Enki organized the marshes, made grow there reeds young
    and old,
Brought fish and birds into the marshes, swamps, and lakes,
15Filled the steppe with breathing creatures as their food and drink,
Charged them with supplying the abundance of the gods.
After Nudimmud, the noble prince, the lord of wide understanding,
Had fashioned the . . .
He filled the canebrake and marsh with fish and bird,
20Assigned them to their stations,
Made them acquainted with the rules.

Unlike other Eridu cosmogonies, this text integrates Enki's (=Nudimmud) act with An's and Enlil's; together they institute the rules. Enki alone, however, creates the world by bringing up the underground waters to the Tigris and Euphrates and their canals. As in other cosmogonic introductions to debates (see II.7ab below), the text focuses on the habitat of the two debaters, the bird and the fish (the marsh). In the area fertilized by the waters, Enki establishes herders and founds cities and kings to rule them. Then Enki makes marshes for birds and fishes.

The three myths just discussed imply rather than state in detail that Enki created human society in the course of making the earth fertile. The fourth myth, *Enki and Ninmah,* specifically narrates the creation of man from clay moistened with water. Its first section tells how the god at the behest of the mother goddess Nammu, and with her and Ninmah's help, created humans as substitute workers for the minor gods who were unhappy at having to work.

1In[59] those days
  once heaven and earth [were split apart],
in those nights
  once heaven and earth [were severed],
in those years,
  the years after the fates have been decreed,
once the Anunna were born,
5once the goddesses were joined in wedlock,
once the goddesses had been allotted their shares
  of heaven and earth,
after the goddesses . . . had been impregnated [?],
  had given birth,
after the gods had been forced to . . . their food
  . . . for their own dining halls,
the great gods labor,
  the young gods carry baskets,
10the gods dig canals,
  heap up their dirt *ḫarali,*
the gods grind away,
  grumble about their life:
In those days, the one with the cunning grasp,
  fashioner of all the gods that exist,
Enki, in the deep billowing sea—
  into whose midst no one dares to gaze—
is lolling in his bed,
  will not stir from sleep,
15[while] the gods wail [and] mutter.
To the one who is lying in the deep,
  to the one who will not stir from his bed,
Nammu, primeval mother,
  who had given birth to all the great gods,

---

[59] The translation is that of S. N. Kramer in Kramer and Meier, *Myths of Enki,* 31–33. For the Sumerian text, see C. Benito, "'Enki and Ninmah,'" 21–25, lines 1–37. Other translations are in van Dijk, "Le motif cosmique," 24–31; Pettinato, *Menschenbild,* 70–71, 24–31; and Jacobsen, *The Harp that once. . . ,* 153–66. Commentary is in Kramer, *Sumerian Mythology,* 68–72, and "Sumerian Mythology Reviewed and Revised," 292–93; Jacobsen, *JNES* 5 (1946) 129, 143 (*TIT,* 106, 120–1); Wilcke, *Kindlers,* 6.2152; and R. Borger, "Einige Texte religiösen Inhalts," *Or* 54 (1985) 18–22. Van Dijk, in a private communication, suggests the following: line 10, Ḫarali is a place-name, so *in* Ḫarali; line 21, "are beaten on their back parts," reading the verb udu. . .dub$_x$, "to beat the flesh"; line 23, "Create servants replacing the gods."

carried the wailing of the gods—to her son:
"You who are lying about,
      you who are sleeping,
20you who will not stir from your sleep:
the gods—my handiwork—are beating their . . . .
Rise up, my son, from your bed,
      practice your skill perceptively.
Create servants[?] for the gods.
      Let them throw their baskets away."
Enki, at the word of his mother, rose up from his bed.
25The god, once he examined a fattened kid . . . ,[60]
the cunning (and) perceptive one,
      the one who guides the seeker,
      the skilled one who fashions the form of things,
         turned out the *sigensigdu*,[61]
Enki had them stand at his side, looks at them intently.
After Enki, form-fashioner, had, by himself,
      put sense in their head,
he says to his mother, Nammu:
30"My mother, the creature whose name you fixed—it exists.
      The corvée of the gods has been forced on it.
Knead the 'heart' of the clay that is over the *abzu*.
The *sigensigdu* will nip off this clay.
      You give it form.
Let Ninmah act as your helper.
Let Ninimma,
   Suzianna,
   Ninmade,
   Ninbara,
35   Ninmug,
   Musargaba,
   Ningunna,
serve you as you form it.

---

[60] Jacobsen in *The Harps that once.* . . , 155, is preferable to Kramer here: "in Halankug, his room for pondering, he smote the thigh," i.e., made a gesture of decision.

[61] The word contains four signs, sig₇-en-sig₇-du₁₀, which are conventionally read as sigensigdu. A later bilingual replaces it with *šassūru* ("womb"), in Benito, "'Enki and Ninmah,'" 155 n. 16. M.-J. Seux points out that *šassūru* in *Atrahasis* designates the creator god Mami and her fourteen helpers. Here, he suggests, they are probably the seven divine helpers mentioned in lines 34–35, in his review of *LD, Or* 60 (1991) 358.

My mother, you decree its fate.
Let Ninmah force upon it the corvée of the gods."

Enki creates human beings, with the help of the mother goddesses, as surrogate laborers for the unwilling gods. Human beings as substitute worker for the gods is also a theme of the Akkadian epic *Atrahasis*.[62] At Nammu's request Enki molds the form of the man and endows him with his wisdom. Enki creates the sigensigdu to help with the birth process. The separation of tasks suggests that Enki is responsible for the rational "form" of man, and the mother goddess for the shaping of the body. Nammu and her helpers assign the man his task—to be a laborer for the unwilling gods. The next scene (not translated here) depicts a banquet, presumably a celebration of the creation of man. Enki and Ninmah, both inebriated, engage in a contest. Ninmah creates seven deformed humans and challenges Enki to find useful employment for them. Enki succeeds in finding them places. He then makes a helpless creature, *umul,* as a challenge to Ninmah.[63] The tale shows how Enki created man as a substitute for worker gods and also how he found uses for human misfits.[64]

In the fifth and last myth of Enki the creator, the *Sumerian Flood Story,* the human race is created in two stages. Other two-stage creation texts will also be dealt with here. The story is extant in the lower third of a six column tablet, apparently from Nippur, which is dated no earlier than the late Old Babylonian period. Some scholars suppose it to be based on an Akkadian version of the story, though it lists the antediluvian cities in the same way that the *Sumerian King List* does.[65] Each of its five legible sections are interrupted by damaged sections: the legible parts of cols. i and ii narrate the situation before the flood; cols. iii-iv describe the hero Ziusudra whom Enki helped; col. v tells of the actual flood and its recession; and col. vi concerns the granting of eternal life to Ziusudra and his settlement in Dilmun. Jacobsen supplements the Old Babylonian tablet

[62] The motif occurs in the standard version of *Gilgamesh* I, where Enkidu is created by the gods as a response to the problem of Gilgamesh, who is terrorizing Uruk.

[63] A. D. Kilmer, "Speculations on Umul, the First Baby," in *Kramer Anniversary Volume* (ed. B. L. Eichler et al.; AOAT 25; Neukirchen-Vluyn: Butzon & Bercker, 1976) 265–70.

[64] One cannot argue from this myth that creation of man is separate from creation of the world. The text tells of the origin of man as a toiler within the world.

[65] Dalley, *MFM,* 6.

with two other tablets (a fragment of the same period and a bilingual of ca. 600 B.C.), entitling the resulting combination "The Eridu Genesis."[66]

After a lost opening of about 36 lines, a god (probably Enki who elsewhere shows parental love for his creatures) resolves to rescue humankind so that they might "come back to their dwelling grounds," build cities and temples, and celebrate rituals:

> [38]I want to [. . .] the destruction of my human race,
> For Nintu, I want to *stop* the annih[ilation of] my creatures,
> [40]I want the people to come back to their dwelling grounds.
> Let all their cities be built, I want their shade to be restful.
> Let the bricks of all cities be laid on holy places,
> Let all . . . rest on holy places,

When the text resumes after a break of some 40 to 50 lines, kingship descends from heaven and five cities are founded (ii. 86–100):

> [88][When the . . .] of kingship had come down from heaven,
> After the lofty crown and the throne of kingship had come down from heaven . . .

A god names the cities, assigning each to a god, and establishes canals. Jacobsen inserts his bilingual fragment at this point to begin col. iii as a list of nine kings of five cities (Eridu, Badtibira, Larak, Sippar, and Shuruppak). The kings' ages are also given: they live from 10,800 to 64,800 years.[67] The list ends ominously: "Enlil took a dislike to mankind (17′) the clamor of their shouting . . . kept him sleepless." When col. iii of the Nippur text resumes, the gods have already decided to send the flood, provoking Enki's secret warning to the pious Ziusudra. On the basis of *Atrahasis* and *Gilgamesh* XI, one may assume that Ziusudra built a boat at Enki's urging, since col. v describes the flood and Ziusudra emerging

[66] T. Jacobsen, "The Eridu Genesis," *JBL* 100 (1981) 513–29, and *The Harps that once. . .* , 143–50; see P. D. Miller, "Eridu, Dunnu, and Babel: A Study in Comparative Mythology," *HAR* 9 (1985) 227–51. I use the translation of M. Civil in Lambert-Millard, *Atra-hasis,* 138–45. A translation and discussion are given by Kramer, "The Sumerian Deluge Myth," *Anatolian Studies* 33 (1983) 115–21; and by Pettinato, *Menschenbild,* 34–35, 97–100. See D. O. Edzard, *Kindlers,* 10.9111.

[67] The great ages of the kings here and in the Sumerian King List resemble the great ages of the ten ancestors in Genesis 5. Jacobsen suggests that the great ages show ancient worthies' slow rate of development, which might explain why the biblical ancestors beget children so late, e.g., Methuselah at 187 and Lamech at 182 (in "The Eridu Genesis," 520–21).

from the boat to offer sacrifice. After a break, col. vi shows Ziusudra prostrating himself before An and Enlil and receiving life like a god's and a dwelling in Dilmun: "[An and Enlil] gave him life like a god. / At that time, the king Ziusudra / Who protected the seed of mankind at the time (?) of destruction, / They settled in an overseas country, in the orient, in Dilmun." The end is broken.

The gist of cols. iii–vi is clear if it is read together with *Atrahasis* and *Gilgamesh* XI: the gods decide to send a flood, and Enki warns the pious king Ziusudra to build a boat. When the flood abates the king makes a sacrifice and receives eternal life. The puzzle is cols. i–ii. What is the "annihilation" of the race that Enki resolves to end? The most plausible answer is to suppose that the situation resembles that in *Ewe and Wheat* and *Rulers of Lagash:* the human race was originally created animallike, with no cities and culture, and only subsequently was it given the arts making life humane and bearable. The "destruction" cited in i.38 would then be the miserable state of humanity before the gods gave man culture. Creation thus occurred in two stages: first bare existence and then civilized life.

On the basis of his supplementation of the original six-column Nippur tablet with two others, Jacobsen proposes that the original story had three parts, each with its own theme and purpose. The first part was concerned with nature versus culture, and demonstrated the superiority of culture. The second part was modeled on the *Sumerian King List*[68] and reflected the composer's historical interest. The third part narrated the near destruction of the human race by the flood. The tone was not pessimistic or macabre but rather optimistic; after all the human beings were able to survive a catastrophe, and the gods learned that they need the human race to run the world. The author was aware of historical cause and effect; the story moved from nature to civilization with cities; from organization necessary for irrigation to increased food supply and population increase. From this comes the confrontation with Enlil. "Now, this arrangement along a line of time as cause and effect is striking, for it is much the way a historian arranges his data, and since the data here are mythological we may assign both traditions to a new and separate genre as mythohistorical accounts."[69] Though Jacobsen's reconstruction

[68] For a translation see *ANET,* 265–66, which depends on Jacobsen's standard edition, *The Sumerian King List* (Assyriological Studies 11; Chicago: University of Chicago, 1939).
[69] Jacobsen, "The Eridu Genesis," 528.

is speculative it is quite plausible. His composite story displays an anthological impulse, an expansion of stories about the beginning in order to explore basic questions. This impulse will be even more apparent in the Akkadian epics *Atrahasis* and *Enūma elish*.

The clearest text on the primitive state of man is the cosmogonic introduction to *Ewe and Wheat* (U_8 *and Asnan*).

> [1]Upon[70] the Hill of Heaven and Earth
> When An had spawned the divine Godlings,
> Since godly Wheat had not been spawned with them, not been created with them,—
> Nor had been fashioned in the Land the yarn of the godly Weaver,
> [5]Nor had the loom of the godly Weaver ever been pegged out—
> And Ewe had not appeared, so that there were not numerous kids,
> For Ewe did not drop her twin lambs,
> And Goat did not drop her triplet kids,
> [10]The names even of Wheat, the holy blade, and of Ewe
> Were unknown to the Godlings and the great Divinities.
> There was no wheat-of-thirty-days;
> here was no wheat-of-forty-days;
> There was no wheat-of-fifty-days,
> [15]Nor small wheat, nor mountain wheat, nor wheat of the goodly villages.
> And there was no cloth to wear:
> The godly Weaver had not been born, so no royal cap was worn,
> And lord Herald, the precious lord, had not been born;
> Shakkan did not go out to the arid lands.
> [20]The people of those distant days,
> They knew not bread to eat;
> They knew not cloth to wear;
> They went about with naked limbs in the Land,
> And like sheep they ate grass with their mouth,
> [25]Drinking water from the ditches.

[70] Translation of B. Alster and H. Vanstiphout, "Lahar and Ashnan: Presentation and Analysis of a Sumerian Disputation," *ASJ* 9 (1987) 1–43. See also Falkenstein, *BO* 5 (1948) 165; E. I. Gordon, "A New Look at the Wisdom of Sumer and Akkad," *BO* 17 (1960) 145; Kramer, *Sumerian Mythology* (rev. ed.; Westport, CT: Greenwood, 1972) 39; Pettinato, *Menschenbild*, 88–89; Wilcke, "Kollationen zu der sumerischen literarischen Texten," 69–70; and J. Bauer, "Leben in der Urzeit Mesopotamiens," *28. Rencontre assyriologique internationale in Wien* (*AfO* Beiheft 19 [1982] 377–83).

At that time, and at the birth-place of the Gods,
In their own home, the Holy Hill, they fashioned Ewe and Wheat.
Then, *gathering* in the divine dining hall,
Of the bounty of Ewe and Wheat
30The Godlings of the Holy Hill
Partook, but were not sated.
Of the sweet milk of their goodly sheepfold
The Godlings of the Holy Hill
Then drank, but were not sated.
35And so, for their own well-being in the goodly sheepfold
They gave them to mankind as sustenance.
Then Enki spoke to Enlil:
"Father Enlil, Ewe and Wheat
Being well settled on the Holy Hill,
40Let us now send them down from the Holy Hill."
Enki and Enlil, having agreed on this as their sacred word,
Sent down Ewe and Wheat from the Holy Hill.

The text begins with An on the hill of heaven and earth generating the gods, who are divided into the great divinities and the lesser gods. The gods are without the sustenance provided by grain and flocks. There were human beings at that time but they were like animals, living without clothing and without the sustenance provided by grain and flocks. The gods discover the advantages of agriculture and animal husbandry for themselves but their human servants, without those means, could not satisfy them. Enki, wishing to increase human efficiency for the ultimate benefit of the gods, persuades Enlil to communicate to the human race the secrets of farming and animal husbandry.

The fifth and last myth on Enki the creator, *The Sumerian Flood Story* (and *Ewe and Wheat*), preserved the tradition of the human race appearing in stages, first culture and second with the instruments of culture. The appearance of the human race in two distinct stages is attested often in mythology and folklore. In explaining the phenomenon, the anthropologists A. O. Lovejoy and B. Boas employ the terms primitivism and antiprimitivism. According to primitivism, early times were the best. In the "soft" version of primitivism, early times were full of ease and enjoyment; in the "hard" version, life was difficult but simple and virtuous. Antiprimitivism, on the other hand, portrays humans' earliest days as brutal and arduous.[71] *Ewe and Wheat* is an example of antiprimitivism.

[71] A. O. Lovejoy and B. Boas, *Primitivism and Related Ideas in Antiquity* (Baltimore:

Another example of antiprimitivism is the obscure text, *How Grain Came to Sumer,* which begins, "At[72] that time, humans ate only grass like sheep: / It was then, of old, that An made cereals (Ashnan), barley, and flax descended from heaven." Enlil then came down to the mountain and stored the grain on it. Two gods of lesser rank considered bringing the cereals to Sumer but decided instead to seek help from Utu the sun god.

A fourth Sumerian text speaks of creation in two stages, though it was originally written in Akkadian. The *Rulers of Lagash* is an Old Babylonian text, described by its editor as "a politico-satirical work written by a Lagash scribe in answer to the author(s) of the *Sumerian King List,* who had ignored the rulers of Lagas." The prologue speaks of postdiluvian new creation.

> 1After[73] the Flood had swept over
> and had brought about the destruction of the land—
> As mankind had been made to endure,
> as the seed of mankind had been left,
> 5as the black-headed people had risen in their clay—
> When An (and) Enlil,
> the name of mankind having been called
> and Rulership established,
> 10as they had not (yet) sent forth from above
> 9kingship, the crown of the city,

Johns Hopkins University, 1935). For this reference, I am indebted to W. L. Moran, "Ovid's *blanda voluptas* and the Humanization of Enkidu," *JNES* 50 (1991) 122. Moran mentions two further instances of antiprimitivism: the *Sumerian King List,* where a pre-kingship ruler's name may suggest a period of anarchy and savagery, and the *Myth of Etana.* M.-J. Seux summarizes relevant data in "La création," in *La création,* 64–67.

72 My rendering of the French translation of S. N. Kramer in Bottéro, *LD,* 514.

73 Edmond Sollberger, "The Rulers of Lagaš," *JCS* 21 (1967) 279–86. The line numbering is his. The quotation appears on p. 279. Van Dijk suggests that the picture is like the flood in Lugal-e, lines 334–35; "that day, the wholesome water, no longer issuing from the earth, did not go up to the fields: / since the ice, heaped up everywhere, the day it began to melt carried the destruction into the Mountain, / since (on account of that) the gods of the land were subject to slavery, / they had to carry the hoe and the basket." Both texts describe the famine of prehistory; see *LUGAL UD ME-LÁM-bi NIR-ĜÁL: Le récit épique et didactique des Travaux de Ninurta, du Déluge et de la nouvelle Création* (Leiden: Brill, 1983) 31. For a naturalistic explanation of the same text, see W. Heimpel, "The Natural History of the Tigris according to the Sumerian Literary Composition LUGAL," *JNES* 46 (1987) 309–17.

¹³(and) they had not (yet) established (for) the countless
   overwhelmed people
¹¹Nin-Girsu, the spade, the hoe,
¹²the basket, (and) the plough (which are) the life of the land:
In those days, man in his carefree youth
   acted for 100 years,
   (and) from his coming of age acted for (another) 100 years.
   (However,) he did not perform the prescribed tasks,
   he became small, he became very small, . . . ,
   his sheep were felled in the sheepfold.

According to *Rulers,* a group of human beings survive the flood. An
and Enlil had "called the name of mankind," i.e., created human beings,
but had not bestowed kingship and the instruments of culture. Human
beings later declined because they did not perform their tasks well and
"the water of Lagash was held back" (line 20), forcing people to rely on
rain alone. Their decline is only reversed by An's and Enlil's bestowal
of the spade, hoe, basket, and plough, "which are the life of the land"
(lines 56, 54, 55) and presumably underground water in prior missing lines.
For the race to live and expand, the gods had to give them kingship and
tools.

Transposition of two-stage creation to an individual is found in tablet I
of the Akkadian epic *Gilgamesh,* which is derived in part from Sumerian
sources. When Enkidu first appears, he is described by the Sumerian loan-
word *lullû,* which is translated neutrally by *CAD* as "man" but by *AHW*
as "ursprünglicher Mensch."[74] Enkidu lives like an animal before meeting
the prostitute (I.iv.3–5): "With the gazelles he feeds on grass, / With the
wild beasts he drinks at the watering place. / With the creeping creatures
his heart delights in water." The lines are repeated when Aruru, the mother
goddess, creates him (I.ii.34–36): "When Aruru heard this [the gods' command to create Enkidu], a double (*zikru*) of Anu she conceived within
her. Aruru washed her hands, pinched off clay and cast it on the

---

[74] Von Soden translates the word *Wildmensch* in his revision of A. Schott's *Das
Gilgamesch-Epos* (Stuttgart: Reclam, 1984). A recently published Akkadian text distinguishes *lullû,* "primal man," from *maliku,* "thinking-deciding man" (=the king), in
W. Mayer, "Ein Mythos von der Erschaffung des Menschen und des Königs," *Or* 56 (1987)
55–68.

[75] Translation and line numbering of E. A. Speiser, *ANET,* 74.

steppe.[76] / [On the step]pe she created valiant . . . [sha]ggy with hair is his whole body, he is endowed with head hair like a woman. / . . . / He knows neither people nor land; / Garbed is he like Sumuqan [god of cattle]." Enkidu leaves his animal-like existence when he enters the city and accepts kingship in the person of King Gilgamesh (especially II.vi); in so accepting kingship he becomes fully human. An echo of the same tradition is found in the hellenistic writer Berossus ("in Babylon there was an immense mass of people, and these lived in disorder [*ataktos*], like the animals").[77]

In summary, the Eridu tradition makes Enki, the god of wisdom, creator (sometimes with the help of mother goddesses). He brings underground waters to earth's surface, making it fertile and populous. In some myths the human race is presupposed in the cities along the river and canal banks that are watered; other myths are specifically devoted to the creation of human beings from clay and water.

D. KAR 4: A Unique Text

The Sumerian creation text *KAR 4* is idiosyncratic, outside both the Nippur and Eridu traditions. It draws on traditional elements, but its story is unparalleled. The main tablet is from Asshur and is dated ca. 1100 B.C. Whether Akkadian or Sumerian was the original language of the bilingual tablet is not known.

> [1]When[78] Heaven had been separated from Earth
> —hitherto they were joined firmly together—
> After the earth-mothers had appeared;
> When the earth had been founded and set in place;
> After the gods had established the plan of the universe,
> [5]And, to prepare the irrigation system,
> Had determined the course of the Tigris and Euphrates,

[76] J. Van Dijk suggests that the casting on the steppe of the *zikru* of Anu that later emerges as Enkidu is an instance of *emersio*. In the Nippur tradition, man emerges from the ground out of An's seed. Akkadian *zikru* means: (1) "image, counterpart, replica; (2) idea, concept (?)" (*CAD* z). (Private communication.)

[77] S. M. Burstein, *The Babyloniaca of Berossus* (SANE 1/5; Malibu: Undena, 1978) 155.

[78] My rendering of the French translation by S. N. Kramer, in Bottéro, *LD*, 503–5. See also Pettinato, *Menschenbild*, 77–79. The scribe wrote "break" in lines 33–34, showing that his copy was broken.

Then An, Enlil, Ninmah (correction) and Enki, the chief gods,
With the other great gods, the Anunna,
Took their place on the high dais,
    And held an assembly.
10As they had already established the plan of the universe,
And with the intention of preparing the irrigation system
That was determined by the course of the Tigris and Euphrates,
⟨Enlil asked them,⟩ "And now what are we going to do?
    What are we going to make now?
O Anunna, great gods, what are we going to do now?
15What are we going to create?"
And the great gods who were present there,
    With the Anunna who assign destinies,
Responded in chorus to Enlil:
"In the 'Flesh-Growing Place' of Duranki (Nippur),
We are going to slay two divine *Alla* (NAGAR, reading uncertain),
20And from their blood give birth to human beings!
The corvée of the gods will be their corvée:
    They will fix the boundaries of the fields once and for all,
And take in their hands hoes and baskets,
To benefit the House of the great gods,
    Worthy seat of their high Dais!
They will add plot to plot;
25They will fix the boundaries of the fields once and for all.
They will install the irrigation system
{They will fix the boundaries of the fields.} [dittography]
To provide water everywhere
And thus make all kinds of plants grow.
30. . . rains . . .
They will fix the boundaries of the fields and pile up sheaves.
break   break
break   break
35Thus they will cultivate the fields of the Anunna,
Increasing the riches of the land,
And diverting the fresh water to the Great Residence,
    Worthy seat of the high Dais!
They will be named Ullegarra and Annegarra [=first humans].
40And they will multiply, for the prosperity of the land,
Cattle, sheep, (other) animals, fish, and birds.
This is what they decided by their sacred mouth—
    Enul and Ninul [=primal gods].

And of it Aruru [Akkadian *Bêlit-ilî*], worthy sovereign,
    has approved the full plan!
Learned person after learned person, unlearned after unlearned
Will spring up like the grain:
[45]And no more than the eternal stars of heaven
    will they ever change!
Then will be celebrated worthily, day and night,
    the feasts of the gods,
According to the full plan that they have established—
An, Enlil, Enki, and Ninmah, the chief gods."
And right there where human beings had been created,
Nisaba was installed as their sovereign [=grain goddess].
  —It is there a secret doctrine:[79]
    One ought to speak of it only among the initiate.

The text is eclectic, echoing the Nippur tradition in its cosmic marriage (line 1, except that heaven and earth were originally united rather than separated), Uzumua and Duranki (line 18), and *emersio* (line 44), and echoing Akkadian cosmogonies in the prominence given to Anu, Enlil, and Enki, and to the gods' planning. Divine design is prominent; the Sumerian word giš-ḫur, literally "wood-scratch," means the plan of the universe. Heaven and earth are founded without reference to the gods' activity. As usual in Mesopotamian cosmogonies, much is implicit. The gods act by implementing a plan and creating the Tigris and Euphrates Rivers, which are essential for life in Mesopotamia. The mention of the rivers suggests that workers are needed to bring their waters to the fields. The text assumes that worker-gods (the NAGAR-gods, reading unclear) are unwilling to care for the world and have rebelled. The gods deliberate about creating humans from the NAGAR-gods. Creation takes place proleptically at the sacred site in Nippur, Duranki, as in The Praise of the Pickax.

Conclusions from the Sumerian Material

The Sumerian cosmogonic traditions belonged to either the Nippur ("cosmic") or the Eridu ("chthonic") *systems*. Even the pickax in the *Praise of the Pickax* was celebrated not for itself but because it freed humans deposited in the earth by the cosmic marriage and because it was the

---

[79] The last two lines are probably a rubric regarding prospective readers.

quintessential instrument of labor. Creation of human beings was not a separate tradition. *Emersio* presumed an earth inseminated by heaven, and *formatio* presumed clay made pliable by the underground water of Enki.

The Nippur tradition imagined a period before creation, when father/mother gods represented inchoate culture (to judge by their names); from them arose the executive great gods. An and Ki created by their marriage act; Enlil of Nippur, their first begotten, separated them. Humans grew up from the earth. *Emersio* survived vestigially in Akkadian literature with Aruru's casting a piece of clay onto the steppe that will blossom into Enkidu.

Creation in the Eridu tradition was accomplished by Enki, the personification of underground spring water, who impregnated the rivers and fertilized the earth. The tradition presumed the bare existence of earth and focused on the moment when abundant waters made life bloom upon it—vegetative, animate, human. Enki's act was portrayed in sexual terms—the insemination of rivers and canals with his semen, which is water from beneath the earth. The world that Enki's act created includes human beings (herders, cities, and kings) but the Enki traditions also comprised his separate formation of human beings as composites of body and "something more" (*formatio*). Akkadian cosmogonies will take up *formatio* and add to the clay mixture the blood of a slaughtered rebel god.

The tradition of Enki as creator, precisely because he is the god of fertility *and* wisdom, allowed for two stages of creation—a blooming of the earth of which man is a natural part, and the advent of culture. It thus differed from the Nippur tradition, in which everything issued all at once from the marriage act. *Enki and the World Order* speaks of culture in the second speech, after the insemination described in the first speech. *Enki and Ninmah* shows a particular interest in social order; Enki's incest in the myth may be an instance of antiprimitivism. The cosmogonic introduction to the disputation *Bird and Fish* depicts culture apart from the fertilizing waters. In *Enki and Ninmah* the first stage occurs when the gods have to work, and the second stage, when human substitutes have been created by Enki. The *Sumerian Flood Story* indicates a pre-Flood phase of human existence, as does the *Sumerian King List, Ewe and Wheat,* and the idiosyncratic *KAR 4.* Akkadian reflections of the same tradition appear in the *Rulers of Lagash* and *Atrahasis.* The two stages are portrayed with great variety, either as primitivism in the "hard" and "soft" versions, or as antiprimitivism.

The *Sumerian Flood Story* shows a tendency, which will continue in the Akkadian "anthological" cosmogonies, to incorporate several traditions into a single long story. The author is sufficiently aware of historical cause and effect to construct a plot, which will become a model for the Akkadian *Atrahasis* (assuming that the composition of the *Sumerian Flood Story* is prior). Though the lengthy plot is new, it merely draws out what is already implicit in cosmogonies, for creation is concerned with human society and human culture.

Very important in both cosmogonic systems is the gods' assigning to each person or thing a "destiny" or share (namtar = Akkadian *šīmtu*) and their determining the giš-hur, or plan of the universe. There is no exact English equivalent; destiny or fate are inaccurate English equivalents. The universe is a given, simply there. The development of beings from simple to complex, which is a basic assumption of modern evolution, is unknown in Sumer. The origin is the defining moment; that is why people took cosmogonies so seriously.

CHAPTER 3

Creation Accounts in Mesopotamia: Akkadian Texts

The previous chapter examined cosmogonies written in Sumerian, and asserted that no neat distinction can be drawn between Sumerian and Akkadian texts. This chapter looks at cosmogonies preserved in Akkadian. They date from the Old Babylonian period (ca. eighteenth century B.C.) to the late first millennium. They can be roughly classified as follows:

A) minor cosmogonies;
B) the anthological cosmogonies *Atrahasis* and *Enūma elish;*
C) the *Dunnu Theogony.*

Several Sumerian genres and themes are found also in the Akkadian material: cosmogonic introductions to debates, the formation of human beings by Ea (=Sumerian Enki), the importance of the destiny (Akkadian *šimtu*=Sumerian namtar) assigned on the first day, and the temple as the site of creation. As in Sumerian texts, the intent is not to convey historical and scientific information (in a modern sense) about creation but rather to ground or explain a contemporary reality or system. There are differences, however: the Nippur (cosmic) system of cosmic marriage is not continued in Akkadian; in *formatio* the blood of a god rather than water is used to moisten the clay from which human beings are made. A final difference: the Akkadian language, which belongs to the Semitic family of languages, is far better understood than Sumerian.

Akkadian cosmogonies are found in both short ritual texts (A below) and in compositions that incorporate a number of traditions (B below).

The latter develop a tendency already noted in the *Sumerian Flood Story*—literary expansion of the act of creation. Bottéro calls the short texts "minor cosmogonies," which is a useful term for distinguishing between short and anthological cosmogonies.[1] The following pages translate and comment on the cosmogonies.

A. Minor Cosmogonies

1. Incantations. Several prologues to incantations show how cosmogonies functioned in rituals.

1a. In the incantation against a toothache the sufferer goes to a magician, who prays to the god Ea to call the worm back to the function assigned it in the order of creation.

> [1]After[2] Anu [had created heaven],
> Heaven had created (*banû*) [the earth],
> The earth had created the rivers,
> The rivers had created the canals,
> The canals had created the marsh,
> (And) the marsh had created the worm—
> The worm went, weeping, before Shamash [the sun god],
> His tears flowing before Ea:
> "What wilt thou give me for my food?
> What wilt thou give me for my sucking?"
> "I shall give thee the ripe fig
> (And) the apricot."
> "Of what use are they to me, the ripe fig,
> and the apricot?

---

[1] "Antiquités Assyro-Babyloniennes," *AEPHE*, 85135, reprinted in *Mythes et rites de Babylone* (Bibliothèque de l'École des hautes études, Sec. 4, Sciences historiques et philologiques 328; Paris: Slatkine-Champion, 1985) 279–328, revised in *LD*. My treatment owes much to Bottéro. All the minor cosmogonies except no. 7b are from first-millennium manuscripts. They are probably older than that but an earlier date cannot be proven.

[2] Translation of E. A. Speiser in *ANET*, 100–1. The chief manuscript is Neo-Babylonian, but two Old Babylonian fragments in Hurrian exist. See A. Heidel, *The Babylonian Genesis* (2d ed.; Chicago: University of Chicago, 1951) 72–73; and Bottéro, *AEPHE* 88–91; and *LD*, 483–85. The Akkadian transcription is given in F. Thureau-Dangin, "Tablettes Hurrites provenant de Mâri," *RA* 36 (1939) 3. For a similar incantation, see J. van Dijk et al., *Early Mesopotamian Incantations and Rituals* (Yale Oriental Series 11; New Haven, CT: Yale University, 1985), 19, no. 5.

10Lift me up among the teeth
And the gums cause me to dwell!
The blood of the tooth I will suck,
And of the gum I will gnaw
Its *roots!*"
    Fix the pin and seize its foot.
Because thou hast said this, O worm,
May Ea smite thee with the might
Of his hand.

The text was used by an *āšipu* (magician) who went to the afflicted person's home, using formulas such as "The god sent me" to legitimate himself. He examined the patient and through a rite described the power involved in order to control it. Here the magician recalls that when the world was created the worm was destined to eat overripe fruit, in the hope that Ea will now punish the worm for deviating from its original destiny by eating human gums.

Creation in the text is a sequence of acts, initiated by Anu the god of heaven and then continued by each newly created element in turn, down to the marsh that creates the worm. The newly created worm came before Shamash, the sun god who oversaw justice, and Ea, the organizer of the universe, to receive its destiny. The verb for creating throughout is *banû* (to build, to beget), the most common Akkadian term for creation. Though the creation of the human race is not mentioned because of the focus on the worm, it is presupposed since the *human* tooth is the basic concern. The incantation illustrates how deeply rooted was the belief that the destiny of things were fixed on the day of creation.

The same assumption operates in two other incantations, both against the ergot, a dark sclerotium of fungi that occurs as a tiny body replacing the seed of grass. The sufferer prays that deviation from the original order be corrected.

1b:

> 51Incantation:[3] In the beginning, before creation (*bašāmu*), the
> work-song came down to the land;
> the seeder plough bore (ù tu=*alādu*) the seed furrow, the
> furrow (bore) the germ,

[3] Translation of B. Landsberger, "Corrections to the Article, 'An Old Babylonian Charm against *Merḫu*,'" *JNES* 17 (1958) 56.

the germ the root-stock, the root-stock the node, the node the
   ear, the ear
the ergot. The Sun-god reaped, the Moon-god gleaned; when the
   Sun-god was reaping, the Moon-god was gleaning,
55the ergot entered into the eye of the man; Sun-god and
   Moon-god stand by, so that the ergot may come out!

1c is also against the ergot:

The earth[4] — they tell — was. The earth
bore (*alādu*) the dirt,
the dirt
bore the stalk,
the stalk bore
the ear,
the ear bore
the ergot.
In — they tell — the field of Enlil,
the square
seven *bur* [a measure of ca. fifteen acres] field,
the Moon-god
was reaping
the Sun-god was gathering;
(then) into — they tell — the flesh
the ergot
entered.
Whom shall I send
and (whom) shall I order
to the daughters of the god . . . . ?
May they fetch
the pot-stand of carnelian,
the pot of *chalcedony*,
may they draw up
the water of the sea,
the pure; the ergot
may they drive out
from the flesh!

The strategy of these cosmogonies is the same as in the incantation
against the worm — to provide a rational framework for interpreting the

[4] Translation of B. Landsberger and T. Jacobsen, "An Old Babylonian Charm against
Merḫu," *JNES* 14 (1955) 15–16.

eye disease. The analogy used is that of the alien ergot entering the seed of grass and spoiling it. In the cosmogonies each element begets (*alādu*) the next in an orderly sequence. Only the intrusion of the ergot into the human disturbs the original harmony. Both cosmogonies end with a prayer that the gods restore the coherence of creation. The mode of creation is begetting but no sexual union is mentioned. The second text has seven generations: seeder plough, seed furrow, germ, root stock, node, the ear, the ergot.[5]

2. Creation accounts occur in another kind of ritual, Namburbi texts. These "are standardized but non-canonical handbooks for the performance of private apotropaic rites (including both action-rites and word-rites, *agenda* and *dicenda*), . . . distinguished from other Akkadian apotropaic rites . . . in that their purpose is to "undo" or "avert" *portended* evil."[6] Many of these extremely repetitious texts refer to the river as a creator, some expanding the theme of River as creator with insignificant variations. The following text is typical.

2'Before[7] the river [you recite as follows]:

Incantation: you [River, are the creator of everything ((*banû*)].
When [the great gods dug you (*ḫerû*)],
5'on your bank [they placed prosperity].
In your midst [Ea, king of the *apsû* built his residence].
He endowed you with fe[arsomeness, splendor, (and) awesomeness].
You are the storm-flood (*abu‹bu›*), not to be opposed.
9'The gods Ea and Bel en[dowed] you with wisdom.
r.1[You are the one who gives judgment on peoples].

The great gods (Anu, Enlil, and Ea) created River by digging its channel, as Anu in text no. 1a above had (mediately) created the rivers. River as cosmic water (*apsû*) is the locale of Ea's temple. The rite presumes that the river water will carry away the evil. The river has a dual quality: as running water it absorbs and carries off the evil laid on substitute figurines;

[5] Landsberger, "Corrections," 56, n. 4. The *Dunnu Theogony* (II.C below) also has a seven-member genealogy and mentions the plow in the first generation.

[6] R. Caplice, *The Akkadian Namburbi Texts: An Introduction* (SANE 1/1; Los Angeles: Undena, 1974) 7. Italics his.

[7] Translation of R. Caplice, "Namburbi Texts in the British Museum," *Or* 34 (1965) 130; and see the similar text 10 in his "Namburbi Texts in the British Museum," *Or* 39 (1970) 138. See Bottéro, *AEPHE*, 95–98; and 486–87.

as a form of Ea, the underground waters, it is endowed with divine splendor (*melammu,* line 5).

3. The next four cosmogonies are found in dedications used in founding or refounding (through repairing) the temple. A ritual text from Babylon for the repair of a temple (ca. 500 B.C.), not well preserved, prefaces a prayer by the *kalû* priest. It was recited before a brick of the temple that was ritually destroyed and rebuilt.

> [1]After[8] Anu had engendered (*reḫû*) heaven,
> (And) Ea had founded (*kunnu*) earth,
> Sin the valiant threw the dice:
> "O Shamash (he says to this god), the totality of "omens(?)"
> [5]Has been put in the hands [. . .]
> [(Teach me then(?)] by what [   ] that which fits (the cure? of)
>   the present illness . . .

There are two creators—Anu for heaven and Ea for earth. Sin the moongod casts the dice to determine the various gods' spheres of influence. From him the priest seeks to find out which god has power over the illness. Bottéro suggests that the verb "engendered" (*reḫû*) may be an echo of the cosmic marriage of Sumerian texts; sometimes synonymous with *alādu,* its literal meaning is "to pour out (seed)."

4. A Seleucid prayer for the reconstruction of a temple, entitled after its opening line "When Anu created the heavens," was recited by the *kalû* priest.

> When[9] the god Anu created (*banû*) heaven,
> [25](When) the god Nudimmud [Ea] created (*banû*) the *apsû*-ocean, his dwelling,
> The god Ea pinched off a piece of clay (*karāṣu ṭiṭṭa*) in the *apsû* ocean,
> Created (*banû*) (the brick god) Kulla for the restoration of [temples]
> Created (*banû*) the reed marsh and the forest for the work of
>   their construction,
> Created (*banû*) the gods Ninildu, Ninsimug and Arazu to be the
>   completers of their construction,

[8] My rendering of Bottéro's translation, *AEPHE,* 98–100.

[9] Translation of A. Sachs, *ANET,* 341–42. Heidel, *Babylonian Genesis,* 65–66; Bottéro, *AEPHE,* 100–06; and 488–91, to whom my remarks are greatly indebted. An Akkadian transcription appears in F. Thureau-Dangin, *Rituels accadiens* (Paris: E. Leroux, 1921) 44 ff.

30Created (*banû*) mountains and oceans for everything . . . ,
Created (*banû*) the deities Gushkinbanda, Ninagal, Ninzadim and
  Ninkurra for their work,
(Created) the abundant products (of mountain and ocean) to be
  offerings . . . ,
Created (*banû*) the deities Ashnan, Lahar, Siris, Ningizzida,
  Ninsar, . . .
For making their revenues abundant . . . ,
35Created (*banû*) the deities Umunmutamku and Umunmutamnag
  to be givers of offerings,
Created (*banû*) the god Kusug, high priest of the great gods,
  to be the one who completes their rites and ceremonies.
Created (*patāqu*) the king to be the provider . . . ,
Created (*banû*) men to be the makers . . . ,
. . . the gods Anu, Enlil, Ea . . .
40. . .

Heaven, created by Anu, and *apsû,* created by Ea, are the two parts
of the universe, expressed by the hendiadys heaven and earth. Earth
evidently comes into being at the same time as heaven and *apsû,* since
the reed marsh and the forest already exist in line 28. It is not clear whether
the phrase "his [Ea's] dwelling" in line 25 implies that Ea already has his
temple in *apsû* and then acts to ensure that the other gods have their
own dwellings without which they cannot carry on their lives (Bottéro's
view) or whether *apsû* is simply where Ea is, with no implication that
he has a temple. At any rate, the cosmogony is theocentric and templocentric.

The verb *banû,* "to build," describes the making of heaven and earth
as well as temples. Ea creates the architect god Kulla from moist clay,
the reed marsh and forest (the raw materials for the temple), and finally
the artisan gods Ninildu for wood, Ninsimug for metal, and Arazu
(specialty unknown). The second group of gods (line 31) embellishes the
temple and makes the all-important images of the gods, which mediate
their presence to their human servants. Then Ea creates "the mountains
and oceans," the sources of the offerings that feed the gods. Ashnan is
the god of grains, Lahar of cattle, Siris of beer, Ningizzida of dates and
probably all arboriculture, and Ninsar of garden plants. The names of
the two deities in line 35 mean "What does Sire wish to eat?" and "What
does Sire wish to drink?" Kusug is created to oversee court ceremonies.

Finally, to ensure that the temple is actually built and maintained, the king is created to oversee the human servants.[10] The great gods are by vocation idle. The last line (39), introduces the actual prayer with the names of the three great gods. Creation here is entirely the work of Anu and Ea; Enlil plays no role though he is mentioned at this point.

The temple is important in creation because there the gods receive the services and goods for which they created the human race. It is, as it were, the concrete expression of the finality of the creation. There were deposited the food offerings to satisfy their hunger and there the ceremonies giving them honor took place. The dedicatory prayers at the temple founding (probably at the New Year festival) or refounding (probably when the building was brought back from neglect) show just how constitutive the temple was.

5. A prayer to dedicate the foundation brick of a temple has the same theocentric and templocentric perspective as no. 4. Difficult to interpret, it apparently accompanied the manufacture of statues and their burial with the foundation brick of the temple. The section below is preceded by a fragmentary speech ("when humans were created . . . when cities . . . law to humans . . . the shrines of the great gods") and by references to mountains and rivers, to Anu, Enlil, and Ea, and to the assignments they made.

[71]When[11] Anu, Enlil and Ea had a (first) idea (*i-ḫu-zu*)
Of heaven and earth,
They found a wise means
  Of providing for the support of the gods:
They prepared, in the land, a pleasant dwelling,
[75]And the gods were installed (?) in this dwelling:
  Their principal temple.
Then they entrusted (?) to the king the responsibility (?)
  Of assuring them regular choice offerings.
And for the feast of the gods,
  They established the required food offering!
The gods loved this dwelling!

---

[10] The king is likewise placed over the gods' human servants in nos. 7b and 9 below.
[11] The text was published by R. Borger, in "Tonmännchen und Puppen," *BO* 30 (1973) 176–83. My rendering of Bottéro, *LD*, 491–93 and see *AEPHE*, 106–8. Nos. 7a and 9a below also describe the gods planning before creating.

Thus did they institute their hold
Over what became the principal land of humans.

The Akkadian word translated as "have the first idea" is uncertain. Anu, Enlil, and Ea provide a dwelling for the other gods, which constitutes an act of authority over them. The human king is given the responsibility of seeing to their food offerings from the people. Ownership of the temple gives the gods a claim on the surrounding land. The *bīt qudmi ilī* (line 75), "their principal temple," makes the surrounding territory into "the principal land of humans" (*māt qudmi-šin,* line 78). The last line is tentative; Borger does not even attempt to translate it. What was said of temples under text no. 4 applies here.

6. The last text directly relevant to creation and temples was discovered in 1882 at Sippar. It is the preamble to a now-lost prayer of the Seleucid era for the foundation of a temple and is known as the *Chaldean Cosmogony* and the *Foundation of Eridu.* It was recited during a procession during the Akitu festival at Uruk. The text is a bilingual, the inferior Sumerian apparently translated from the Akkadian.

1A[12] holy house, a house of the gods, had not been built in
　　(its) holy place;
A reed had not come forth, a tree had not been produced;
A brick had not been laid, a brick mold had not been built;
A house had not been made (*epēšu*), a city had not been built (*banû*);
5A city had not been made, a living creature had not been
　　placed (in it);
Nippur had not been made, Ekur [main temple of Nippur] had not
　　been built;
Uruk had not been made, Eanna [main temple of Uruk] had not
　　been built;
The *apsû* had not been made, Eridu had not been built;
A holy house, a house of the gods (and) its foundation, had not
　　been made.

[12] My translation. Other translations are given in Bottéro, *AEPHE,* 110–111; and *LD,* 497–502 (he rearranges the verses thus: 29+28+31); and Heidel, *The Babylonian Genesis,* 62–63. For the Akkadian transcription, see P. Jensen, *Assyrisch-Babylonische Mythen und Epen* (Berlin: Reuther & Reichard, 1900–01) 38–43. A new Sippar text has been announced by F. N. H. Al-Rawi and A. R. George, in *Iraq* 52 (1990) 149, n. 1. Van Dijk suggests the text is not strictly a cosmogony but an etiological introduction to "a ritual of purification of the mouth" for a city; etiologies are concerned with the foundations of temples and cities ("Existe-t-il un 'poème de la Création' Sumérien?" 127).

10All the lands were sea,

The spring in the midst of the sea was only a channel.[13]

Then Eridu was made, Esagil was built,

Esagil that Lugaldukuga erected (*ramû*) in the heart of *apsû*,
    Babylon was made, Esagil was completed.

15The gods, the Anunnaki, he divided into (two) equal parts,

They called (it) the preeminent city of the gods, the
    dwelling pleasing to them.

Marduk constructed (*rakāšu*) a raft on the waters;

He created (*banû*) dirt and piled it on the raft.

In order to settle the gods in the dwelling pleasing to them

20He created (*banû*) humankind.

Aruru created (*banû*) the seed of humankind with him.

He created (*banû*) the wild animals and all the animals of the steppe.

He created the Tigris and the Euphrates and set (them) in place,

Giving them a favorable name.

25He created the grass, the rush of the marsh, the reed, and the woods;

He created the green herb of the field,

The lands, marshes, and canebrakes,

The cow (and) her young, the calf; the ewe (and) her lamb, the sheep
    of the fold;

The orchards and forests,

30The wild sheep, the ibex . . . to them.

He made an embankment along the sea.

. . . dried up (?) the swamp.

He caused to appear . . .

He creat[ed (*banû*) the reed], he created (*banû*) the tree;

35[. . .] in the place he built,

[Bricks he laid, the br]ick mold he built;

---

[13] Line 11 (*i-nu ša qereb tâmtim rātumma*) is difficult. The context suggests that it is parallel to line 10, since line 9 (an *inclusio* of line 1) concludes the nonexistence phase, and line 12 ("then") begins a new section. Perhaps the channel bringing up the fertilizing waters of the *apsû* was not operational in the precreation period. Bottéro proposes, "Lors donc que le contenu de cette Mer ne formait encore qu'un fossé (?)" (*LD,* 498), against Heidel's "the spring, which is in the sea, was a water pipe." Heidel's interpretation of *i-nu* (=*înu*) as freshwater springs in the sea around the island Bahrain in the Persian Gulf (Heidel, *Babylonian Genesis,* 62, n. 7) is rejected by Bottéro on the grounds that the outlook is too universal for such a local allusion. His own suggestion that the line refers to a freshwater sea unconstrained by banks is unsatisfactory, since *înu* does not mean "content" but "source." *CAD* has *sub rāṭum:* "The spring in the middle of the lake was nothing more than an irrigation pot."

[Houses he built,] cities he built;
[Cities he made,] living creatures he placed (therein);
[Nippur he built], Ekur he built;
40[Uruk he built, Eann]a he built.

Line 9 reprises line 1, a literary device (*inclusio*) to conclude the description of noncreation; lines 10–11 make the transition from the description of nonexistence to the act of creation beginning in line 12. Finally, lines 34–40 reprise lines 2–7, repeating the temple-cities Nippur, Ekur, Uruk and Eanna (but not Esagil/Babylon and *apsû*/Eridu). The text uses *epēšu* "to make" and *banû* "to build" interchangeably; each verb has as its direct object cities or temples.

The precreation period is described concretely as a period when temples and cities (in this poem the primary symbols of existence) had not yet come into being (lines 1–5). The cosmogonies do not express nonexistence abstractly as nothingness, but as a period when essential institutions did not yet exist. Lines 6–7, reversing the sequence of city + temple, mention two cities and their temples, and line 8 (again reversing the temple + city order) mentions in third and climactic place, *apsû* and Eridu. As in texts 4 and 5, the perspective is templocentric; reed and brick, human servants, and sacrificial animals in lines 28–29 are for the gods' palaces. The temples in lines 1–8 belong to the traditional divine triad: Ekur of Enlil in Nippur, Eanna of Anu in Uruk, and Apsû of Ea in Eridu (lines 6–8).

Marduk constructs his own temple first (lines 12–15), building the other gods' temple-cities (presumably through the agency of the human race) only at the end (lines 36–40). After building his own house, he divides the gods (division is an act of political power) and *they* proclaim his dwelling supreme (line 16). Only then does he create earth, the human race, animals, marshes, and the gods' temples. In a sentence: at first, no temples, then Marduk's temple, then the earth and the human race, and then the other gods' temples.

Marduk takes over Ea's position and temple in lines 12–20, as he does in *Enūma elish* VII.140, where Ea acknowledges that Marduk has taken over his name. By making Marduk the creator and assigning to him Ea's functions, the text echoes *Enūma elish,* which also exalts Marduk by assigning to him the functions of Anu and Ea. There are some differences, however. In the *Chaldean Cosmogony,* there is only *tâmtu* (sea) prior to creation but in *Enūma elish, apsû* and *tâmtu* are an undifferentiated mass of water and are personified. In *Enūma elish* the dividing of the gods into two categories (VI.40–44, 69) follows the construction of the universe (IV.135–V.65) and the creation of humans (VI.1–28); in this text the division comes first. Also the *materia ex qua* here is not the carcass of Tiamat as in *Enūma elish* IV; rather Marduk constructs a reed raft upon which he piles dirt. In both texts Marduk creates humans to serve the gods, but here he does so with the help of the goddess Aruru (lines 19–20). After the human builders of the temples have been created, creatures necessary for the temples and their maintenance are formed. The world is created not for human beings but for "cult," the housing and feeding of the gods.

7. Derived quite possibly from the Sumerian genre discussed in the previous chapter, cosmogonies appear in the prefaces of disputations between creatures giving the disputants' origin. Of the six extant Babylonian examples of the genre, only three preserve cosmogonic introductions: *Two Insects, Tamarisk and Palm, Ox and Horse.*[14]

7a. The disputation *Two Insects* (of uncertain species) is fragmentary.

> [1]When[15] the gods, met in their assembly (*puḫrum*), had created (*banû*)
>   [heaven and earth],
> formed (*kašāru*) heaven, consolidated [the sun (?) . . .],
> they brought into being (*šūpû*) the animals [   ]:
> large wild animals, wild animals, small wi[ld] animals[   ];
> [5]and once they had [   ] (to) these animals,
> they allot[ted (?) their respective domains (?)]
> to the cattle and to the small domestic animals. . .

The divine assembly[16] makes important decisions regarding the world, as in text 5, line 1. Heaven and earth are created, then various animals; the series presumably ends with the two insect disputants. Wild animals

---

[14] For a list of extant Akkadian disputations, see *RLA* 7. 58. For discussion, see Lambert, *BWL,* 175–85, M. E. Vogelzang, "Some Questions about the Akkadian Disputes," in *Dispute Poems and Dialogues,* 47–58, and H. J. L. Vanstiphout, "The Mesopotamian Debate Poems: A General Presentation (Part I)," *AS* 12 (1990) 276–78.

[15] My rendering of Bottéro, *LD,* 495 and cf. *AEPHE,* 121. See also Heidel, *Babylonian Genesis,* 64.

[16] For a review of the assembly of the gods see E. T. Mullen, Jr., *The Assembly of the Gods in Canaanite and Early Hebrew Literature,* (HSM 24; Chico: Scholars Press, 1980) chap. 1.

are classed by size (line 4), and tame animals are classed as work or domesticated animals. The human race is is not mentioned, except implicitly in the distinction between wild and domesticated animals, which is a distinction vis-à-vis human society.

7b. The introduction to the disputation *Palm and Tamarisk* tells of the creation of the two plant contestants. From new fragments found at Emar (modern Meskene in Syria), Claus Wilcke has reconstructed a single tablet and compared it with the already-known Old Babylonian and Assyrian recensions. He concludes there were four versions of a still fluid tradition derived from Sumerian traditions.[17] Here is the Emar version.

> 1–5In light-filled days, in dark n[ights], in [far-off] years, when the gods had founded (*kunnu*) the land, had built (*epēšu*) cities for far-off humans, when they had heaped up the mountains and dug the canals that give life to the land, the gods of the land met in assembly. Anu, Enlil, (and) Ea deliberated together; among them sat Shamash, and in their midst sat the great Mistress of the gods.
> 6–11Formerly kingship did not exist in the land, and rule was given to the gods. But the gods grew fond of the black-headed people and g[ave? them a king. The people] of the land of Kish assembled around him so that he might protect (? them). The king planted a date palm in his palace, the space around it he filled with tamarisk(s). In the shadow of the tamarisks, meals were served; in the shadow of the date palm, the crafts were grouped, the drum was beaten — the people rejoiced, the palace exulted.[18]

The cosmogony culminates in the king's planting the date palm and tamarisk on his palace grounds. The king is prominent because the genre

---

[17] The Emar text was published by Daniel Arnaud, in *Recherches au pays d'Astarta: Emar* (Mission Archéologique de Myskene-Emar; Paris: Editions Recherche sur les civilizations, 1985) 6/4, nos. 783–84, and reedited by Wilcke, in "Die Emar-Version von 'Dattel-palme und Tamariske'– ein Rekonstructionsversuch," *ZA* 79 (1989) 161–90. Lambert's texts a, b, and c appear in his *BWL,* 155, 163. The translation presented here is my rendering of Wilcke.

[18] The Old Babylonian version from Tell Harmal (Lambert's text A, Wilcke's THa) differs from the Emar version, and is translated by Wilcke: 1–5"[In] those days, in far off years, when the Igigu established the land, then the gods exerted themselves for humans. In an assembly they agreed to bestow upon them a rich legacy. 6–11At the beginning they appointed a king who would provide order for the land, strengthen the people, govern the city of Kish, the black-headed ones, the numerous people. The [king] planted a date palm in his palace," etc. (The translation is my rendering of Wilcke, "Die Emar-Version," 183).

was, after all, a royal entertainment. Wilcke suggests that the phrase "in light-filled days, in dark nights" parodies Sumerian u_4-ri-a, "in that day."[19] Early man[20] had no king. The date palm and tamarisk are part of the "cultural" environment. In the following sixty lines the two plants debate their usefulness. The origin of the debaters is part of the debate about which of the two cultural elements is the more valuable. Like other disputations, this is a witty exercise of erudite scribes designed for entertainment. It also contains an important presupposition: destinies or characterizations were fixed on the day of creation.

The text is doubly interesting because Emar was a center of east-west trade, and the Baal-malik library, in which the disputation was found, dates between ca. 1320 and 1187 B.C. Emar linked Mesopotamia to the Levant, and the Hittite Empire to Egypt. Many such literary texts (including a fragment of *Gilgamesh*) were found in the library, which was not a repository of training tablets but Baal-malik's own collection. The find illustrates the wide distribution in the Levant of canonical writings from Assyria.[21]

8. The next two cosmogonies function as prologues to the *Great Astrological Treatise,* a work that describes in twenty-two tablets the movements of the moon, and in its later tablets, the movements of the sun, planets, stars, and meteors. No. *8a,* a bilingual, attributes the genesis of the astral movements to the designs of the gods. The Sumerian version, given first, differs from the Akkadian.

> [1]When[22] An, Enlil, and Enki, the great gods,
>> in their infallible counsel,
>> among the great laws (me) of heaven and earth,
> had established the crescent of the moon,
> which brought forth day, established the months
>> and furnished the omens
>> drawn from heaven and earth,
> This crescent shone in heaven,
>> and one saw the stars shining in highest heaven!
> [5]In other words [=the Akkadian version]:

[19] Wilcke, "Die Emar-Version," 184.

[20] The meaning of "far off"; the same adjective modifies "years" in line 1.

[21] Arnaud, "La bibliothèque d'un devin syrien à Myskéné-Emar (Syrie)," *CRAIBL* (1980) 375–87, especially 383–84.

[22] My rendering of Bottéro, *LD,* 493. Cf. *AEPHE,* 123–24.

When Anu, Enlil, and Ea, the great gods,
Had in their counsel
    established the plans (*uṣurātu*) of heaven and earth,
    and when they had charged the great astral gods
to produce (*banû*) day,
    and to assure the regular sequence of months,
    for the (astrological) observation of humans,
one saw then the sun rising
    and the stars shone (*šūpû*) forever in highest heaven!

Text 8b, the second prologue, in Akkadian, is at the end of tablet XXII.[23]

1When Anu, Enlil, and Ea, the great gods,
Had created (*banû*) heaven and earth, had made manifest (*uddû*)
    the token (=[German] "*Wahrzeichen*"),
Had established (*kunnu*) the "stand," had fixed (*šuršudu*) the "station,"
Had appointed (*uddû*) the gods of the night, had distributed (*zu'uzu*)
    the courses,
5Had [installed] stars as (astral) counterparts, had designed the "images,"
Had [measured] the length of day and night, had created (*banû*) month
    and year,
Had [ordered] the path for Sin and Šamaš (and) had made the decrees
    concerning heaven and earth. . .

The cosmogonies introduce the astrological texts, narrating how the gods put in the skies signs of the course of time visible to the human race. The gods intend human beings to observe those signs in the sky (no. 8a, line 7) and direct their lives according to the divine will writ in the heavens. These cosmogonies are concerned exclusively with sun, moon, and stars.[24] No. 8a does not mention creation explicitly but only the assigning of functions to the heavenly bodies (Sumerian me and Akkadian *uṣurātu*). No. 8b, though mentioning creation of heaven and earth, is chiefly concerned with the functions of the heavenly bodies. Divine planning is explicit in nos. 5 and 7a above. Planning or design

[23] Translation of B. Landsberger and J. V. Kinnier Wilson, "The Fifth Tablet of ʿEnūma elish," *JNES* 20 (1961) 172. See *LD,* 494.

[24] Cf. Psalm 148:5–6: "Let [angels, sun and moon, stars, heavens, waters above the heavens, vv. 2–4] praise Yahweh's name; for Yahweh commanded and they were created, assigned them duties forever, gave them tasks [*ḥōq*] that will never end."

by the great gods, however, seems implicit in most cosmogonies, because cosmogonies were often recited to persuade the gods to reassert the original *design* of creation.

9. A Neo-Babylonian tablet on the creation of humans (VAT 17019) was published by Werner Mayer in 1987. Approximately three-quarters of its original forty-five lines are preserved.[25] Its final exhortation to loyalty to the king is so similar to Assurbanipal's coronation prayer as to suggest that the function of the text was to ground reverence for the king in creation.

²[*tur*]*ned away* was [their (=the laboring gods)] *coun*[*tenance . . .*]
Bēlet-ilī [their] mistress, *was fri*[*ghtened at*] their (oppressed) *silence;*
to Ea, her twin brother, she sp[eaks] a word:
⁵"Labor has [become burden]some to them:
brought near is . . [. . . . .] . . the belt [. . .]
Turned away is [*their countenance, and*] hostility has [broken] out.
Let us create (*banû*) a clay figure on which to impose [*the labor*];
from weariness let us give them (=the gods) rest fo[rever]."
¹⁰Ea rose to speak, [directing a wo]rd to *Bēlet-ilī:*
"[Bēlet]-ilī, you are the mistress of the great gods.
[. . . . . . .] . . . . later;
[. .] . . . . [. . .] . . his hands."
Then Bēlet-ilī snipped off the clay (*karāṣu ṭiṭṭa*) for him (=the man);
¹⁵[. . . . . .] . . she acted skillfully.
[. . . . *she pur*]*ified and* mixed the clay for him.
[. . . . .] adorned his body,
[. . . . .] his entire form.
[. . . . . . .] . . . he/she placed,
²⁰[. . . . . . .] . . . he/she placed,
[. . . . . . .] . . . he/she placed,
[. . . . . . .] . . . placed [*his*] body.
[. . . . . . .] Ellil, the hero of the great gods,
[when . . . . . .]. . he saw him, [*his*] *fa*[*ce*] shone,
²⁵[. . . . . *in the ass*]*embly* of the gods he looked at [. . .] from all sides,
[. . . . . . .] . . he *com*[*pleted*] his bodily form.
[. . . . . .El]lil, the hero of the great gods,

[25] "Ein Mythos von der Erschaffung des Menschen und des Königs," *Or* 56 (1987) 55–68. The upper fourth of the tablet is broken off, and the left half of the lower fourth is damaged on the obverse and reverse. Uncertain words are in italics. My rendering of Mayer's translation.

[*lullû-man*(?)] *he made* its name;
[the lab]or of the gods he ordered to be imposed on him.
30Ea rose to speak, directing a word to Bēlet-ilī
"Bēlet-ilī, you are the mistress of the great gods.
You have created (*banû*) lullû-man (*lullû*[-*amēlu*]):
form (*patāqu*) now the king, the thinking-deciding man!
With excellence cover his whole form,
35form (*banû*) his features in harmony, make his whole body beautiful!"
Then Bēlet-ilī formed the king, the thinking-deciding man.
The great gods gave the king the battle.
Anu gave him the crown, Ellil ga[ve him the throne],
Nergal gave him the weapons, Ninurta ga[ve him shining splendor],
40Bēlet-ilī gave [him a handsome appea]rance.
Nusku gave instruction, imparted counsel *and sto*[*od by him in service*].
Whoever speaks [falsehood and deception] to the king,
if it is an . . . . , [he will . . . .]

The text presupposes that the lower class of gods have rebelled against
their servitude. Human beings are being created as substitute workers.
The same story is told in the Sumerian tale of *Enki and Ninmah* and
the Akkadian *Atrahasis*. In those stories Ea and the mother goddess create,
Ea providing the "form" and the mother goddess doing the actual shaping. New in this text is the detailed readying of the man in lines 17–22
(presuming Enlil is the subject in lines 23 and 27), Enlil's prominence
in naming and defining human tasks, and the sharp distinction between
(ordinary) human beings and the king. Mayer points to a number of verbal
correspondences to other works: "to nip off clay"=*Gilgamesh* I.ii.34b,
and see *Atrahasis* ("to mix clay"=I.211, 226, 231 (Old Babylonian); "to
impose compulsory labor"=*Gilgamesh* I.241, II.vii.31 (Old Babylonian),
and cf. "to bear compulsory labor" in *Atrahasis* I.191, 197, G.ii.12 (Old
Babylonian), and *dulla emēdu* in *Enūma elish* VI.8, 34, 36, 130); "to make
lullû-man"=*Enūma elish* VI.7, *Atrahasis* I.195 and G.ii.9 (Old Babylonian); "to give rest from weariness"=*Enūma elish* VI.8, 12, 130.

The text is especially concerned with the creation of the king and his
endowment with every virtue needed to rule. He is distinguished from
lullû, presumably man in the primitive state before culture, for Enkidu
in *Gilgamesh* is called *lullû* before he enters the city and submits to the
king. Several royal inscriptions and hymns describe the gods endowing
the king for rule. The translation of the royal epithet *maliku-amēlu* is

uncertain. It can be translated simply as "prince, king" (*mal[i]ku*) but Mayer prefers to take *maliku* as the participle of *malāku* ("the thinking-deciding man"), a special kind of man. The final warning to be loyal is paralleled in Assurbanipal's throne prayer.

Conclusions from the Minor Cosmogonies[26]

The minor cosmogonies are all "function-bound," i.e., part of an operation or ritual. They provide the setting or essential information for an operation. They are not exploratory as in the next section.

The creator gods. The creator is distinct from the created, indicating genuine creation rather than evolution or spontaneous generation. Anu is sole creator in text no. 1, and Marduk (evidently displacing Ea) in no. 6. Nos. 3 and 4 have two creators—Anu and Ea, each creating his half of the world. There are three creators in nos. 2, 5, 7 (and presumably 8a and 8b)—the triad Anu, Enlil, and Ea. Creation takes place in a single act (nos. 1, 2, 3, 4, 6, probably 8b), though in nos. 5, 7a, and 8a prior planning is mentioned, like the planning of Marduk in *Enūma elish* IV.135–136 and VI.2–4.

Several texts depict "secondary causes" creating rather than the great gods creating directly. Nos. 1a and 1b have a sequence of creations: Anu creates the heavens, the heavens create the earth, earth creates the rivers, the rivers create the canals, the canals create the marsh, and the marsh creates the worm. How each element creates is not explained. In no. 2, River is "creator of everything" though the gods created the riverbed and banks; Ea endowed River with godly splendor and Ea and Marduk gave him wise judgment.

The gods create directly in nos. 4 and 6. In no. 3 the gods create their proper domain—Anu creates heaven and Ea creates Apsu. In no. 5 the gods plan and create but hand over to the king responsibility for maintenance (line 76). In nos. 5 and 8a the gods plan and assign astral roles, and in no. 8b they create and design. In Nos. 4, 5, 7b (both versions), and 9 the gods create the king, presumably to oversee their human servants.

Modes of creation. There is no single underlying concept as is shown by the wide variety of verbs of creation, e.g., *šūpû*, "to make appear" (7a; 8a:8; see *Enūma elish* V:12); *zu'uzu*, "to distribute, allot" (8b:4);

---

[26] These remarks are indebted to Bottéro, *AEPHE*, 128–35.

uddû, "to design" (8b:2m 4; see *Enūma elish* I:76; V:3). The phrase *šuma nabû,* "to give a name" (6:16, 24, see *Enūma elish* I.1), occurs in creation contexts.

Many verbs come from the area of architecture and building: *šuršudu,* "to found, establish a foundation" (8b:3, see *Enūma elish* I.77; V.6); *ramû,* "to raise high (a building)" (6:13); *kašāru,* "to repair (ruined walls, buildings, and especially temples)" (7a:2); *bašāmu,* "to fashion, form, build, design, lay out (a building, arable land)"; "to create (plan, dust, bow)" (1b:1, see *Enūma elish* V.122); *kunnu,* "to establish solidly" (3:2; 7b:2; 8b:3; see *Enūma elish* I.71; 5:8, 62); *epēšu,* "make" (often of buildings)" (6; 7b:2; see *Enūma elish* V.122); *patāqu* (4.36; 9:33, 36), "to form, shape (walls, temples; heaven and earth, humans)." By far the most common verb is *banû,* "to build," which sometimes alternates with *epēšu* (1a; 2; 4; 6; 7a; 8a; 8b; 9; see *Enūma elish* I.9, 12, 45, 105; IV.145; V.48, etc.). The verb *banû,* however, means not only "to construct" but also "to beget, generate."[27]

Different manual activity can be included under creation: *ḫerû,* "to dig a canal or cistern" (2:2); *karāṣu ṭiṭṭa,* "to pinch off a fistful of clay" (4:26; 9:14); *rakāšu,* "to tie together (a raft)" (6:17); *mullû,* "to heap up a pile" (6:31). Two verbs in their literal meaning imply sexual generation (possibly a vestige of Sumerian cosmic marriage): *reḫû,* "to engender" (3:1; see *Enūma elish* I.80), and *(w)alādu,* "to beget" (1bc; see *Enūma elish* I.16, 115).

There is no evidence of a precreation period as in the Sumerian Nippur tradition. The verbs of building (the majority) imply a *materia ex qua.* Nos. 4 and 9 say that man was nipped from clay; no. 6 says that before creation all was sea (*tâmtu*), but sea is not personalized like Apsu and Tiamat in *Enūma elish.*

Context of creation. Presupposed in the cosmogonies is that destinies or characterizations were fixed on the day of creation. This presupposition is especially clear in the incantations (texts no. 1), disputations (no. 7), astrological treatises (no. 8), and the creation and endowing of the king (no. 9). The first time is the authority-filled moment, for then divine intent is freshest and most visible. The worm was meant to eat rotten fruit, the character of the tamarisk and palm was set so that their *essential* traits can play off one another in the ensuing debate, the heavenly

---

[27] It has the same wide range as **banaya,* "to build," in Ugaritic.

bodies were arranged for the human race to measure time by, and the king has been endowed with special authority over his human subjects.

The temple is central to nos. 4–6. Why? Because the gods created the human race for their service and the temple is the place where they collect their due. The king is also central for the same reason — the human race has to be organized to deliver their services to the gods and the temple has to built as the site of divine-human encounter. In texts 4–6, the gods first form the marshes, where the raw materials of the archaic temples (reeds and clay) are to be found.

The minor Akkadian cosmogonies thus reveal no one invariable mode of creation, though Anu, Enlil, and Ea, or heaven and earth, invariably initiate it. Despite a uniform belief that the world was created by the gods for their own benefit, the articulations of that belief differed greatly. Composers worked with great freedom.

B. Anthological Cosmogonies

In sharp contrast to the single-scene Akkadian cosmogonies discussed above are two lengthy narratives — *Atrahasis* (1,245 lines according to the third tablet of the Nur-Aya edition) and *Enūma elish* (ca. 1,100 lines in seven tablets). In each the actual fashioning of the world is one part of a lengthy story. In *Atrahasis* the formation of humans occupies only lines +189–260+ of tablet I. In *Enūma elish* the opening theogony takes up only the first twenty lines of tablet I, and Marduk's formation of the cosmos fills the latter part of tablet IV to the middle of tablet VI. Yet one cannot remove these texts of actual fashioning from their narrative context without misrepresenting the view of creation in these narratives. In *Atrahasis* the creation of man is the climax of section one — the rebellion of the lesser gods — and the indispensable preface to section two on the flood and restoration. The opening theogony of *Enūma elish* introduces the two rival royal lines (Anshar-Anu-Ea-Marduk and Apsu-Tiamat-Kingu) that are central to the story, and Marduk's construction of the universe in tablets IV–VI constitutes the basis for his rule over gods and human beings.

The single-scene cosmogonies of section A are functional in a strict sense. They are bound to a single operation, giving essential information for its performance, e.g., how to cure an ailment, dedicate a temple properly, provide the context for an entertaining debate, show that heavenly bodies are divine signs determining the times for rituals.[28] Anthological cosmogonies on the other hand occur within a story. The story explores broad questions such as divine governance and the purpose of human society, in addition to cultural themes such as knowledge, social boundaries, and mortality. One might say that the single-scene cosmogony is explanatory and the anthological cosmogony is exploratory. The entire epics of *Atrahasis* and *Enūma elish* become cosmogonies from the creation accounts within them. When applied to the epics, "anthological" and "compendious" do not imply a bundle of traditions but a coherent whole. Any discussion of the two epics must reckon with their narrative contexts.

The tendency to develop Sumerian stories into lengthy narrative marks Old and Middle Babylonian literature. Jeffrey Tigay has demonstrated that the Old Babylonian *Gilgamesh* has transformed Sumerian tales of the legendary king of Uruk into a unified epic.[29] *Atrahasis* formed a new story from the Sumerian myth of *Enki and Ninmah* and the *Sumerian Flood Story,* and *Enūma elish* did the same with the Ninurta traditions, among other sources.

1. Atrahasis

The myth begins in the period when only gods existed and lesser gods, the Igigu, did the menial labor for the senior Anunnaki gods. After laboring for many years the Igigu refused to serve. The crisis was resolved by Enki and the mother goddess by creating human surrogate-workers from clay and the flesh and blood of an Igigu god. After 600 years the human race increased in such numbers that their noise kept Enlil and the other gods from sleep; he and his fellows took steps to destroy the human race by a series of plagues culminating in a world-wide flood. Only Atrahasis and his family survived, building at Enki's suggestion a boat to ride out the flood. The gods, deprived of their human servants, realized how

[28] According to Bottéro, minor cosmogonies are neither doctrinal "treatises" nor objective, disinterested, didactic reports. They typically occur in the *legomena* of prayers or in prefaces to *dromena* (*AEPHE,* 87).

[29] J. Tigay, *The Evolution of the Gilgamesh Epic* (Philadelphia: University of Pennsylvania, 1982). Bottéro sees *Atrahasis, Enūma elish,* and the *Erra Epic* as the three great literary works after Hammurabi (1792–1750 B.C.). They differ from earlier works not only by their length but also by their new vision of the world and interpretation of the myths, *LD,* 526.

dependent on their human workers they had become. Therefore they relented and allowed repopulation while adding safeguards against over-population — mortality and limits on reproduction.[30]

The epic is most completely preserved in the Old Babylonian version written by the scribe Nur-Aya in the eleventh and twelfth year of the reign of Ammi-saduqa of Babylon (ca. 1685 B.C.). Other manuscripts of the same or later periods, Middle and Late Babylonian as well as Late Assyrian, agree with the version of Nur-Aya, though a few diverge widely. The tablets were not fully published in their proper sequence until 1969, though fragments had been known for over a century.[31] Over 700 lines of the Old Babylonian recension have now been published in addition to other recensions. Lacunae remain and some issues are still controverted but the plot and meaning of the whole are fairly clear.

Old traditions were incorporated into the epic. The first part of the epic — the rebellion of the Igigu gods and the formation of human beings as substitute workers — draws on the Eridu story of *Enki and Ninmah*.[32] In the Sumerian myth, the *formatio* of man is followed by a bibulous feast at which Ninmah creates seven defective humans, with Enki finding useful occupations for each. The second part of *Atrahasis*, the flood, uses a flood tradition (in a short or long version) attested in the *Sumerian Flood Story*, in some versions of the *Sumerian King List*,[33] in the standard

[30] That the main issue was overpopulation is argued by the following: A. D. Kilmer, in "The Mesopotamian Concept of Overpopulation and Its Solution as Reflected in Mythology," *Or* 41 (1972) 160–77; W. L. Moran, "Atrahasis: The Babylonian Story of the Flood," *Bib* 40 (1971) 51–61 and see n. 31; T. Frymer-Kensky, "The Atrahasis Epic and Its Significance for Our Understanding of Genesis 1–9," *BA* 40 (1977) 147–55; and V. Fritz, "'Solange die Erde steht'—Vom Sinn der jahwistischen Fluterzählung," *ZAW* 94 (1982) 599–614.

[31] Lambert-Millard, *Atra-hasis*, give a history of interpretation on pp. 1–5. I follow their line numbering. The following should be noted in the large bibliography: W. L. Moran's review of Lambert and Millard in *Bib* 52 (1971) 51–61, and his "Some Considerations of Form and Interpretation in *Atra-Hasis*," in *Language, Literature, and History: Philological and Historical Studies Presented to Erica Reiner* (ed. F. Rochberg-Halton; AOS Monograph 67; Winona Lake, IN: Eisenbrauns, 1987) 245–55; R. A. Oden, "Divine Aspirations in Genesis 1–11," *ZAW* 93 (1981) 197–216; and Dalley, *MFM*, 1–38, for the most recent English translation.

[32] The *formatio* of man by Enki and the mother goddess is also attested in VAT 17019, but it is late (the beginning of the first millennium) according to its editor, W. Mayer, "Ein Mythos von der Erschaffung," 55.

[33] According to Jacobsen's standard study, *The Sumerian King List*, 5–61, the flood story is an Eridu addition of the Isin-Larsa period (ca. 1969–1700 B.C.) to the king list.

version of *Gilgamesh* XI, and in the *Rulers of Lagash.* Both the Eridu story of *Enki and Ninmah* and the flood traditions were already parts of cosmogonies—*Enki and Ninmah* beginning with the separation of heaven and earth, and the longer version of the flood tradition continuing the story of creation.

The composer of *Atrahasis* vigorously shaped the old traditions into an artistic unity. Cross-references between the two original myths, proportions of lines per scene, and the plot all show artistry and sophistication. The Igigu myth of the rebellious gods is the preface to the myth of the deluge and prefigures its main points: the sleeping Enlil is wakened // the sleepless Enlil; the noise of the Igigu // the noise of human beings; the failure of Nusku's mission // the failure of the plagues and deluge; the resolution of the crisis by Enki and Mami creating man // the resolution of the crisis by Enki and Mami restoring their creation. The distribution of lines among the episodes unifies the action and determines narrative time. The Igigu myth consists of about 320 lines, about the same number as is devoted to the plagues (340); the Igigu rebellion and the plagues take up the first 660 lines, just about the midpoint in this poem of 1245 lines. The proportions have been charted by William Moran.[34]

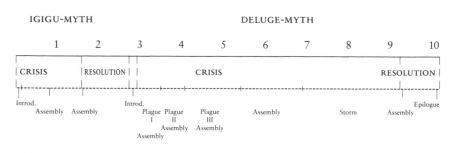

=125 lines

The best indication of artistic design is the plot, which unites diverse traditions into a story. The story begins, "When gods were man, / they bore the toil, the basket lugged. / The basket of the gods being large, / And heavy the toil, the suffering much."[35] The Anunnaki gods (who include Anu, Enlil, and Enki) assigned tasks to the Igigu gods as part

---

[34] Moran, "Some Considerations," 253, for themes; 245–47 for proportions of lines. The chart appears on p. 246.

[35] Translation of Moran, "Some Considerations," 247, with discussion. The exact translation is controverted (a simile or a metaphor?) but not its general import.

of the original settlement by which they "had cast lots and had divided" the universe among themselves (I.i.12, see lines 7–18). Anu took heaven, Enlil took earth, and Enki took the underground waters. After many years the Igigu grow weary of serving the Anunnaki and go on strike, burning their weapons and belligerently surrounding Enlil's dwelling. Enlil hides behind his vizier, Nusku. The Anunnaki demand that the chief rebel god be given up (I.iii.140–41); the Igigu refuse, taking collective responsibility. Anu concedes that the grievances are legitimate: "What are we accusing them of? / Their work was heavy, their distress was much!" (I.iv.176–77).[36] To solve the problem of who will now serve them, the gods ask the mother goddess (called Mami/Mama, Nintu, and *Belet-ilī*) to create man: "Let the birth-goddess create . . . , / And let man bear the toil of the gods" (I.iv.190–1). Enki and the birth goddess together create man (fourteen males and fourteen females in the later Assyrian recension) from clay and the flesh and blood of the slaughtered god.

The second section can be entitled (from its fourth and climactic plague) "the deluge." It begins with a thirty-line introduction (I.vi.321–vii.351). The creation of man has not been entirely successful. Human beings indeed toil in place of the Igigu, making new picks and spades and constructing canals (lines 337–338), but their noise (*rigmu // ḫubūru*) has disturbed Enlil, god of the earth. "600 years, less than 600 years, passed" and "the country was as noisy as a bellowing bull" (I.vii.354).[37] The gods send a plague of disease to wipe human beings out but Enki thwarts it by advising Atrahasis to direct all the people's offerings exclusively to Namtara (I.vii.352–415). His plan is successful: Namtara averts the plague. The gods' second plague, drought (ca. 30 lines longer than the first plague), is again nullified by Enki's advice to humans to direct their attention to Adad (II.i.1–ii; ca. 36 lines), that he might "rain down a mist in the mornings and may furtively rain down a dew in the night, so that fields will furtively bear ninefold" (II.ii.16–19). Enlil devises a third plague, renewing the drought somehow, but this too is foiled.[38] There follows the fourth and climactic plague, the flood (II.ii.ca. 37–v.5; ca. 65 lines longer than the second). Enki, now under oath not to leak any more secrets

[36] Anu quotes the opening lines of the poem: "heavy the toil, the suffering much" (I.i.3–4). The gods admit that their original creation was flawed, preparing the reader for the revision of creation.

[37] Dalley, *MFM*.

[38] The text is broken off and the course of action unclear. See Lambert-Millard, *Atra-hasis*, 10–11.

to human beings,[39] addresses the wall rather than Atrahasis who sits behind it; he speaks of a boat large enough to ride out the impending deluge. Atrahasis takes the hint and built a boat. Enki's subversion of the gods' plan causes a crisis in the assembly (ca. 175 lines). Although the gods denounce him for voiding the plagues, Enki is too much the parent to destroy the human beings whom he helped to create.

The loss of their human servants brings home to the gods that they cannot do without the human race and that its destruction was ill-advised. As Enki and the mother goddess resolved the first crisis by creating human substitutes for the gods, so they resolve the second by revising their creation. At Enlil's command, Enki summons Nintu (III.vi.43–44). In the first part of Enki's instruction to the mother goddess, Lambert plausibly restores (from the similar, and dependent, *Gilgamesh* X.vi.30–32), "[You] birth-goddess, creatress of destinies, / [Assign death] to the peoples" (III.vi.47–48).[40] In the revised creation human population cannot be without limit, and so death is to be part of the new order. Human beings were, of course, always capable of dying violently, "unnaturally," as in the flood; even an Igigu god could be killed. But in the preflood era, there was no innate mortality.[41]

Enki further revises his creation to limit the population:

> vii.1In addition let there be one-third of the people,
> Among the people the woman who gives birth yet does
> Not give birth (successfully);
> Let there be the *pašittu*-demon among the people,
> To snatch the baby from its mother's lap.
> Establish *ugbabtu, entu, egisītu*-women:
> They shall be taboo, and thus control childbirth.[42]

[39] Moran, "Some Considerations," 251.

[40] "The Theology of Death," in *Death in Mesopotamia* (ed. B. Alster; Mesopotamia 8; XXVI Rencontre assyriologique internationale; Copenhagen: Akademisk, 1980) 58. Mortality is a postdiluvian innovation in both *Atrahasis* and *Gilgamesh*. Lambert's restoration and interpretation has been accepted by Jacobsen in the abstract of his talk in *Death in Mesopotamia*; Moran, "Some Considerations," 254, by C. Wilcke, "Göttliche und menschliche Weisheit im Alten Orient," *Weisheit: Archäologie der literarischen Kommunikation III* (Munich: Fink, 1991) 260, and by J. Bottéro, *LD*, 528.

[41] In Gilgamesh XI, Utnapishtim is immortal by virtue of belonging to the preflood generation. Enlil allows him and his wife to live "at the mouth of the rivers" (XI.193–96), but does not need to give them immortality.

[42] Dalley, *MFM*, 35. There are twenty-nine lines missing at the end of col. vii and eight

The human population will be limited by infertile women, demons who attack infants, groups of celibate women, and perhaps other means also. A brief epilogue concludes the piece (III.viii.11–19). The coherent plot just outlined thus demonstrates that ancient traditions have been woven into a unity.

The creation of man in Atrahasis: The most remarkable aspect of creation in *Atrahasis* is the creation of humans (I.iv–v). It continues the Sumerian tradition of *formatio* from moistened clay, adding to the material the blood and "ghost" of a god. The epic is "the most important single witness to Babylonian speculation on the origins and nature of man."[43] The lines on the creation of man (192–248) constitutes a unit: a separate scene precedes (the gods deciding to create) and follows it (the birth goddess creating); key words form lines 192–193 reappear in lines 246–248 to form an *inclusio*. The text is exceptionally difficult even though the ordinary meaning of the words is known.

The broad context is the rebellion of the Igigu gods, which requires a new creature to labor in their stead. The gods command Mami, a birth goddess (called Nintu here), to create *lullû*-man to bear the yoke assigned by Enlil (lines 194–197). She agrees on condition that Enki provide the purified clay (lines 198–203). He draws a bath to cleanse the gods from the impurity, a result probably of the death of the god in lines 204–209. Enki speaks.

> "On[44] the first, seventh, and fifteenth of the month
> I shall make a purification by washing.
> Then one god should be slaughtered.
> And the gods can be purified by immersion.
> Nintu shall mix clay
> With his flesh and his blood.
> Then a god and a man
> Will be mixed together in clay.
> Let us hear the drumbeat forever after,

---

lines missing at the beginning of col. viii. Obviously, much is missing from the directives of the renewed creation.

[43] Moran, "The Creation of Man in Atrahasis I 192–248," *BASOR* 200 (1970) 48–56. The quote is from p. 48. My discussion is much indebted to him and to Bottéro, "La création de l'homme et sa nature dans le poème d'Atrahasis," *Societies and Languages of the Ancient Near East: Studies in Honor of I. M. Diakonoff* (ed. M. A. Dandamaer; Jersey, 1982) 24–32.

[44] Translation of Dalley, *MFM*, 15.

Let a ghost come into existence from the god's flesh,
Let her proclaim it as his living sign,
And let the ghost exist so as not to forget (the slain god)."
They answered "Yes!" in the assembly,
The great Anunnaki who assign the fates.

Enki commands Nintu to mix the slaughtered god's flesh and blood with the clay he will supply. The Akkadian phrase "forever" usually occurs in contexts where something is to be commemorated; the drum (heartbeat, pulse?) will commemorate, it seems, the dead god for all time. The next stanza describes how the ghost (*etemmu*) of the dead god, instead of wandering about, will remain in the god's flesh, which now (with the blood) becomes the *materia ex qua* of man. There seems to be a play on *etemmu* ("ghost") and *ṭēmu* ("intelligence") of the dead god; the intelligence (and heartbeat?) of man comes from the god. The clever Enki determines the "formula" for man: clay from the terrestrial world and intelligence from the gods.[45]

There is a new emphasis on human beings in the epic. *Formatio* is the climax and resolution of the Igigu story, and the spread of the human race is the cause of the deluge. The length and subtlety of the account of man's origin is particularly striking, since Mesopotamian cosmogonies routinely portrayed human beings simply as slaves of the gods, cogs in the machinery for divine care and feeding. Human beings are important to the plot; even when offstage they move the action forward. The opening words are "When gods were man," and the resolution of the gods' strike is a statement of the essential purpose of the human race. The second section further explores the nature of man. Mortality and limited procreation are the conditions for living peacefully with the gods in the postdiluvian age. Without such limits, the human race will expand beyond the capacity of the land to support it. The immediate issue is overpopulation, perhaps more precisely problems attendant upon early-second-

---

[45] Bottéro, "La creation de l'homme," 25. On pp. 26–27, he effectively refutes Wolfram von Soden's unwillingness to read *etemmu* in its ordinary meaning of "ghost" on the grounds that a ghost is not necessarily a disturbing demon and can have a benign meaning. See von Soden, "Der Mensch bescheidet sich nicht: Überlegungen zu Schöpfungserzählungen in Babylonien und Israel," in *Symbolae Biblicae et Mesopotamicae Francisco Mario Theodoro de Liagre Böhl dedicatae* (ed. M. A. Beek et al.; Leiden: Brill, 1973) 349–58, reprinted in *Bibel und Alter Orient* (BZAW 162; Berlin: de Gruyter, 1985) 165–73.

millennium urbanization, but the deeper question concerns the uneasy relationship between the gods and the human population.

Atrahasis cannot be reduced to an anthropology, however, for it also speaks about the gods, often savagely.[46] The sovereign freedom of the gods is limited by their need for the human race. Creation of humankind was necessary for peace in the divine world, and its restoration was necessary for the gods to live in the idleness that befits them. The scornful portrait of Enlil goes a step further. He is cowardly and incompetent (even the other gods recognize it), willing to destroy the human race for short-term comfort without giving a thought to the consequences. Yet his will prevails. The relationship between man and gods is an uneasy tradeoff; the human race is too essential to be annihilated even though its entire purpose is to serve the gods. The picture is not entirely black and white, however. Enki and the mother goddess are committed to the human race and individuals like Atrahasis have special access to heaven.

Atrahasis and Genesis 2–11: It has been widely recognized, especially since the edition of W. G. Lambert and A. R. Millard, that the plot of *Atrahasis* resembles Genesis 2–11.[47] The sequence of events in both is the same: the creation of humans, their offending of the god(s), the flood and the privileged survivor, the restoration. Further comments will be made under Genesis 1–11, but one issue must be discussed here because it is proper to *Atrahasis* — the nature of the noise that offended Enlil and brought upon the human race the plagues and flood. Many scholars believe that the noise (*rigmu* // *ḫubūru*) made by the human race is not morally neutral (a simple result of overpopulation) but symbolizes the exceeding of divinely assigned limits; the race is in some way guilty.[48]

---

[46] Only the *gods'* behavior is subjected to psychological scrutiny; their interaction in the assembly is drawn with mordant realism. No human being receives the same scrutiny.

[47] Already pointed out by Moran in *Bib* 52 (1971) 61–62, and developed by Oden, in "Divine Aspirations," 197–216, and in "Transformations in Near Eastern Myths: Genesis 1–11 and the Old Babylonian Epic of Atrahasis," *Religion* 11 (1981) 21–37; R. Albertz, "Die Kulturarbeit im Atramhasis-Epos im Vergleich zur biblischen Urgeschichte," in *Werden und Wirken des Alten Testaments: Festschrift Claus Westermann* (ed. R. Albertz et al.; Neukirchen-Vluyn: Vandenhoeck & Ruprecht, 1980) 38–57; and C. Westermann, *Genesis 1–11: A Commentary* (Minneapolis: Augsburg, 1984) 68–69.

[48] The argument for moral fault in *rigmu* is well summarized by Oden, "Divine Aspirations," 204–10, and answered by Moran, "Some Considerations," 251–55. Those holding that noise does not imply moral fault include, among others, Moran (nn. 3 and 4), Kilmer (n. 3), Jacobsen (n. 12) and Albertz (n. 19).

The main arguments that *rigmu* is a moral fault are: (1) the issue cannot be overpopulation alone, since overpopulation is not elsewhere mentioned as a problem in Mesopotamian literature; (2) biblical and classical texts suggest that the deluge was a punishment for sin; (3) the noise of humans in section two echoes the rebellious noise of the Igigu in section one; (4) Enki advises Atrahasis to deflect the plagues by refusing sacrifice; (5) man is made from a rebel god and must be likewise rebellious. Each can be rebutted: (1) *Atrahasis* presents overpopulation as a problem of the *antediluvian* rather than postdiluvian period; (2) *rigmu* retains its ordinary meaning—"noise" as a sign of population (its absence signifying desolation and its presence, a crowd); (3) biblical and classical examples cannot alter the fact that in *this* literary work no human fault is mentioned; (4) Enki does not suggest refusal of sacrifice *per se* but rather concentration of all sacrifices on the god most likely to avert the particular plague; (5) the similarities between parts one and two of the epic are only suggestive not determinative. In short, the weight of evidence strongly suggests that the human race committed no other fault than expanding beyond the capacity of the land to support it.

One last question: is the creation of man separate from the creation of the world? No, the creation of man is part and parcel of the creation of the world. The dividing of domains (I.i.1–18) by Anu, Enlil, and Enki is part of creation, as it is in the opening lines of the cosmogonic introduction to the Sumerian composition *Gilgamesh, Enkidu, and the Underworld*. Like its Sumerian model, *Enki and Ninmah, Atrahasis* begins with a problem: the earth and its canals have just been created, but who will maintain them—the lesser gods or a new kind of creature, man? *Menschenschöpfung* is not an afterthought; it is intrinsically related to *Weltschöpfung*.

2. Enūma elish

Enūma elish, a work in seven tablets, is sometimes called the standard Mesopotamian creation text.[49] Its story begins before there were any

[49] E. A. Speiser entitles it "The Creation Epic" in *ANET,* 60–72; J. Bottéro calls it "L'Epopée de la Création ou les Hautfaits de Marduk et son sacre," in *AEPHE,* 77–126, reprinted in Bottéro, *Mythes et rites de Babylone,* 113–62; Dalley names it "The Epic of Creation," *MFM,* 228–77. Biblical scholars routinely so term it, e.g., L. Fisher, "Creation at Ugarit and in the Old Testament," *VT* 15 (1965) 320–21; A. Kapelrud, "Creation in

gods—when the primordial waters Apsu and Tiamat were an undifferentiated mass and neither land nor gods existed. Then gods were born: the pairs Lahmu and Lahamu, Anshar and Kishar, Anu and then Ea. The gods' activity provokes Apsu's hostility, but before he takes any action Ea slays the sleeping Apsu with a spell and builds a palace on the corpse. Settled in the palace, Ea and Damkina give birth to Marduk, who turns out to be greater than any predecessor. His noisy play wakens Tiamat to vengeful rage; she commissions Kingu to destroy the gods, arming him with the Tablet of Destinies. Anshar in response invites first Anu and then Ea to lead the army, but both turn back in fear. Ea proposes Marduk as leader. He accepts on the condition that the assembly transfer to him its power of fixing destinies (*šīmātu*). So assured, Marduk marches forth and in single combat kills Tiamat, making from her split body the upper and lower halves of the universe. The grateful gods give Marduk "Anuship." He announces that Babylon will henceforth be their residence, and commands Ea to form from the blood of the slain Kingu a new creature, man, to manage the universe. The gods build Marduk a city and a temple and glorify him with fifty names.

Thanks to new advances in dating and identifying its sources, it is possible to interpret *Enūma elish* and its cosmogonies with more precision than before. The Old Babylonian date once generally assigned to *Enūma elish*[50] is now recognized to be too early; most scholars today prefer either a late Kassite (fourteenth to twelfth centuries B.C.) or Isin II (Nebuchadnezzar I, 1125–1104 B.C.) date. Scholars point out that the supremacy of Marduk over all the gods attested in *Enūma elish* is not attested in Old Babylonian times; in the late eighteenth-century B.C. Code of Hammurabi, Marduk is supreme over the earth but not over the gods. Only in the reign of Nebuchadnezzar I of Babylon (1125–1104 B.C.) did the old triad of Anu, Enlil, and Ea yield completely to Marduk.[51] He replaced the

the Ras Shamra Texts," *ST* 34 (1980) 1, 5–6; B. Margalit, "The Ugaritic Creation Myth: Fact or Fiction," *UF* 13 (1981), *passim*. Heidel, *Babylonian Genesis*, pp. 10–11, denies that it is primarily a creation epic; it is first and foremost a literary monument in honor of Marduk as the champion of the gods and the creator of heaven and earth.

[50] So Heidel, *Babylonian Genesis*, 14; Speiser, *ANET*, 60; Edzard, *WM*, 122. Line numbers for *Enūma elish* are according to *ANET* except for tablet II, which is numbered according to F. N. H. Al-Rawi and A. R. George, "Tablets from the Sippar Library: II. Tablet II of the Babylonian Creation Epic," *Iraq* 52 (1990) 149–57, especially n. 5.

[51] Lambert, "The Reign of Nebuchadnezzar I: A Turning Point in the History of Ancient

triad of Anu, Enlil, and Ea rather than joining it, since Semites (unlike Sumerians) preferred to worship very few high gods.[52] Originally without a place in the pantheon and lacking a mythology, Marduk had to appropriate other gods' traditions to become supreme. Inevitably, therefore, *Enūma elish* is an anthology of traditions about other gods.

The epic became a much copied sacred text; its sixth and seventh tablets containing Marduk's fifty names were favorites of commentators. It was recited in its entirety on the fourth day of the New Year festival. Its influence extended down to Berossus' third-century B.C. digest *Babylonaica* and even to the Neoplatonist Damascius' *Aporia* of the fifth century A.D.

Enūma elish depends on Ninurta traditions, especially those found in the Akkadian *Myth of Anzu*. The *Myth of Anzu* is extant in a fragmentary Old Babylonian and relatively complete standard version.[53] The plots of both versions of Anzu are similar to that of *Enūma elish:* after the failure of the old gods to stand up to the monster, a young hero defeats him and is honored by the assembly with new names. The hero can vary; in the Old Babylonian *Anzu* it is Ningirsu, and in the standard version of *Anzu* it is Ninurta; in the Babylonian version of *Enūma elish* it is Marduk and in the Assyrian version of *Enūma elish* it is Assur.

The standard version of *Anzu* begins with a crisis—the absence of water; springs have not yet supplied the Tigris and the Euphrates with water. The strange monster Anzu enters the service of Enlil only to steal the Tablet of Destinies. Anu pleads for a general to lead an army to recover them but his pleas are rejected in turn by Adad, Girra, and Shara; all claim that victory is impossible without the Tablets. Finally, the young

---

Mesopotamian History," in *The Seed of Wisdom: Essays in Honor of T. J. Meek* (ed. W. S. McCollough; Toronto: University of Toronto, 1964) 3–13. The first evidence of total supremacy comes from the reign of Nebuchadnezzar I, when a boundary stone of the period calls Marduk *šar ilāni*, "the king of the gods"; thereafter his kingship over the gods is commonly attested. A date in the Kassite period is defended by W. Sommerfeld, *Der Aufstieg Marduks: die Stellung Marduks in der babylonischen Religion des zweiten Jahrtausends v. Chr.* (AOAT 213; Kevelaer: Butzon & Bercker, 1982) 174, and "Marduk," *RLA* 7:368. Dalley, *MFM*, 228–30, also argues against a post-Kassite date.

[52] W. Sommerfeld, "Marduk," 368.

[53] Dalley, *MFM*, incorporates the important new tablet GM (published by H. W. F. Saggs, in "Additions to Anzu," *AfO* 33 [1986] 1–29), which provides I.67–93, 139–48, 211–13; II.1–155 [complete]; III.1–48, x+50-x+75, 113–69, 175–81. W. L. Moran, "Notes on Anzu," *AfO* 35 (1988) 24–29, makes important corrections to Saggs.

god Ninurta marches forth, ordered by Mami the mother goddess. Ninurta's first volley of arrows is repelled by Anzu, using the Tablets. Ninurta's personified weapon Sharur returns to Ea for instructions and is told that Ninurta should lop off Anzu's wings with his arrows.[54] The strategy achieves victory, and Ninurta brings abundant water to the fields. The gods welcome him back, granting him dominion and acclaiming him with many names.

Lambert has clearly demonstrated direct dependence of *Enūma elish* on the Old Babylonian version of *Anzu* by pointing to specific borrowings: in *Anzu* three gods turn down the invitation to fight Anzu before Ninurta accepts, and in *Enūma elish* Ea and Anu refuse to march before Marduk accepts; in Sumerian traditions eleven monsters oppose Ninurta, and the same number appear in *Enūma elish* I.146 even though *Enūma elish* I.133–146 names only eight, indicating that the number eleven is a borrowing; the Tablet of Destinies fits awkwardly in *Enūma elish* but not in *Anzu,* where its disappearance initiates the dramatic action; the stock epithet of Ninurta *mutīr gimilli abīšu* ("renderer of the service of his father"), which is applied to Marduk in *Enūma elish* II.123, is unnatural Akkadian and best explained as a wooden rendering of a Sumerian original; Marduk's net (IV.95) is not a natural weapon against the monster Tiamat but perfectly appropriate against the birdlike Anzu; the blood borne on the north wind that signals victory over Tiamat (*Enūma elish* IV.131–2) is an awkward adaptation of wind-borne feathers from the defeated birdlike Anzu ("let the winds carry the feathers to give the news," in Old Babylonian *Anzu* II 70=72). The direct borrowing in *Enūma elish* from the *Myth of Anzu* in effect makes Marduk not only the new Anu, Enlil, and Ea, but the new Ninurta as well.[55]

The borrowed Ninurta traditions shed light on Marduk's battle with Tiamat, "Sea." On the grounds that the sea is not prominent in Mesopotamian literature, Jacobsen explained Marduk's battle with Tiamat in *Enūma elish* as an import via the Amorites of the West Semitic combat

---

[54] Moran, "Notes on Anzu," 27.

[55] Lambert, "Ninurta Mythology in the Babylonian Epic of Creation," *Keilschriftliche Literaturen. Ausgewählte Vorträge der XXXII. Rencontre assyriologique internationale* (ed. K. Hecker and W. Sommerfeld; Berliner Beiträge zum Vorderen Orient 6; Berlin, 1986) 55–60. See also Bottéro, "L'Epopée de la Création," *Mythes et rites,* 154–56, and S. Goldfless, "Babylonian Theogonies: Divine Origins in Ancient Mesopotamian Religion and Literature" (unpublished Ph.D. dissertation, Harvard University, 1980) 125–26.

myth between the storm god Baal and Sea, or (his later suggestion) as a reflex of the history of Kassite Babylonia in relation to the southern Sea-Land Kingdom.[56] To postulate West Semitic borrowing is unnecessary in view of Ninurta's close links to *tâmtu* attested already in the Old Babylonian and Sumerian traditions; his enemies are found in the *tâmtu*, which are bodies of water in the mountains east and northeast of the sources of the Tigris.[57] *Tâmtu* can thus be used of bodies of fresh water in mountain country and does not always refer to the salt sea. In some texts the word has a cosmological meaning, "the sea of the underworld," as in *Erra* I.152 and *Atrahasis*.[58] *Tâmtu* thus at times carries the same range of meaning as *apsû*. The implications of the meaning of Tiamat for *Enūma elish* are important.

There is no saltwater-fresh water duality in the opening lines of *Enūma elish* (I.1–20). Rather, Apsu and Tiamat are both undifferentiated primordial water. Sanford Goldfless is correct in interpreting Tiamat in this epic as the personified doublet of Apsu, created for the sake of creating rival kingships; it is not salt sea to Apsu's sweet water.[59] The poet is more interested in politics — rival lines of kingship — than in natural phenomena.

From observations on the date and traditions of the epic, we turn to its structure. There are five sections.

1. I.1–20. Theogony: the rise of the gods from Apsu-Tiamat culminating in Anu and Ea (Nudimmud).

[56] Jacobsen, "The Battle between Marduk and Tiamat," *JAOS* 88 (1968) 104–8, and "Religious Drama in Ancient Mesopotamia," in *Unity and Diversity: Essays in the History, Literature, and Religion of the Ancient Near East* (ed. H. Goedicke and J. J. M. Roberts; Baltimore: Johns Hopkins University, 1975) 63–97, especially 76. Regarding the argument of the latter article, the Kassite period is too poorly known for the argument to be convincing.

[57] Tiamat is the absolute state of the noun *tâmtu*. *Tâmat Na'iri* is Lake Van, and *tâmtu elītu* (lit. the "upper sea") is Lake Urmia as well as the Mediterranean, *CAD* E 113b s.v. *elû*. In the standard version of the *Myth of Anzu* (I.ii.20–23), Ea explains that "water of the spate" (*ellūti mê*, line 21) begot Anzu and Earth conceived him, probably meaning that "the fresh waters at the sources of the Tigris and Euphrates had once fecundated the earth, but they had remained blocked within her until released by the birth of Anzu." So W. W. Hallo and W. L. Moran, in "The First Tablet of the standard Babylonian Recension of the Anzu-Myth," *JCS* 31 (1979) 70.

[58] Lambert-Millard, *Atra-hasis*, 110, lines 1, 10; p. 118, lines 4, 11, 18; and p. 120, lines 34. For references, see Goldfless, "Babylonian Theogonies," 123–30.

[59] "Babylonian Theogonies," 127–30.

Apsu and Tiamat are separate beings, distinguished from the other pairs in I.1–13 in not having the dingir determinative of divinity. Their power is exercised first by Apsu and, after Apsu's death, by Tiamat and Kingu. This royal line is contrasted throughout the epic with another, that of Lahmu and Lahamu, Anshar and Kishar, Anu, Ea, and Marduk.

2. I.21–78. The first confrontation, between Apsu and Ea, and its resolution by Ea's victory over Apsu and his building of his shrine.

This section foreshadows the far greater conflict between Marduk and Tiamat. The new gods' activity irritates the primordial pair, who seek to destroy them. Ea slays Apsu with a magic spell and builds his shrine on his corpse.

3. I.79–VI.121. The second confrontation, between Marduk the son of Ea and Tiamat the spouse of Apsu, and its resolution.

The assembly (Anshar and Kishar, Anu, and Ea, and other unspecified gods) is unable to oppose Tiamat as once it had opposed Apsu (in the person of Anu). When Ea and Anu prove inadequate, Marduk is commissioned. The assembly proclaims his destiny to be supreme for the duration of the emergency and, after his victory, grants him everlasting supremacy. He constructs the universe (including forming man and building Esagil).

4. VI.122–VII.144. The gods acclaim Marduk supreme by ascribing to him fifty names.

By position and length, the names given to Marduk are the climax of the epic. Especially important are Enlil's bestowing on Marduk his own title "lord of the lands" (the fiftieth name, vii.136) and Ea's granting him the name Ea (vii.140).

5. VII.145–162. Epilogue: exhortation to study the names and to honor Marduk.

Sections 1 and 2 — the theogony and the victory of Ea over Apsu — have no parallel in the *Myth of Anzu.* These sections, which are apparently original to *Enūma elish,* play an important structural role in the plot. Like *Atrahasis,* in which part 1 (the rebellion of the Igigu and the creation of man) prefigures and prepares for part 2 (the human race's offense of the gods, the plagues, and the restoration), the first two sections of

Enūma elish prepare for what follows. The theogony in tablet I presents the rival royal lines that will be in conflict later. Apsu's threat and Ea's victory and temple prefigure the greater threat of Tiamat and Marduk's greater victory and temple. Without sections 1 and 2 the epic would not account for Marduk's replacement of Anu and Ea nor explain how primordial kingship came to be his.

We now turn to an analysis of the creation accounts.

The First Creation Account: the Theogony: I.1–20

[1]When[60] skies above were not yet named
Nor earth below pronounced by name,
Apsu, the first one, their begetter
And maker Tiamat, who bore them all,
[5]Had mixed their waters together,
But had not formed pastures, nor discovered reed-beds;
When yet no gods were manifest,
Nor names pronounced, nor destinies decreed,
Then gods were born within them.
[10]Lahmu and Lahamu emerged, their names pronounced.
As soon as they matured, were fully formed,
Anshar (and) Kishar were born, surpassing them.
They passed the days at length, they added to the years.
Anu, their first-born son, rivalled his forefathers:
[15]Anshar made his son Anu like himself,
And Anu begot Nudimmud in his likeness.
He, Nudimmud, was superior to his forefathers:
Profound of understanding, he was wise, was very strong at arms.
Mightier by far than Anshar, his father's begetter,
[20]He had no rival among the gods his peers.

Lines 1–8 form a section; *enūma,* "when," in line 7 reprises *enūma* of line 1, and lines 7–8 form an *inclusio* by repeating "name(s)" of lines 1–2. Lines 7–8 also point forward by mentioning the gods. Apsu and Tiamat do not have the dingir determinative of deity in contrast to the gods who later arise in their midst. The verbs of lines 1–8 are statives or duratives;

---

[60] Translation of Dalley, *MFM,* 233. The expression "to name" (*šuma nabû/zakāru*) in lines 1–2 are idioms meaning "to create." "Maker Tiamat" is derived by Dalley from *bīt mummi,* a workshop for producing statues. For lines 1–9 see M. Held, "Two Philological Notes on Enūma eliš," *Kramer Anniversary Volume,* 231–37.

preterit verbs begin in line 9 with the actual creation. The first eight lines thus describe a watery mass.[61] There was no dry land (pastures), still less the reed beds that supplied the common building material of Mesopotamia.

Then the gods "were born" (*banû*, line 9); Lahmu and Lahamu "emerged" (*šūpû*), "their names pronounced (line 10)." All these verbs are used for creation elsewhere. The next pair, Anshar and Kishar, greater and larger than Lahmu and Lahamu, begot (implied by "firstborn" of line 14) Anu, and Anu begot (*alādu*) Nudimmud (=Ea). Anshar and Kishar, to judge from their names (An=heaven, Ki=earth, šár="totality"), mean heaven and earth or their horizon. Ea is equal to Anu, a fact that will make Marduk's exceeding of Ea's victory a displacement of Anu as well as Ea. With Ea the theogony ends and the narrative of the gods' conflict begins.

The five-generation theogony of I.1–20 is an invention of the poet to differentiate the gods from the primordial force of sea, and to make of sea a doublet of Apsu and Tiamat.

Apsû - Tiamat

Lahmu - Lahamu

Anšar - Kišar

Anu

Nudimmud (=Ea)

The genealogy is not pure invention, however. In the god list An=*Anum*, Anshar and Kishar precede Lahmu and Lahamu, which suggests that this theogony inverted the order—perhaps to show that the earth was settled on piers before the appearance of horizon.[62] Anshar is important as the origin of legitimate kingship.[63]

---

[61] The precreation picture is echoed in the Babylonian Cosmogony (Akkadian Cosmogony no. 6): "All the lands were sea (*tâmtu*)" (line 10) and "there was no reed (for the temples)."

[62] Lambert suggests that Lahmu and Lahamu are Atlas figures holding up the cosmos, a transposition of a glyptic motif (holding up gateposts and temples) in "The Pair Lahmu-Lahamu in Cosmology," *Or* 54 (1985) 189–202. Jacobsen argues from etymology that they represent silt in the primeval ocean (*TD*, 168 and n. 332).

[63] The de Genouillac god list (TCL XV 10) may have influenced the genealogy of Anu:

^{d}nammu (= ^{d}ama-tu-an-ki)

^{d}uraš (= ^{d}nin-í-li)

^{d}en-uru-ul-la

The theogony makes Tiamat a doublet of Apsu in order to underline the parity of conflicts between Apsu and Ea on the one hand and Tiamat and Marduk on the other. Goldfless explains: "What the poet has done is to take two terms for subterranean waters that are applicable to the point he wishes to make about cosmic realms and their analogues in the temple, personify them, and use one as antagonist in the story of Ea and one as antagonist in the story of Marduk."[64]

The theogony, composed with a good deal of freedom, functions to prepare the reader to see that Marduk's kingship is in opposition to the failed kingships of Anshar, Anu, and Ea. Ea's power, acquired by his killing Apsu, is no match for Tiamat. The rival royal line of Tiamat-Kingu claims power over the *šīmātu,* the fates or destinies. Marduk claims the same: "My own utterance shall fix fate instead of you! / What I create shall never be altered" (II.160–1). Only with the false claimant to the throne out of the way can the definitive world come into being. As long as Tiamat is still at large, the gods cannot have their palaces and human servants. Marduk is not yet recognized as sole king of gods and human beings.

Second creation account (IV.135–V.122). Creation takes place in several scenes. Constant references to the earlier Apsu-Ea conflict, including the persistent parallel between Tiamat/Kingu/assembly and Anu/Marduk/assembly, underline the rival kingships. In I.79–107, Marduk, born of Ea and Damkina, is described as greater in size than his predecessors, continuing the theme of child surpassing parent (I.12, 14, 17, 19–20). His storm wind (prefiguring the later battle) disturbs Tiamat (I.107), just as earlier the gods had disturbed Apsu (I.21–28); Tiamat's assembly explicitly compares the two disturbances (I.112–17). In I.124–II.3, Tiamat's assembly confirms her choice of Kingu as the general of the army, just as the assembly under Anshar commissions Marduk.

Ea (II.4–6) hears of Tiamat's plans and reports them to Anshar (II.7–48)

---

    an-šar-gal
      an

Nammu is called ᵈama-tu-an-ki, "the mother who gave birth to heaven and earth," and elsewhere "she who gave birth to all the gods." Since her epithets resemble Tiamat's — "who bore them all" (I.4) and "Mother Hubur, who fashions all things" (I.132=II.19, 23) — she seems to stand behind the figure of Tiamat in *Enūma elish.* See the discussion of the god lists in chapter 2.

[64] Goldfless, "Babylonian Theogonies," 129.

who sends Ea and then Anu to meet the challenge. Both prove inadequate to the task (II.49–118). Finally, Marduk, invited in third and climactic place to fight Kingu, agrees on condition that the assembly grant to him supreme destiny (II.154–62). But will the assembly take this fateful step and change the way the world is governed? The poet builds suspense by devoting many lines to the preparations for the assembly, e.g., Anshar's carefully instructing his ambassador (III.4–32), and Lahmu and Lahamu's hearing out the long-winded embassy before setting forth (III.67–130). Convoked at last, the assembly recognizes the supremacy of Marduk's word and acclaims him king (III.131 iv.32). He receives the kingship legitimately as handed on through Anshar, Anu, and Ea. His destroying and creating the constellation by his mere word signifies that his kingship is effective (IV.18–28).

Legitimate kingship is further underlined by Marduk's address to Tiamat:

> IV.81 You[65] named Qingu as your lover,
> You appointed him to rites of Anu-power, wrongfully his.
> You sought out evil for Anshar, king of the gods,
> So you have compounded your wickedness against the gods my fathers.
> 85 Let your host prepare! Let them gird themselves with your weapons!
> Stand forth, and you and I shall do single combat!

Marduk marches out to meet Kingu's army and converts the battle to single combat with Tiamat. Tiamat's claims to kingship are false because of the prior demonstration of Marduk's effective word.

Marduk wins and majestically looks in triumph on the carcass of his slain enemy (IV.135–136). He creates (*banû*) marvels from her body. He splits her in two as a fish is split for drying, roofing the heavens with her upper half. He arranges the heavens to mark years, months, and days (V.1–24+), which is one of the purposes of creation attested in the minor cosmogonies nos. 8 and 9. Tiamat's body becomes the basis for the formation of the earth:

> V.53 He[66] placed her head, heaped up [   ]
> Opened up springs: water gushed out.

[65] Dalley, *MFM*, 253.
[66] Dalley, *MFM*, 257. *Înu* in Akkadian means both "spring" and "eye."

> He opened the Euphrates and the Tigris from her eyes,
> Closed her nostrils, [   ].
> He piled up clear-cut mountains from her udder,
> Bored waterholes to drain off the catchwater.

Her natural outlets become vents for the fertilizing streams to flow through into the rivers, and her body becomes the foundation of the mountains.

Marduk gives the Tablet of Destinies to Anu (V.69–70), an act expressing at once his own authority and his graciousness to Anu; he exercises his royal office while the gods rejoice (V.71–114). They acknowledge that Marduk is the patron of their sanctuaries (V.115), which is equivalent to acclaiming his lordship, thereby providing Marduk with the occasion to announce the building of his temple at Babylon (V.119–130). The temple concretizes Marduk's kingship. The old dwellings of the gods in Apsu, the underground waters, will be replaced with new dwellings assigned by Marduk—a sign of his authority over them. Marduk's own temple becomes their assembly point.

The mention of dwellings for the gods leads directly to the creation of man (VI.1–34), since a new creature is needed to build and maintain them (apart from Babylon and Esagila, which are built by the gods) and supply offerings.

> VI.5Let[67] me put blood together, and make bones too.
> Let me set up primeval man (*lullû*): Man shall be his name.
> Let me create a primeval man.
> The work of the gods shall be imposed (on him), and so they shall be
>   at leisure.

The rebel god Kingu is summoned, and from his blood Ea creates (*banû*) man. As part of the "Marduk settlement," human beings will do the labor of the gods (VI.34, 36). Marduk then divides the gods, assigning 300 Anunnaki to the underworld and 300 to the heavens (VI.39–46). The grateful gods construct for Marduk his great sanctuary Esagil in Babylon as their final labor (VI.47–64). This temple symbolizes their total deference to him and his replacement of Anu, Enlil, and Ea.

Marduk gives a banquet for the gods, announcing: "This is Babylon, the place that is your home. Make merry in its precincts, occupy its broad [places]" (VI.72–73). They praise his weapons and, vowing fealty, praise

---

[67] Dalley, *MFM*, 260–61.

him with fifty names. By virtue of the climactic fiftieth name, Marduk replaces Enlil.

Marduk replaces Anu, Enlil, and Ea by defeating Tiamat, the great threat to the gods. His victory and resultant kingship are enshrined in his temple Esagil, which expresses his new rank in architectural form. The gods' building of this temple, and his providing them with their own temples, is another way of stating his sole kingship. The creation of humankind is necessary for the reconciliation of the rebel gods[68] and for the construction of the gods' temples and their upkeep. A variety of old traditions has been used, but the overriding theme — the primacy of Marduk — is maintained throughout.

The sequence of actions in other cosmogonies — primordial waters as the first state, creation of heaven and earth; solar, lunar, and astral arrangements; temples; creation of the human race; marshes, forests, and animals for the gods' sustenance — occurs in two phases in *Enūma elish*. The primordial waters and origin of the first gods are narrated separately from the rest. The purpose of dividing creation into two parts is to show Marduk repeating on a grander scale his father Ea's cosmogonic victory over Apsu (I.65–75). Marduk thus replaces Ea, indeed the entire triad (though Enlil is inexplicably shadowy) and becomes sole ruler of Babylon, the center of the world. Like other great claims, this claim must be grounded "in the beginning." Thus, prior creation traditions are rearranged to make Marduk supreme over the other gods. His supremacy is derived from his having wrested primordial power from the line of Apsu-Tiamat-Kingu and created the universe, the dwellings of the gods, and the human race as the gods's servants. The epic should thus be entitled *The Exaltation of Marduk* rather than *The Creation Epic*.

A final word on style. In breaking up the traditional cosmogony into two parts, the poet has blended cosmogonic account and narrative of the gods' politics. Politics among the gods is shrewdly observed. The whole epic, then, may be called a political cosmogony.

---

[68] Marduk's sixteenth name, Agaku, recalls that he "showed mercy even to the captured gods, / Who removed the yoke imposed upon the gods his enemies, / Who created mankind to set them free" (VII.27–29).

C. The Dunnu Theogony

In 1965, W. G. Lambert and P. Walcot published a Late Babylonian manuscript of a theogony. Some forty lines, not all complete, are preserved on the obverse, while only a few damaged lines remain on the reverse.[69]

1At the very beginning (?) [Plough married Earth]
And they [decided to establish(?)] a family (?) and dominion.
"We shall break up the virgin soil of the land into clods."
In the clods of their virgin soil (?), they created Sea.
5The Furrows, of their own accord, begot the Cattle God.
Together they built Dunnu forever (?) as his refuge (?).
Plough made unrestricted dominion for himself in Dunnu.
Then Earth raised her face to the Cattle God his son
And said to him, "Come and let me love you!"
10The Cattle God married Earth his mother,
And killed Plough his father,
And laid him to rest in Dunnu, which he loved.
Then the Cattle God took over his father's dominion.
He married Sea, his older sister.
15The Flocks God, son of the Cattle God, came
And killed the Cattle God, and in Dunnu
Laid him to rest in the tomb of his father.
He married Sea his mother.
Then Sea slew Earth her mother.
20On the sixteenth day of Kislimu, he took over dominion and rule.
[   ] the son of the Flocks God married River his own sister,
And killed (his) father the Flocks God and Sea his mother,
And laid them to rest in the tomb undisturbed (?).
On the first day of Ṭebet, he seized dominion and rule for himself.
25The Herdsman God son of the Flocks God married his sister Pasture
    and Poplar,
And made Earth's verdure abundant,

[69] "A New Babylonian Theogony and Hesiod," *Kadmos* 4 (1965) 64–72. Other translations and discussions are found in A. K. Grayson, *ANET* 517–18; Jacobsen, in *The Harab Myth* (SANE, 2, fasc. 3; Malibu: Undena, 1984); and Bottéro, in *LD,* 472–478. Jacobsen's translation has been criticized by Lambert for "whimsical restoration of missing words" and for emending "the initial male deity from Hain to Harab (construct state of *ḫarbu* [*sic*], "plough"), which is most unlikely when *ḫarbu* is used twice in the opening lines as a common noun" (*Book List 1985* [Leeds: Society for Old Testament Study, 1985] 121). Bottéro, however, finds plausible Jacobsen's reading of *ḫa-rab* for Lambert's Hain, and his reading U.a.ildak for Ga'um (*LD,* 476). The translation is that of Dalley, *MFM,* 279–81.

Supported sheepfold and pen
To feed (?) forefathers and settlements (?),
And [   ] for the gods' requirements.
30He killed [   ] and River his mother
And made them dwell in the tomb.
On the [   ] day of Shabat, he took over dominion and rule
    for himself.
Haharnum son of the Herdsman God married his sister Bēlet-ṣēri
And killed the Herdsman God and Pasture-and-Poplar his mother,
35And made them dwell in the tomb.
On the sixteenth day of Addar, he took over rule (and) dominion.
[Then Hayyashum] son of Haharnum
Married [   ] his own sister.
At the New Year he took over his father's dominion,
40But did not kill him, and seized him alive.
He ordered his city to imprison his father . . . land

[about 38 lines missing, then 20 fragmentary lines which mention Nusku, Ninurta, and Enlil]

The tablet yields a seven-member genealogy.

Ḫain [or Harab]	Earth
Amakandu	Sea
Laḫar	
Ga'u |or U.a.ildak]	River
X	Pasture-Poplar
Ḫaḫarnim	Ningeštinna
Y	Z

Like other cities in Mesopotamia, Dunnu (location unknown) had its pantheon. As in other cosmogonies, the city is important. Built by the first pair, it was the burial place of the primeval gods and presumably the site of religious celebrations.[70]

The extant text presents a seven-member genealogy of the actual pantheon, which probably consisted of (among others) the deities Nusku, Sharrat-Nippuri, Ninurta, and Enlil (mentioned in the fragmentary reverse).[71] There is no indication of how long each god reigned. Though

[70] P. D. Miller, "Eridu, Dunnu, and Babel: A Study in Comparative Mythology," 238.
[71] Bottéro: "As if, with time, one had gone from ancient and almost forgotten deities to the contemporary pantheon, common to Dunnu and the whole land" (*LD*, 476).

not all the figures are known, the male deities appear to be hypostases of the fertility of the flocks and the females, representatives of vegetation. The closest parallels to the sequence Earth/Sea/River/Vegetation occur in the incantations against a toothache and against the ergot (II.1abc), respectively, heaven/earth/rivers/canals/marsh/worm, earth/dirt/stalk/ear/ergot, seeder plow/seed furrow/germ/root stock/node/ear/ergot.

What is the purpose of the text? It tells how the present world arose from primordial pairs, and associates the transfer of power from the primordial pairs to the deities of the city of Dunnu. What is unusual is that the transfer of power comes about through parricide and incest. Despite the absence of comparable texts from Mesopotamia, there are some Near Eastern parallels. In the Hittite *Kingship in Heaven,* a succession of gods is violently dethroned: Alalu reigns nine years before being dethroned by his servant Anu, who after nine years, is displaced by his servant Kumarbi, who bites off Anu's "manhood"; the seed of a further usurper, the Storm God, is contained in that "manhood."[72] In Hesiod's *Theogony* (late eighth century) Zeus kills his father, Kronos, with the connivance of his mother, Ge (Earth). A similar pattern recurs in the *History of Kronos* in Philo of Byblos's *Phoenician History:* Uranus (Heaven) succeeds his father, "Elioun, called the Most High" and marries his sister, Ge (Earth). Angered by his philandering, Ge persuades their son Kronos to usurp his rule; later Kronos castrates and kills Uranus.

With the unparalleled and fragmentary *Dunnu Theogony,* only hypotheses are possible. Van Dijk suggests that the Eridu tradition, which he sees vestigially preserved in the opening lines of *Enūma elish* and in the *Dunnu Theogony,* was originally a succession theogony like that found in Hesiod's *Theogony.*[73] Goldfless proposes, on the basis of the Nippur deities mentioned on the broken reverse, that the tablet deliberately contrasts chaotic natural succession (e.g., murder and incest) with the ordered and civilized succession of Enlil and his family of gods.[74] Jacobsen

---

[72] *ANET,* 120–21 or H. A. Hoffner, ed., *Hittite Myths* (Atlanta: Scholars Press, 1990) 40–43.

[73] Van Dijk, "Sumerische Religion," 20.

[74] Goldfless, "Babylonian Theogonies," 185. Jacobsen agrees: "The myth shows, furthermore, a gradual change from early barbarous indulgence in parricide and incest to somewhat more restrained divine conduct and is in that sense a history of cosmic morals (*The Harab Myth,* 26). For F. M. Cross, the seven generations are the "olden gods" preceding

concludes that the myth belongs to the tradition of "the lost Babylonian source for the Hittite-Hurrian myth of the Kingship of Heaven, the Phoenician creation story, and the Greek Olympic creation myth, each of these retelling only the last parts of the original story and each selecting different aspects and motifs from it."[75]

Jacobsen further suggests that the text was originally a local cosmogony "reflecting cyclically the manner in which the cosmos first — and repeatedly year for year — came into being."[76] One need not, however, assume from the agricultural gods and feast days that this cosmogony arose from the experience of the agricultural year. Without a legible text of the reverse and more inner-Mesopotamian parallels, it is impossible to go further. Goldfless is properly cautious: "From the perspective of known mythologoumena of divine succession in Mesopotamian literature, the motifs of incest and parricide are entirely novel. Neither the Enlil or Anu ancestries, nor *Enūma elish,* nor the cultic commentaries suggest them."[77]

Conclusions

As it was convenient to organize our analysis of Sumerian cosmogonies according to cosmic (Nippur) and chthonic (Eridu) motifs (van Dijk), it is helpful to arrange cosmogonies in Akkadian according to minor (Bottéro) or function-bound and anthological or exploratory. The latter tendency appears already in Sumerian, particularly in the Eridu traditions, where creation is only one part of a longer story of Ea's activity.

The minor cosmogonies presuppose the originating moment to be decisive for the present. Then were things ineradicably characterized — worms, the river, temples, animate things such as palms and tamarisks or horse and ox, heavenly bodies, kings. The original moment shows the right and intended use of elements within the universe. Rituals, prayers,

---

the great gods, the gods of the cult, in "The 'Olden Gods' in Ancient Near Eastern Creation Myths." See his *Magnalia Dei, The Mighty Acts of God: Essays on the Bible and Archaeology in Memory of G. Ernest Wright* (ed. F. M. Cross et al.; Garden City, NY: Doubleday, 1976) 329–38.

[75] Jacobsen, *The Harab Myth,* 26.

[76] Ibid., 26.

[77] Goldfless, "Babylonian Theogonies," 186. Goldfless further notes that the *Dunnu Theogony* provides Semitic evidence for the motifs of incest and parricide being attracted to theogonic narrative.

prefaces, and stories narrate the origin to validate the original design of the gods.

The anthological cosmogonies, on the other hand, are not tied to an operation and are incorporated into large literary goals. *Atrahasis* is a complex work, considering in the course of its long narrative the nature of the gods and the relationship between them and the human race, mortality and other limits upon the race, and the relation of gods and human beings to the land. The epic begins with the apportionment of domain by Anu, Enlil, and Ea (sometimes part of creation accounts), but concentrates on the creation of the human race, putting into parallel creation and its revision. In so doing, the epic explains the "dignity" of the race (the gods cannot do without them) and its mortality (to make population match resources).

Enūma elish exalts Marduk to the head of the pantheon. To do this, it traces his kingship back to the origin of the world, before any god existed. A fundamental contrast (always a rhetorically effective device in the semitic world) underscores the antiquity and legitimacy of his kingship rather than Tiamat's. The opening theogony shows the rival royal houses and the cosmogony of tablets IV and V allows the now victorious Marduk to construct the world and assign a place to the human race. All the Akkadian creation accounts (and the Sumerian for that matter) show no interest in creation as a historical event in the modern sense but only as validating or exploring present reality.

CHAPTER 4

Creation Accounts
in Egyptian Thought

Egypt was the major Near Eastern power geographically closest to Israel; on the Bible's own witness, it played a major role in Israel's formation. Egyptian thinkers avoided the subject-object distinction of Western thought and preferred concrete imagery over abstract concepts in elaborating their thought. As in Mesopotamia, cosmogonies played a major role in prayers and rituals, and also (unlike Mesopotamia) in distinctively Egyptian religious-philosophical speculations. The primary interest was not creation for its own sake. Like the cosmogonies in neighboring cultures, there was no one standard account to which other versions had to conform.[1]

A history of Egyptian religion is beyond the limits of this chapter but a few remarks are necessary. Cosmogonies were developed at important

---

[1] The distinctive Egyptian approach has been stated most recently by J. Allen, in *Genesis,* ix–x and 56–63. The English equivalents of Egyptian names given here follow Lichtheim, *AEL,* except where other translations diverge. Any study of Egyptian cosmogony is indebted to the fundamental work by S. Sauneron and J. Yoyotte, "La naissance du monde selon l'Égypte ancienne," in *La naissance du monde* (Sources Orientales 1; Paris: Seuil, 1959), 17–91. Recent syntheses are by S. Morenz, *Egyptian Religion* (Ithaca: Cornell University, 1973), chapter 8; P. Derchain, "Kosmogonie," *LÄ* 3:747–55; J. Assmann, "Schöpfung," *LÄ* 5:677–90; Allen, *Genesis;* E. Iverson, *Egyptian and Hermetic Doctrine* (Opuscula Graeco-latina 27; Copenhagen: Museum Tusculanum, 1984); and B. Menu, "Les cosmogonies de l'ancienne Egypte," in *La création,* 97–116. V. Notter, *Biblischer Schöpfungsbericht und ägyptische Schöpfungsmythen* (SBS 68; Stuttgart: KBW, 1974), which collects every conceivable Egyptian parallel to Gen 1:1–2:4 with little critical comment, did not prove useful for this study.

cities to exalt the principal local deity—Re, Atum, Ptah, or Amun—to the rank of universal and officially recognized god of state, undergirding the city's claims to importance. The Old Kingdom (ca. 2686–2160 B.C.) had as its capital Memphis, just south of modern Cairo, which remained the capital until the Middle Kingdom (2040–1633 B.C.). The *Memphite Theology* expresses the preeminence of the creator god Ptah. During the Fifth Dynasty (ca. 2440–2315 B.C.) the priesthood of Heliopolis, north of Memphis, rose to power. Its god, Atum, generated the Ogdoad, the eight primeval gods. The relevant cosmogonies are preserved in the *Pyramid Texts* of the mid-third millennium, the *Coffin Texts* of the late third millennium, and the *Book of the Dead* of the second millennium. The social unrest and weakening of centralized royal authority during the First Intermediate Period (ca. 2160–2040 B.C.) was resolved by the time of the Middle Kingdom. Another period of decline, the Second Intermediate Period (ca. 1786–1603 B.C.), was reversed during the New Kingdom (ca. 1558–1085 B.C.). It had its capital at Thebes in middle Egypt and famous temples at nearby Luxor and Karnak. The previously-obscure god Amun became prominent in a new cosmogony that borrowed from Hermopolis. The subsequent course of Egyptian history is not significant for this chapter.

Egyptian religion is extraordinarily difficult for modern students to understand. Gods and systems indigenous to different regions were combined in an ongoing syncretism for nearly three millennia. The resulting religion is a complicated array of gods and divine functions.

Contemporary Egyptologists agree that the different systems of Heliopolis, Memphis, Hermopolis, and other centers rested on remarkably similar underlying ideas.[2] These systems were not in competition as many older scholars believed. Before looking at each of the local cosmogonies, we will review the elements common to all the systems: conditions before creation, the creator god, the primordial mound, the modes of manifestation of the creator god, and the process of creation.

[2] Allen, *Genesis,* chapter 6; and Iverson, "The Egyptian Tradition," in *Egyptian and Hermetic Doctrine,* 7–25.

I. Elements Common to All Cosmogonies

A. *The Period before Creation*

Egyptian thinking about the "nothingness" prior to creation is allusive and difficult. I will draw on Erik Hornung's careful systematizing of the period.[3] There were two ways of characterizing the world before creation—through negation and through affirmation. The negative way made use of a special negative verb form, *n sḏmt.f*; in creation contexts it can be translated as "when X had not yet . . ." or "before X existed." The negative verb form is a good starting point for understanding non-existence in the texts. The phrase "before the sky existed, before the earth existed" frequently introduces a series of nonexistent entities, e.g., "before men existed, before the gods were born, before death existed" (*Pyramid Text* 1466)[4]; "before that which was to be made firm existed, before turmoil,[5] before that fear which arose on account of the eye of Horus existed" (*Pyramid Text* 1040); "when I [Atum] was alone with Nu [=Nun] in lassitude, and I could find no place on which to stand or sit, when On had not yet been founded that I might dwell in it, when my throne(?) had not been put together that I might sit on it; before I made Nut that she might be above me, before the first generation had been born, before the Primeval Ennead had come into being that they might dwell with me" (*Coffin Text* 2:33g).[6]

Especially significant among the negative characterizations of the precreation world is the phrase "before there were two things" (Hornung's

---

[3] Hornung, *Conceptions of God in Ancient Egypt* (trans. J. Baines; London: Routledge & Kegan Paul, 1983) 172–84, and "Chaotische Bereiche in der geordneten Welt," *ZÄS* 81 (1956) 28–32. Allen, *Genesis,* 56–57, discusses the same ideas. In his preface to *Conceptions of God,* Hornung states his preference for the English translation (in which he was involved) over the original German edition.

[4] All translations of the *Pyramid Texts* are taken from R. O. Faulkner, *The Ancient Egyptian Pyramid Texts* (Oxford: Clarendon, 1969).

[5] "Turmoil," according to Hornung, is "a specific allusion to the conflict of Horus and Seth, that is, to the figures and situations of myth, but at the same time it is far more generally a negation of all positive struggle, as can be seen from the affirmative description of this state as being 'weary' or 'inert': there is nothing that would move or begin to struggle—there is total repose" (*Conceptions of God,* 176).

[6] All translations of *Coffin Texts* are from R. O. Faulkner, *The Ancient Egyptian Coffin Texts, Volume 1: Spells 1–354* (Warminster: Aris and Phillips, 1969). For further citations, see Assmann, "Schöpfung," *LÄ* 5:677–78.

translation of *Coffin Text* 2.396b).[7] To Hornung the phrase is "an apparently unnecessary repetition, since there was in any case 'no thing at all.' But this statement is an explicit expression of the Egyptian view that before creation there was a unity, which could not be divided into two things, just as the creator god is often called 'one who made himself into millions.'"[8] "Two things" and "millions" both express the same thing—the diversity of the existent—which is denied for nonexistence; nonexistence is one and undifferentiated. The creator god mediates between it and the existent, and separates them. He is the original one who emerges from the nonexistent and marks the "beginning" of the process of coming into being by differentiating himself into the plurality of "millions"—the multiplicity of the existent and of the gods. Hornung states: "This is the intellectual foundation of Egyptian polytheism: insofar as it exists, the divine must be differentiated. In order to refer to a unity in the realm of the existent, the Egyptians use the dual to juxtapose two complementary concepts: Egypt is the 'Two Lands' or 'Upper and Lower Egypt', space is 'sky and earth'; time is *nḥḥ* and *ḏt;* the totality of what is conceivable is 'the existent and the nonexistent.'"[9]

In positive terms, the time before creation was imagined as one of limitless waters (personified as Nun), the primeval flood, and total darkness. These images were partially derived from people's experience of the Nile, which was the perennial source of all life and movement in Egypt. Where the Nile did not flow was sterile and silent desert. When the annual inundation receded from flood levels, it left behind small mounds teeming with new life. These mounds, as well as the frogs, lotuses, and eggs accompanying the new life left by the receding river, occur frequently as images of creation. But the nonexistent is *not* transformed into the existent and eliminated. This postcreation remainder is eternal and never transformed into existence. Precreation elements—primeval flood, Stygian darkness, inertness, and negation—remain in the created world in two ways—as the final limit, the place outside the limited world of being; and as present within the ordered world of creation.

---

[7] Hornung translates the version that Faulkner (*Coffin Texts* 1:140) puts in note 7. Faulkner himself translates the text as "the second in his land of (?) the south, north, west and east winds."

[8] Hornung, *Conceptions of God*, 170.

[9] Ibid., 176.

The first mode of presence — that outside all boundaries — is illustrated in chapter 175 of the *Book of the Dead,* which describes the underworld (closely related to the nonexistent) as "utterly deep, utterly dark, utterly endless." Once the deceased is assigned to destruction at the post-mortem judgment, he becomes "the nonexistent one." In the limitless depths lives the snake-headed Apophis who seeks to take away the life of Re as he crosses the underworld ocean in his night bark. The snake in the form of a coil in which the head joins the tail — the "tail swallower"— surrounds the world. It developed into a symbol of the nonexistent that outlasts the existent world. It eventually found its way into Gnostic writings.

The second way in which precreation elements are present — within the created world — is alluded to in a New Kingdom text: "The distant region of the sky is in total darkness. Its limits to south, north, west and east are not known. These (ordinal points) are fixed in the primeval waters as 'weary ones.' Its land is not known . . . by the gods and spirits. There is no light there at all, *(and) it stretches under every place . . .*"[10] Hence the Egyptian encounters the nonexistent in the events of everyday life: in the waters of a foundation trench, in the annual flood when "the earth is Nun" (as a Twenty-Fifth Dynasty text has it), and in the night that makes faces unrecognizable, extinguishing all forms.

Encounter with the nonexistent has two sides, one hostile and the other regenerative. When the powers invading creation are hostile, they must be driven out. One example of expulsion of such primeval nonexistence is an epithet of Ramses II, "he who makes rebellious foreign lands nonexistent"; it is said of other kings that they make rebellious foreigners "nonexistent" or "uncreated." Another is the well-known "negative confession" at the judgment after death in chapter 125 of the *Book of the Dead,* which includes the claim "I do not know the nonexistent," averring that the person has not overstepped the limits of the created order.

The regenerative side of the nonexistent is illustrated by the sun's nightly journey through the primeval ocean, which purifies it and enables it to renew the earth. The annual inundation of the Nile, which reenacts the primeval flood, brings new life and fertility as it recedes. The same rejuvenating aspect appears in the familiar Egyptian preparations for death — mummification, burial, and grave goods — which appeal to the

[10] Cited in Hornung, *Conceptions of God,* 168 (italics his).

renewing aspect of the nonexistent to facilitate the deceased's entry into life in the next world.

Hornung sums it up: "In Egypt 'the nonexistent' signified quite generally that which is inchoate, undifferentiated, unarticulated, and unlimited; or, in affirmative form, the entirety of what is possible, the absolute, the definitive. In comparison with the nonexistent, the existent is clearly defined, and articulated by boundaries and discriminations."[11]

B. *The Creator God*

Different gods play the role of creator in Egyptian cosmogonies — Ptah, Re, Amun, Atum, and Khnum — but each cosmogony has only one creator god. The primeval god, whoever he may be, is in the beginning one, and then, with creation and diversity, becomes many. The epithet "the one who made himself into millions" (or a variant) is applied to the creator god from the New Kingdom onward. The created world originates by diversification of the one, or by the separation of previously united elements. Earth and sky, once united, are separated by Shu; light emerges from darkness, land from primeval water. Hence the creator god is always one and creation is self-generated.

The statement "god created the gods" occurs frequently in early periods. Later texts make the human race parallel to the gods, e.g., "he who created everything that exists, who built men and created the gods," or "bringing mankind into being, forming the gods and created all that exists."[12] A *Coffin Text* states, "I brought the gods into being from my sweat [i.e., fragrance] emanating from the god; men are from the tears of my eye" (7.464–65a Faulkner). The wordplay on "humankind" (*rmṯ*) and "tears" (*rmỉt*) is common.

The universally worshiped sun god Re appears in almost every creation account, though his role varies from actually creating to sustaining the fresh beginnings of each day by his warm and illuminating rays. For Re's creating activity the word *ḫpr* is generally employed. Depending on context, it can mean "to be born," "to come into existence," "to exist," "to become," "to be transformed," "to be manifest in." Meaning at once

---

[11] Ibid., 183.

[12] The first text dates from the Twentieth Dynasty. The second is from Edfu. Both are cited by Hornung, ibid.

existence and transformation, it describes not a true *creatio ex nihilo* but the realization of an entity existing virtually in Nun.

Ptah creates by his action as befits the god of sculptors and artisans; he creates in the *Memphite Theology* according to a plan devised in the heart and realized by a word. Khnum likewise creates through his activity, shaping individual persons and things like a potter. Amun, whose name ("the hidden one") suggests transcendence, was part of the Hermopolis cosmogony; he became preeminent with the rise of the New Kingdom.

Each major system added its own nuances. Memphis emphasized the chthonic aspect over the solar; Ptah of Memphis bore the epithet of the primordial mound, Ta-tenen, which means "the land that rises." In the Heliopolitan tradition, on the other hand, the sun (under the names of Re, Atum, Khepri, or Re-Harakhti) was the most ancient demiurge, and gods of other sanctuaries, e.g., Amun, Khnum, were given solar traits.

The creator god is always self-generated within Nun. And from the single creator god issues the hierarchy of gods. Even the Ennead, the nine gods incarnating the elements of the cosmos, is a manifestation of the creator god as he unfolds over three generations. Atum generates the cosmic divine pairs, Shu and Tefnut, Geb and Nut, and then the individual gods Osiris, Isis, Seth, and Nephthys.

C. The Primordial Mound

From their experience of new life rising in the wake of the receding annual Nile flood, Egyptians developed the idea of the primordial mound (German, *Urhügel*) from which arose all life. The hieroglyph of this idea shows the primeval flood with the sun rising over it, stylized as a mound, often stepped. It represented not emerging land in general but the world contained entire in one tiny island.

The mound played an important role in the major cosmological systems. At Heliopolis Atum himself appeared as the primordial mound, which was sometimes called the *benben*. At Memphis the chthonic god Ta-tenen, "the land that rises," was combined with Ptah beginning with the New Kingdom period. In Hermopolis the Ogdoad was placed in or alongside the "island of flames," the mound exploding with life. Other shrines, too, located the primordial mound within their precincts.

Related to the primeval mound were the temple and the throne. Creation was renewed every day in the temple, which thereby became a primordial mound. Temples were built on special sand foundations, with the holy of holies at a higher level than the other rooms. "The king, who represented on earth the god and his life-bringing actions, played the creator role *in parvo.* Like the creator, he ascended the stylized primordial mound. The pedestal (generally stepped) of the throne, functioned as the primordial mound. And every time the king seated himself on it — especially significant in enthronements and on the Sed feast — he repeated the creation symbolically."[13]

D. Modes of Manifestation of the Creator God

Nun and the primordial mound were preliminary and passive. The creator appeared in several forms. If life was imagined as an explosion of vitality, then biological images were used: an egg cracking open, or a water-rooted lotus opening in the morning and closing at night. Serpents also could be manifestations of creative power: perhaps earth was incarnated in a reptile. Another image was the sacred gander who breaks the cosmic egg. According to Serge Sauneron, behind every image lies one of two basic types — Ptah, the god of earth who imposes himself on the liquid element and draws from it animate and inanimate things; or Re-Atum, the sun, whose brilliance is the very condition for all creation (either the spurt from his penis or the gaze from his eyes that dissipates darkness).[14]

E. The Process of Creation

There were three modes of creating. One was the creator's generation of the divine couple Shu and Tefnut from the semen produced by masturbation or, in a variant tradition, from his spittle. A similar idea is conveyed through the wordplay in which the human race (Egyptian *rmṯ*) came from the creator's god's tears (Egyptian *rmĭt*).

The second type was creation by uttering a word. Ptah conceived in his heart the things he intended to create and gave them existence by means of his tongue. One should not draw an overly sharp distinction between creation by physical emanation and by utterance, for theologians interpreted the physical as symbolic of the spiritual; the seed and the hands

---

[13] K. Martin, "Urhügel," *LÄ* 2:874 (my translation).

[14] Sauneron and Yoyotte, *La naissance,* 38–39.

of Atum (in masturbation) were the teeth and lips of Ptah (in creation by utterance).[15]

The third type was modeled on the artisan's activity of building and fashioning. One example is Khnum, the artisan god, the potter-god, and fashioner of human beings who placed babies in the womb of their mother.

II. The Local Systems

The cities with the most venerable cosmogonies were Heliopolis, Memphis, and Hermopolis. The Heliopolis and Memphis systems were contemporary but not in rivalry. These three preeminent systems influenced each other as well as other cosmogonies such as those of Crocodilopolis, Thebes, and Edfu.

A. The Cosmogony of Heliopolis

Heliopolis (Greek for "Sun city," biblical On), south of modern Cairo, was the cult center of the sun god Re. As early as the Old Kingdom, Re was widely known as a creator. His name was frequently joined to that of other creators, e.g., Amun-Re and Re-Atum.[16] He was creator of heaven and earth by virtue of being the sun god, by his light and warmth daily awakening human beings, animals, and plants. Hence he was the god of seasons and his birthday fell on New Year's Day.[17] Re was not, however, the major deity in the Heliopolis cosmogony.

The major roles in the Heliopolis cosmogony were played by Atum and the Ennead (="nine gods"). Atum generated from himself, either

---

[15] Ibid., 40.

[16] The hyphen does not mean that the two gods merged their identities, but rather that Egyptians recognized Re in the other god; Re "inhabited" that deity. Hans Bonnet uses the term "indwelling" ("als Einwohnung des einen im anderen") to describe the phenomenon. The name Re-Atum does not mean that one god is subsumed in the other, nor that Atum is equal to Re, but that Atum is in Re without being lost in Re. He remains himself with the ability to appear separately or in other combinations. *Reallexikon der Ägyptischen Religionsgeschichte* (Berlin: de Gruyter, 1952) s.v. "Götterglauber."

[17] "O Re-Atum, O Kopri, I am one who was born on the First of the Year" (Coffin Text 2.183b). In the New Kingdom story of Isis and Re, the sun god says of his daily course: "I am Khepri in the morning, Re at noon, and Atum who is in the evening" (*ANET* 13). Khepri is depicted as a beetle pushing a dung ball, which was a symbol of renewal, since Egyptians regarded them as the eggs of a new generation.

by masturbation or spitting, the first divine couple, Shu (atmosphere) and Tefnut, who gave birth to Geb (earth) and Nut (sky), who were then separated from each other by Shu. Subsequently there were born Osiris and Isis, and Nephthys and Seth, to complete the Great Ennead. Only the first five gods were cosmic. The famous shrine at Heliopolis *ḥwt bnbn* (lit., "mansion of the top of the obelisk"; also called the Phoenix House) was a place of Atum worship. Atum's symbol, the *bnbn* stone, symbolized the primordial mound.

The Heliopolis doctrine is best expressed in the *Pyramid Texts* of the mid-third millennium, the *Coffin Texts* of the late-third millennium, and the *Book of the Dead* from the mid-second millennium. One *Pyramid Text* prays that the creator's blessing come upon the king and that primordial creative power be given by the god's embrace.

> Atum-Khoprer,[18] you became high on the height, you rose up as on the *bnbn*-stone in the Mansion of the 'Phoenix' in On, you spat out Shu, you expectorated Tefenet, and you set your arms about them as the arms of a *ka*-symbol, that your essence might be in them. O Atum, set your arms about the King, about this construction, and about this pyramid as the arms of a *ka*-symbol, that the king's essence may be in it, enduring for ever . . .
>
> O you Great Ennead which is in On, (namely) Atum, Shu, Tefenet, Geb, Nut, Osiris, Isis, Seth, and Nephthys; O you children of Atum, extend his goodwill(?) to his child in your name of Nine Bows. Let his back be turned(?) from you toward Atum, that he may protect this King, that he may protect this pyramid of the King and protect this construction of his from all the gods and from all the dead and prevent anything from happening evilly against it for ever.

Two *Coffin Texts* describe the roles of Atum and of Shu, who was begotten of Atum like the other gods of the Ennead but endowed with greater importance. In the text the dead person takes on the identity of the god Shu, hoping thereby to share in his power over death.

---

[18] Faulkner, *Pyramid Texts,* 246–47, sections 1652–53 and 1655–56. Faulkner remarks (in n. 2) that "the first *k3* [in the first text cited] is the reference to the actual U-sign with its upraised open arms; the second has here the meaning 'essence' or the like, referring to the divine nature passed on by Atum to his offspring." Faulkner's spelling of Tefnut as Tefenet has been retained.

I [the dead person] am this soul of Shu which is in the flame of the fiery blast which Atum has kindled with his own hand. He created orgasm and fluid(?) fell from his mouth. He spat me out as Shu together with Tefenet, who came forth after me as the Great Ennead, the daughter of Atum, who shines on the gods. I was set in it as son and daughter of Nut, she with the braided hair who bore the gods. Such am I.[19]

In another *Coffin Text* a person seeks to be identified with Shu, who is occasionally credited with separating Geb (earth) and Nut (sky).

I am the soul of Shu, from whom Nut was placed above and Geb under his feet, and I am between them.[20]

The text below from the *Book of the Dead* clarifies Atum's relation to Nun. The first paragraph insists on one creator god, Re-Atum. The second paragraph suggests there was another god besides Nun in the beginning. It transmits the tradition that Re came into being by himself and attributes creation to both Nun and Re, thus resolving the problem of Nun's inertness. The third paragraph identifies the eight gods, the Ogdoad, as aspects of Re, i.e., parts of his body.

I am Atum when I was alone in Nun: I am Re in his (first) appearances, when he began to rule that which he had made. Who is he? This "Re, when he began to rule that which he had made" means that he began to appear as a king, as one who was before the liftings of Shu had taken place, when he was on the hill which is in Hermopolis. . .
"I am the great god who came into being by himself." Who is he? "The great god who came into being by himself" is water; he is Nun, the father of the gods. Another version: He is Re.
"He who created his names, the Lord of the Ennead."
Who is he? He is Re, who created the names of the parts of his body. That is how these gods who follow him came into being.[21]

The Heliopolis cosmogony clearly asserts that the world developed from the monad. The monad is the simple source from which all existence is derived; it is personified in the god Atum. The Hermopolis and

[19] Faulkner, *Coffin Text* 2.18, Spell 77). The sun and daughter of Nut are "presumably Osiris and Isis."
[20] Coffin Text 2.19, Spell 77. The deceased is Shu (air) placed between earth and sky.
[21] *ANET* 3–4.

Memphite cosmogonies assert the same development from the one, but they inquire further about the process—how did it came about?

B. The Cosmogony of Memphis

Memphis, the capital during the Old and Middle Kingdoms, was the most important urban center in Egypt. Ptah, like Amun at Thebes, was important because he was the god of a capital city. In all probability he was first considered a creator by virtue of being the divine craftsman (the Greeks identified him with Hephaistos); only later was creation through word or sex ascribed to him.[22] From the thirteenth century, he was associated with, and even identified with, the Memphite god Ta-tenen, the primordial mound. Creation at Memphis was conceived on the model of artistic activity rather than natural processes, which was the tendency at Heliopolis.[23]

The famous *Memphite Theology* is an extremely reflective statement of Ptah's creative role and merits some discussion.[24] Its unusual diversity of ideas have persuaded some scholars that the text is an anthology of different sources linking Ptah to creative activity only extrinsically. James Allen, however, finds a single train of thought and a consistent analogy in which mind directs all activity. Since Ptah is the patron of artisans, particularly of stonemasons and sculptors, it is not surprising that descriptions of his creative activity combine the material and the nonmaterial. Sculptors "in-form" or imprint a stone with their mental image. Their action makes an immaterial image into a material statue.

> 1 Through[25] the heart and through the tongue something
>   developed into Atum's image.

[22] The earliest reference to Ptah creating through his word occurs in *Coffin Text* (6:268) from the twentieth century B.C.; it was probably borrowed from the Heliopolis theology of Atum. See further H. T. V. Groningen, "Ptah," *LÄ* 4.1178.

[23] J. Assmann, "Schöpfung," *LÄ* 5.687–689.

[24] Pharaoh Shabaka around 710 B.C. had the venerable worm-eaten manuscript of the *Memphite Theology* copied on stone to preserve it. The stone was later defaced from being used as a millstone. The period of composition is disputed. Some date it to the Old Kingdom, but a date no earlier than the thirteenth century is increasingly finding favor. See H. Alenmüller, "Denkmal memphitischer Theologie," *LÄ* 1:1065–69; and Allen, *Genesis,* 43. Translations are in *ANET* 4–6; Lichtheim, *AEL* 1. 51–57; and Allen, *Genesis,* 43–44 (partial).

[25] Translation of Allen, in *Genesis,* 43. I am indebted to his analysis on pp. 45–46.

And great and important is Ptah,
> who gave life to all the gods and their *ka*s as well
> through this heart and this tongue
5   through which Horus and Thoth became Ptah.

The first verse states the thesis: the creator's thought and command ("heart" and "tongue") operated on the primordial monad so that forces and elements of the world ("something") emerged that reflected the material from which they came ("Atum's image"). In line 2 the intellectual creative principle is essentially embodied in Ptah, though components of it can be found in the gods Horus (command) and Thoth (perception).

10His Ennead is before him, in teeth and lips—
> that seed and those hands of Atum:
> for it is through his seed and his fingers that Atum's Ennead
> developed,
> but the Ennead is teeth and lips in this mouth
> that pronounced the identity of everything,
15and from which Shu and Tefnut emerged
> and gave birth to the Ennead.

All created things, represented here by the Ennead, are the means by which the concept is realized. The idea, which comes first, "pronounced the identity of everything." The Heliopolis doctrine of Atum's creating through masturbation ("through his seed and his fingers") is analogous to Ptah's creating through concept and speech ("teeth and lips in this mouth").

20So were all the gods born.
> Atum and his Ennead as well,
> for it is through what the heart plans and the tongue
> commands that every divine speech has developed.

As a result of the process of creating, all created reality ("Atum and his Ennead as well") is both the product and the image of the primordial source from which it came. The same idea is expressed by "Atum's image" in line 1 and repeated in the "divine speech" of line 22. Allen points out that "image" and "divine speech" are terms used in hieroglyphic writing, which for the Egyptians was "a means for capturing reality through symbols. In effect, all creation is a hieroglyphic text of the creator's original concept (lines 20–22) . . ."[26] The power above Atum is Ptah; the creative

[26] Ibid., 45.

function of thought and "in-formation" is conceptualized in him. Allen concludes: "In general, the *Memphite Theology* is concerned less with the creator's actions than with explaining the means through which his concept of the world became transformed into reality. That means is the principle embodied in Ptah."[27]

D. The Cosmogony of Hermopolis

Hermopolis in middle Egypt was so named by the Greeks, who identified the city's chief god, Thoth, with their Hermes. Thoth was not, however, part of the local creation doctrine. The Egyptian name of the city, *Ḥmnw* ("city of eight [primeval gods]"), underlines the Ogdoad's major role in the local cosmogony.

The Ogdoad consisted of four pairs of gods: Nun and his female partner Naunet (primeval waters), Huh and Hauhet (flood), Kuk and Kauket (darkness), and Amun and Amaunet (concealed dynamism). The males were pictured as frog-headed and the females, as snake-headed. The goddesses had no independent existence, and no couple except Amun and Amaunet had a cult. The Ogdoad represented conditions before creation, being present at the first appearance of the sun. Prominent also in the cosmogonic imagery of Hermopolis was the egg from which all things were born, and the sun, in its first appearance, as a child bursting from a lotus.

A ritual for the presentation of a bejeweled lotus to a god explains the significance of the lotus.

> Accept the lotus that came into being at the beginning, which dispelled the heavy cloud, so that no one saw it any longer. You [the Eight] made a seed from a fluid expelled from you, and you poured over the (lotus) this seed, while spilling the seminal fluid; you put it in Nun, condensed into a single form and your descendant is born radiant in the form of an infant.[28]

The significance of the egg in the Great Pool at Hermopolis is revealed in an inscription of a certain Petosiris of Hermopolis.

> I reserved a zone around the Great Pool to prevent it from being contaminated by the common people, for it is the place where Re was born

[27] Ibid., 47.
[28] Sauneron, "La naissance," 585 (my translation).

in the First Time, when the land was still immersed in Nun, for it is the place of birth of all the gods who began to exist at the beginning, for it is in this spot that every being was born, for half the egg was buried in this spot, and there also are all the beings that issued from the egg.[29]

Especially in New Kingdom texts from Hermopolis, Amun figures as primordial god, creative principle, and ruler over what exists. His name, derived from the verb *imn* ("to conceal, to be hidden"), suggests transcendence. An impressive statement of his role is given in the thirteenth-century *Papyrus Leiden* I 350; twenty-two of its original twenty-six chapters are preserved. According to the "200th Chapter,"[30] Amun is manifested in the sun, the primeval mound (Ta-tenen), and the precreation universe. Both his immanence and transcendence are caught in line 29: "Manifest one whose identity is hidden, inasmuch as it is accessible."[31] The "300th Chapter" states clearly that all things are manifestations of a single transcendent deity:

> All[32] the gods are three:
> Amun, the Sun, and Ptah, without their seconds.
> His identity is hidden in Amun,
> 5his is the Sun as face, his body is Ptah.

These are three expressions of one underlying deity, since the singular pronoun "his" is used. The deity is transcendent ("his identity is hidden in Amun"), he is manifest through the greatest force in nature ("his is the Sun as face"), and he extends his form or essence into the multiple "developments" of the created world ("his body is Ptah").[33] Earlier hints at Amun's role come to a climactic conclusion here; he is the ultimate cause.

III. Egyptian Cosmogonies and the Bible

Did Egyptian cosmogonies influence the biblical creation stories? The universe of Genesis 1 certainly resembles in a general way the Egyptian

---

[29] Ibid., 61 (my translation).
[30] The chapters are numbered by ones or tens or hundreds.
[31] Allen, *Genesis,* 53.
[32] Translation of Allen, *Genesis,* 54.
[33] Ibid., 54–55.

universe: "To the Egyptians, the world of experience was a finite 'box' of light, space, and order within an infinite expanse of dark, formless waters. The limits of this space were defined by the earth below and the surface of the outer waters above, held off the earth by the atmosphere. Earth is the domain of the mortal: man, animals, plants, 'fish and the crawling things.'"[34] In Genesis 1:2, all is boundless darkness and waters, and creation is by God's word. Hence many scholars believe that the process of creation described in the *Memphite Theology*—creation by the word of a single deity—influenced Genesis 1 either directly or indirectly through Phoenician models.[35] Egyptian influence on Genesis 1 is possible, especially if allowance is made for mediation through Phoenician cosmogonies like that of Philo of Byblos.[36]

Important differences between Egyptian and biblical cosmogonies must be mentioned. In Egyptian cosmogonies everything is contained within the inert monad, even the creator god. The creation process is sometimes depicted as a self-development from within Nun, at other times the creator is independent of his creation; these depictions may represent two sides of the same coin. In Genesis 1 the creator is unequivocally distinct from the *materia,* the distinction being underlined by repetition of the divine name and by the variety of the verbs of creating. The manner of creating in Genesis—speaking a word to darkness and waters—may have been at the inspiration of the *Memphite Theology,* but the assumptions behind each text are quite different.

One biblical text has been influenced by Egyptian cosmogonies—Psalm 104. Though the psalm opens with a description of a cosmogony in vv 5–9 (in which the verbs are preterit), it is primarily "a panorama of the natural world, conducted with a view to praising the creator for his superlative wisdom in conceiving and producing such an astonishing place."[37] There are parallels between the two hymns, both in phrasing

---

[34] Ibid., 56, and see pp. 6–7.

[35] K. Koch, "Wort und Einheit des Schöpfergottes in Memphis und Jerusalem," *ZTK* 62 (1965) 251–93; J. Ebach, *Weltentstehung und Kulturentwicklung bei Philo von Byblos: Ein Beitrag zur Überlieferung der biblischen Urgeschichte im Rahmen des altorientalischen und antiken Schöpfungsglauben* (BWANT 108; Stuttgart: Kohlhammer, 1979) 35–37; M. Fishbane, *Biblical Interpretation in Ancient Israel* (Oxford: Clarendon, 1985) 322–26; C. Westermann, *Genesis 1—11* (Minneapolis: Augsburg, 1984) 38–40.

[36] See "Creation Accounts in Canaanite Texts" below.

[37] J. D. Levenson, *Creation and the Persistence of Evil: The Jewish Drama of Divine Omnipotence* (San Francisco: Harper & Row, 1988) 57. He discusses the psalms and its

and concept; both poems open with a description of the deity wrapped in light, regard the night as the time for human beings to sleep and lions to prowl, underline divine care for the human race in daily life, and express wonder in the midst of their description. Even here one should not overlook different assumptions in the Egyptian poem about divine presence in the rays of the sun and about the connection of the divine rays with the new dynasty.

Even if Egyptian influence on the Bible is not nearly so pronounced as that of Mesopotamia on Genesis 2–11 or Canaan on Psalms, Job, and Second Isaiah, there are similarities. Both Egyptian and biblical texts witness to several "systems" or narratives of origins, though the Bible does not have the number and variations found in Egyptian literature. Regarding the place of the human community in creation, Egyptian texts stand apart from both the Bible and Mesopotamian literature. "The existence of men side by side with the gods at the time of their sojourn on earth is assumed everywhere, but so far no detailed account of the creation of man is known."[38] From the time of the New Kingdom the creator god is celebrated as "he who created the gods." Only late texts show human beings parallel to the gods in formulas such as "he who created everything that exists, who built men and created the gods," and "bringing mankind into being; forming the gods and creating all that exists."[39] A few early texts say that the human race was created from the tears of Re: "They [Shu and Tefnut] brought to me [Re] my eye with them. After I had joined my members together, I wept over them. That is how men came into being from the tears which came forth from my eye";[40] and "I created the gods from my sweat, and mankind from the tears of my eye" (*Coffin Text* 7. 465, Spell 1130). There is a play on the words for "humankind" and "tears." The gods are made from the divine aroma emanating from the creator god but humans are made from an imperfectly seeing, tear-filled eye. Human beings are created like everything else and

---

parallels with the *Hymn to the Aten* on pp. 57–65. The is found in *ANET* 369–71 and Lichtheim, *AEL* 2. 96–100.

[38] J. Cerny, *Ancient Egyptian Religion* (1952; reprinted Westport, CT: Greenwood, 1979) 48.

[39] Texts cited from Hornung, *Conceptions of God,* 149.

[40] "The Repulsing of the Dragon and Creation," *ANET* 6.

are called "cattle of the god" (*Instruction to King Merikare*) or "cattle of Re," but it is the gods who occupy center state in the cosmogonies.

Another difference concerns the finality of creation. No Egyptian text gives clear and unambiguous answers to the question why the world was created.[41] Amid the variety of biblical accounts, Yahweh always creates for a purpose—the divine honor.

[41] Hornung, *Conceptions of God,* 198.

CHAPTER 5

Creation Accounts
in Canaanite Texts

"Canaanite" refers to the culture common to the east coast of the Mediterranean in antiquity. The languages of the area, among them Ugaritic, Phoenician, Moabite, Ammonite, and Hebrew, are classed as Northwest Semitic. There existed also a common poetic tradition of themes and techniques, which is discernible in the extant literatures.[1]

There are three main sources (outside the Bible) for Canaanite cosmogonies: the Ugaritic texts of the Late Bronze Age (pre-1200 B.C.); the divine epithet "creator of (heaven) and earth," which occurs in Phoenician, Aramaic, and Punic inscriptions from the eighth century B.C. to the second century A.D.; and a late first- or early second-century A.D. compendium of mythology by a certain Philo of Byblos. The contribution of extant Canaanite literature if compared with Mesopotamia is disappointing. Ugaritic literature has no undisputed cosmogonies. The inscriptions only allude to cosmogonies in divine epithets. Philo's brief cosmogony is elliptical and its contents are undatable.

I. Ugaritic Texts

The evidence consists of epithets of El and Asherah, a text in which El begets a pair of gods, and the Baal cycle.

---

[1] For a recent discussion of the main issues in comparing Canaanite religion and cultures, see N. P. Lemche, *The Canaanites and Their Land: The Traditions of the Canaanites* (JSOTSup 110; Sheffield: JSOT, 1991).

A. Epithets of El and Asherah

El, old and bearded, chief of the pantheon, is five times called *bny bnwt*[2] (participle governing a substantive), "the creator of creation/creatures." Like Akkadian *banû*, Ugaritic **banaya* has a wide range of meanings — from constructing buildings to begetting gods or humans (in the latter meaning sometimes with *'b* "father").[3] The epithet usually occurs in the context of divine or human appeals to El's mercy (sometimes parallel to *'l d p'd,* "El who is merciful") to emphasize the supplicant's claim on El based on his fatherhood, something like "Do not abandon the person you have fathered." Another epithet of El in the Keret Epic, *'b 'dm,* "Father of Man,"[4] is also an expression of intimacy and dependence, as in such sentences as "Does [Keret] ask for the kingship of Bull his father / dominion like the Father of Man?" (*KTU* 1.14.1.43).[5]

El's wife Asherah has an analogous epithet *qnyt 'lm,* "creator of the gods."[6] The root **qny* is common Semitic for "to possess"; in Ugaritic, Phoenician, and Hebrew it also means "to create."[7] Its five instances in the Baal cycle characterize Asherah whose children ask her to obtain her husband El's permission to build palace for Baal. The nuance is something like "Help those whom you have borne!"

KTU 1.23 is a seventy-six-line poem in which El becomes sexually aroused and impregnates two women who then give birth to the two gods Shahar and Shalim. The text opens with repeated invitations, which suggests that it originally reflected or accompanied a ritual. A few scholars

---

[2] The instances are *KTU* 1.4.ii.11; iii.32; 1.6.iii.5, 11; 1.17.i.25. *Bnwt* alone is found in RS 24.244=*KTU* 1.100.62 (*w ttkl bnwth*) and RS 23.251=*KTU* 1.107.41 (broken context).

[3] For the Akkadian, see *CAD,* s.v. *banû.* The root has the same meaning in Amorite proper names. See H. B. Huffmon, *Amorite Personal Names in the Mari Texts: A Structural and Lexical Study* (Baltimore: Johns Hopkins University, 1965) 176. Hebrew *banâ,* on the other hand, never means "to beget."

[4] *KTU* 1.14.i.37, 43; iii.136, 151; v.259; vi.278, 297.

[5] In the Bible Yahweh is the father of the king by adoption, e.g., "You are my son, today I have begotten you" (Ps 2:7). Other instances are Ps 89:27–28 and 2 Sam 7:14 (see 1 Chr 28:6).

[6] The phrase occurs in *KTU* 1.4.i.23; iii.26, 30, 35; iv.32; 1.8.2. When it occurs as a fixed pair with *rbt atrt ym,* "Lady Asherah of the Sea," it occurs in second place.

[7] Bruce Vawter has denied that **qny* ever means create, but his argument is forced, particularly so in Deut 32:6 ("Surely He is your father who created you [*qānĕkā*], // He made you and established you"). See his "Prov 8:22: Wisdom and Creation," *JBL* 99 (1980) 205–16.

see the text as a theogony in which two gods are the firstborn of all the gods of Ugarit. Gregorio del Olmo Lete properly rejects this interpretation, taking the poem as a ritual, a *hieros logos* turned into literature and used at a festival under the patronage of the two gods who are personifications of Venus and Ashtar.[8]

From these epithets and from *KTU* 1.23, J. C. de Moor concludes: "To the Canaanites creation and procreation were aspects of one and the same concept."[9] El created the world, the gods, and human beings. Unfortunaely, the details of El's creative acts are not presented in the extant texts; we have only the epithets.

B. The Baal Cycle

The only other important Ugaritic evidence bearing on cosmogonies is the so-called Baal cycle, six tablets describing the storm god's battles with *Yammu* (Sea) and with *Môtu* (Death). Are the texts genuine cosmogonies? Many specialists deny it, among them J. C. Greenfield: "The Ugaritic texts record no creation or flood story, although fragments from Akkadian texts excavated at Ugarit deal with elements of these stories."[10] According to John Day, "There are grounds for believing, therefore, that the Canaanites may have associated the creation of the world with Baal's victory over the dragon and the sea, even though the Ugaritic Baal-Yam text (*CTA* =*KTU* 1.2) is not concerned with the creation."[11] Arvid Kapelrud is more emphatic: "Creation is when something new which

---

[8] G. del Olmo Lete, *Mitos y leyendas de Canaan segun la tradición de Ugarit* (Madrid: Ediciones Christiandad, 1981) 437–39. The suggestion of del Olmo Lete (p. 270) and others that El "creates" a being to take away Keret's illness in *KTU* 1.16.28–32 is based, apart from the verb **qaraṣa* ("to pinch off [clay]"), entirely upon conjectural readings.

[9] J. C. de Moor, "El the Creator," in *The Bible World: Essays in Honor of Cyrus H. Gordon* (ed. G. Rendsberg et al.; New York: Ktav, 1980) 187. J.-L. Cunchillos, "Peut-on parler de mythes de création à Ugarit?" in *La Création*, 94–95, attempts to reduce creation in Ugaritic to sexual generation, failing to appreciate that Ugaritic **bny*, like Akkadian *banû*, can mean "build" as well as "beget."

[10] J. C. Greenfield, "The Hebrew Bible and Canaanite Literature," in *The Literary Guide to the Bible* (ed. R. Alter and F. Kermode; Cambridge, MA: Harvard University, 1987) 547 and 557. Similarly skeptical is W. Röllig in "Syrien. Die Mythologie der Ugariter und Phönizier," *WM* (Stuttgart: Klett, 1965) 1. 309.

[11] J. Day, *God's Conflict with the Dragon and the Sea: Echoes of a Canaanite Myth in the Old Testament* (Cambridge: Cambridge University, 1985) 17.

was not there before is produced. Ordering of chaos is thus not creation"; and again: "Is there . . . a Baal creation as cosmogony? . . . the answer is definitely no."[12] According to André Caquot, Maurice Sznycer, and André Herdner, the Baal texts are interpretations of specific phenomena rather than cosmogonies. The conflict between Baal and Sea is a theomachy pure and simple; the story of Baal's death and liberation is a mythic transposition of the annual disappearance of rain in the spring and its return in the autumn.[13]

Others unhesitatingly interpret Baal's battles and victories as cosmogonies. Frank Moore Cross distinguishes "the Ugaritic cosmogonic cycle (in which Baal battles with Sea and Death to secure kingship)" from theogony, which he defines as "the birth and succession of the gods, especially the old gods."[14] Loren Fisher discerns cosmogony in certain key themes:

> Is this conflict theme [between Baal and Sea or Death] related to kingship, temple building, or creation? I think this is an improper question. . . . conflict, kingship, ordering of chaos, and temple building are all related to an overarching theme that I would call "creation." However, this is not a theogony or a creation of the El type. Rather it is cosmogonic and is of the Baal type.[15]

The terms of the debate have not always been clear as is evident when one compares the definitions of Kapelrud and Fisher. One must define cosmogony in ancient rather than modern terms, i.e., as the emergence of the world of gods and of human society, and then rely for proof chiefly on narrative logic rather than on isolated verses or themes. The Baal cycle

---

[12] A. Kapelrud, "Creation in the Ras Shamra Texts," *ST* 34 (1980) 3, 9. Other scholars who deny that there are cosmogonies at Ugarit are M. H. Pope, *El in the Ugaritic Texts* (Leiden: Brill, 1955) 49; and B. Margalit, "The Ugaritic Creation Myth: Fact or Fiction?" *UF* 13 (1981) 137–45, at least in regard the Baal-Mot conflict (p. 140).

[13] *Textes ougaritiques* (LAPO 7; Paris: Cerf, 1974) 116, 234.

[14] F. M. Cross, "The 'Olden Gods' and Ancient Near Eastern Creation Myths," *Magnalia Dei: The Mighty Acts of God: Essays on the Bible and Archaeology in Memory of G. Ernest Wright* (ed. F. M. Cross et al.; Garden City, NY: Doubleday, 1976) 333, 329. See also his *CMHE,* 39–43, 120.

[15] L. Fisher, "Creation at Ugarit and in the Old Testament," *VT* 15 (1965) 316. I originally defended a similar position in "Cosmogonies in the Ugaritic Texts and in the Bible," *Or* 53 (1984) 183–201, but now believe the evidence is insufficient to draw such a firm conclusion.

is a narrative that works through plot and character; the composer does not step outside the story. Hence we must turn to the narrative elements of the cycle for answers to the question about cosmogony.

The major Ugaritic texts telling of Baal's combats with Yam and Mot are in *KTU* 1.1–6 (=*CTA* 1–6). Some of the tablets are too obscure or broken to provide a connected story. Only tablets 1.3–6 are of sufficient size and narrative coherence to be helpful; 1.1. and 1.2 are relevant but fragmentary. A longstanding problem of interpretation is the original sequence of the tablets now designated *KTU* 1.3–6. Of the four tablets (each written on both sides in two, three, or four columns), initial and final columns are preserved only on *KTU* 1.5 and 1.6. Preservation of such final and initial columns is important because the final line of one tablet is repeated in the first line of the next, thus showing the sequence of tablets. The lost beginnings and ends of *KTU* 1.3 and 1.4 make it impossible to know with certainty how the tablets relate to each other and to tablet 1.5–1.6.[16]

Since I have presented my views on the proper sequence elsewhere, I offer only two brief conclusions here.[17] The first is that, contrary to the scholarly consensus, *KTU* 1.4 does *not* immediately precede *KTU* 1.5. My reasons for denying such a sequence of tablets are that Baal's enemy is distinct in each story—Mot in 1.4–1.6 and Yam in 1.2–1.3. In the Bible, too, Yahweh's battles with sea and with desert are not parts of a continuous story but rather different versions.[18] The alleged sequence 1.4+1.5+1.6 yields an inconclusive and implausible seesaw battle first between Baal and Yam and then between Baal and Mot. Further, there is a serious mechanical problem if one proposes that tablet 1.5 follows 1.4: there is not enough space in the final column (viii) of *KTU* 1.4 for the action and words that are presupposed by the messenger speech in the first column of *KTU* 1.5. My second conclusion, that *KTU* 1.3 and

[16] Most scholars hold that tablets 4, 5, and 6 are in sequence but differ on where *KTU* 1.3 belongs. Herdner's sequence (in *CTA* pp. 5–31), *KTU* 1.2.i, iii, iv; 1.3; 1.4, is rearranged by H. L. Ginsberg as *KTU* 1.2.iii, i, iv; 1.4; 1.3 (in *ANET* 129–42). De Moor posits *KTU* 1.3, 1.1., 1.2, 1.4., 1.5, 1.6 in *The Seasonal Pattern in the Ugaritic Myth of Ba'lu* (AOAT 16; Neukirchen-Vluyn: Butzon & Bercker Kevelaer, 1971) 36–43. See also del Olmo Lete, *Mitos y leyendas*, 87–95.

[17] For a full discussion see my "Cosmogonies in the Ugaritic Texts," 188–93.

[18] The Baal-Mot story is reflected in the Bible in Deut 32:7–14 and in Second Isaiah 43:16–21, among other texts. The Baal-Yam story occurs more frequently, e.g., in Exod 15:1–18; Pss 74:12–17; 77:14–21; 89:10–11; 114, etc.

1.4 are variants rather than sequential parts, is suggested by the identical sequence of action in both tablets; the differences arise from the character of the opponents. We turn to the three narratives of the cycle.

1. KTU 1.5–1.6. In the tablet (now missing) that preceded 1.5, Mot in his underworld domain must have instructed Baal's two messengers to deliver to their master on Mount Zaphon an ominous invitation to his banquet: "Indeed summon Baal with my brethren. Invite Haddu with my kinfolk. Eat food with my brethren. Drink wine with my kinfolk."[19] Baal hears it with dread and confesses that he is Mot's vassal "forever" (col. ii). In the fragmentary cols. iii and iv, the gods are summoned to a banquet; the divine assembly makes a decision, apparently to ratify Mot's power over Baal, for in col. v a messenger (or Mot himself) orders Baal and his entourage to the underworld with such authority that Baal descends to his death.

Later, messengers report back to El, "We came upon Baal fallen to the earth. Dead is Aliyan Baal, departed is Prince, Lord of the earth" (vi.8–10). El and Anat engage in mourning rites (vi) and Anat in the next tablet brings the body to Mount Zaphon for burial and sacrifice (1.6.i). El is unable to find among his and Asherah's children a replacement for Baal, making dramatically clear the enormity of Baal's loss (i.32–67). Afterward the bereaved Anat, still passionately devoted to Baal, encounters Mot. In response to her pleas, Mot callously describes how he consumed Baal "like a lamb in my mouth" (ii.22–23). Later, losing control of herself, she seizes Mot, cutting him up and sowing him far and wide (ii.30–37). After a break of forty lines, El declares that "Aliyan Baal lives, existent is Prince, Lord of the earth," for he sees in a dream the signs of Baal's return to life—the heavens raining oil and the wadis running with honey (iii). Anat is sent to ask Shapshu, the sun goddess, to search for Baal, who is presumed to be alive on the basis of the reviving earth in El's dream (iv). After a break of thirty-five lines, Baal defeats rebellious sons of Asherah and takes the throne. In the seventh year of his reign,[20] Mot returns to exact vengeance for the humiliation inflicted on him by Anat: "Because of you, Baal, I experienced winnowing in the sea. Give me one of your brothers to eat" (v). After sixty broken lines, Mot comes back

---

[19] The invitation can be reconstructed from its repetition in 1.5.i.

[20] The number seven in Ugaritic literature can simply mean a climax, as in Keret's march against Udum (*KTU* 1.14.iii.106–9). It may well have nothing to do with agricultural seasons, expressing perhaps only the climactic moment of Mot's revenge.

to Baal on Mount Zaphon to accuse him of offering Mot's own brothers for Mot's consuming: "My brothers you have given, O Baal, for my devouring, the children of my mother for my consuming" (vi.14–16). Baal and Mot fight like animals until both collapse. Shapshu rebukes Mot: "How dare you fight with Aliyan Baal . . . [Bull El your father] will uproot the base of your dwelling. Surely he will overturn your royal throne. Surely he will shatter your scepter of judgment" (vi.24–29). Mot in fear desists, and Baal remounts his throne. The final scene seems to describe a banquet of the gods. The lines laud the sun god, Shapshu, as a judge, and mention Koshar wa-Hasis (vi).[21]

Is the text a cosmogony? Baal dies at the hands of Mot, rises and defeats his enemies, and is finally enthroned in response to El's word.[22] Human life and social order are at stake in Baal's death and return to life. When El and Anat hear that Baal is lying dead in the underworld, they lament: "Baal is dead, what will happen to the people? The son of Dagan, what will happen to the multitudes?" (1.5.vi.23–24; 1.6.i.6–7). Baal's enemy, Mot, is an enemy of life and what makes life possible: "My appetite is in want of humans, my appetite, of the multitudes of the earth" (1.6.ii.17–19). As long as Baal is dead, the fields do not produce (1.6.iv.25–29). El realizes that Baal is alive when he dreams of fertility: "The heavens rain oil, the wadis run with honey" (1.6.iii.6–7, 12–13). At stake, then, in the texts is the existence of the human race and the order of the world.

Although the story concerns the preconditions for life (fertility) and human society (and consequently human kingship), the extant myth does not portray cosmogony in the strict sense. Baal is not shown creating the cosmos, and his dominion is not absolute; in the beginning he is in the power of Death, and at the end El's power (invoked by Shapshu), not his own, rids him of Mot. Thus Baal's dominion is limited.

The root puzzle is the relationship between El and Baal. El hands Baal over to Mot (to Yam in *KTU* 1.2.i) yet rejoices when Baal revives and upholds his reign. Though the same epithet "beloved of El (*ydd 'l*)" is applied to both Yam and Mot, its precise nuance is unknown. Baal appears to rule as El's viceroy, but even El is overruled by fate. Did El (and Asherah) create the world and then assign rule to Baal to govern with as much

---

[21] Shapshu here and in *KTU* 1.2.iii is the guardian of thrones, a function that Astarte and Horon exercise elsewhere (in *KTU* 1.2.iv and 1.16.vi.54–58).

[22] 1.6.vi has the look of a true finale.

power as is possible in an imperfect world?[23] At any rate, only El and Asherah are explicitly said to create (*bny, qny*) in the Ugaritic texts. The fact that in the Bible Yahweh's victories over Sea (e.g., Ps 74:13–17) and the sterile desert (e.g., Deut 32:6–14 and Isa 43:16–21; 51:9–11) are genuine cosmogonies is no argument that the Ugaritic victories of Baal are cosmogonic also. The Bible borrows language belonging both to the storm god Baal and the patriarch El for its portrait of Yahweh. Since Yahweh is the sole deity, his victories over Sea and Death can be cosmogonic, without implying that Baal's victories are. In polytheistic Ugarit, the two gods have different functions.

2. *KTU 1.4.* The opening complaint, "Baal has no palace like the gods, no court like the sons of Asherah," is directed to the artisan god Kothar wa-Hasis. He is asked to fashion gifts for Asherah, the consort of El, to persuade her to intercede with her husband on behalf of Baal's palace. Asherah receives Baal and Anat bearing the gifts and apparently sends off her servant to provide fish for a meal (ii). Thirty-five lines are defective or missing, making it difficult to understand why Baal rebukes a dissolute banquet. Baal and Anat return during a banquet of the gods to persuade Asherah to cooperate (iii).

Asherah agrees to intercede, journeying in grand style toward El "at the sources of the Two Floods." As El greets her affectionately, she reminds him that the gods have acclaimed Baal as king, which implies a palace: "Your decree, O El, is wise, your wisdom is forever, a life of good fortune is your decree. Our king is Aliyan Baal, our judge, there is none above him . . . . Alas, he cries out to Bull El his father . . . Baal has no palace like the gods, no court like the sons of Asherah" (iv.41–51). El accedes to her request: "Let a palace be built for Baal like the gods, a court like the children of Asherah" (iv.62–v.63).

Events move quickly. Anat brings the happy news to Baal, who, after amassing the materials for a large structure, summons Kothar wa-Hasis

---

[23] W. G. Lambert suggests that the Labbu and the Anzu myths in which a junior god does battle with a demonic being or monster on behalf of elders unable to defend themselves who yet retain their power, provides a better model for the Baal cycle than the often-cited *Enūma elish,* in which Marduk is given irrevocable power; see his "Old Testament Mythology in Its Ancient Near Eastern Context," in *Congress Volume* (ed. J. Emerton; VTSup 40; Leiden: Brill, 1988) 140. But the two Mesopotamian myths are very fragmentary and in any case do not explain El's power over Mot (1.6.vi) or his yielding to Mot (1.5) and Yam (1.2).

to be the architect. Kothar insists on building a window in the palace (v). The controversy about whether a window should be installed will not be settled until vii.14–28. The palace is built, Baal declaring at its completion, "My house I have built of silver, my palace of gold" (vi.36–38). A dedicatory banquet for the all the gods follows (vi). In column vii, Baal marches through numerous towns in the vicinity of his Mount Zaphon, and from his palace proclaims his kingship in peals of thunder, scattering his enemies. At this moment of triumph, Baal instructs his messengers to carry his proclamation to the underworld and invite Mot to a banquet (viii). This unusually long tablet (about 480 lines), quite possibly complete in itself, ends with the proclamation to the underworld.

Unlike *KTU* 1.5–1.6, which underlines the momentous consequences of Baal's death and resurrection for the nourishment and security of the human race, 1.4 focuses on the palace of Baal. The palace represents power in the heavens and hence power on earth. Baal can at last leave the household of El, for his own palace gives him autonomy. His hosting of the banquet signals a shift in divine power: "I alone am the one who will rule the gods, who will fatten gods and human beings, who will sate the multitudes of the earth" (vii.49–52). The thunder and lightning that issue from his palace have specific meaning; they accompany the rains that awaken the fertility of the soil. Despite the symbolic importance of the palace, however, the extant myth does not seem to be a cosmogony. Baal's kingship, of course, has implications for the human king and society, but the building of his palace requires permission of El. Obtaining El's permission seems in fact to be the point of the drama.

3. *KTU 1.3*. Cols. i and ii, because of their uncertain context, do little more for us than give *tableaux vivants* of Baal at a banquet (i) and of Anat rampaging as a war goddess (ii). In col. iii Baal sends a message to Anat. Upon seeing his messengers, she assumes that he needs help against the enemies she and Baal once defeated—Yam and his allies, who drove Baal from his throne on Mount Zaphon (iii–iv). Baal's message, however, is a happy one: Anat is invited to join him for a love feast (iv). Baal's offer of love is a bribe, like the gifts offered to Asherah in *KTU* 1.4. And it is likewise effective; Anat agrees to intercede with El for Baal's palace (iv). Poor El! The goddess of war threatens mayhem if he withholds permission (iv). She repeats the complaint that Baal has no palace. El's response to her is not preserved, but about 32 lines later,

someone (probably El or Asherah) instructs messengers to summon Koshar wa-Hasis, no doubt to begin work on the palace.

The contribution of *KTU* 1.3 to our knowledge of cosmogony is similar to that of 1.4, though 1.4 because of its length gives more detail on the palace. The special contribution of 1.3 is to show that Baal's great victory over Sea and his allies preceded the request for a palace. In 1.3 the palace of Baal probably commemorates the victory over Sea (Mount Zaphon is the site of both the palace and the battle), which is not included in the extant Baal-Mot tablets.

The question whether the Baal cycle is a true cosmogony is unanswerable. Some of the elements of cosmogonies are there—the building of a temple, the bestowal of fertility and of kingship (hence of social order); on the other hand, Baal does not make anything and, more importantly, is not ultimately powerful. He sits on the throne through El's decree, as both Anat's and Asherah's intercession for him attest. As long as the relationship of El and Baal in the Ugaritic texts is not fully known, a satisfactory understanding of cosmogony in the Baal cycle is not possible.[24]

II. Phoenician and Punic Inscriptions

In a lengthy eighth-century Phoenician inscription from Karatepe in Cilicia, Azitiwada (apparently a vassal king), after describing his benefactions to Adana, the Danunians, and the royal house of Mopsos, threatens any would-be defacer of his monument: iii.18"May Baal Shamem and El Creator of the Earth (*'l qn 'rṣ*) 19and Eternal Sun and all the assembly of the sons of the gods efface that kingdom and that king and iv.1that man who is a man of renown" (*KAI* 26).[25] A similar phrase appears in Genesis 14:18: *'ēl 'elyôn qōnēh šāmayim wā'āreṣ,* "El Elyon creator of heaven and earth." In Azitiwada's curse, El is named

---

[24] Del Olmo Lete also seems undecided on our precise question, insisting on a primordial ("separation") aspect to Baal's conflicts, even as he allows influence from a seasonal or fertility interpretation, *Mitos y leyendas,* 145–53.

[25] Other epigraphic mentions of "El Creator of the Earth" are not particularly revealing: an eighth/seventh century B.C. Jerusalem fragment, an Aramaic first-century A.D. inscription from Palmyra, four tesserae from Palmyra, an inscription from Hatra, and a Neo-Punic dedicatory plaque of the early second century A.D. See P. D. Miller, "El, the Creator of Earth," *BASOR* 239 (1980) 43–46. In a Hittite myth borrowed from Canaan before 1200 B.C., El is called Elkunirsa, a reflection of *'ēl qōnē 'erṣ(a).*

after Baal Shamem (probably the storm god Baal Hadad)²⁶ and before Eternal Sun and the assembly of the gods.²⁷ Azitiwada invokes Baal at the beginning of the inscription and that priority apparently carries over into the curse at the end. El was the high god of the pre-1200 B.C. Ugaritic pantheon and presumably remained so generally in Phoenician religion, but evidently did not have to be named first in lists. If the first epithet "Lord of Heaven" suggests authority over storms and fertility, El's epithet "Creator of the Earth" locates his authority in the act of creating, which is here distinct from Baal Shamem's activity. The inscription thus supports the conclusions based on the Ugaritic texts, in which El creates and Baal (presuming Baal Shamem is Baal Hadad) is patron of kings and lord of the fertility-bestowing storm.

III. The Cosmogonies of Philo of Byblos

In his apologetic work *Praeparatio evangelica,* the church father Eusebius of Caesarea (ca. A.D. 260–340) reprinted excerpts from *The Phoenician History* of Philo of Byblos (ca. A.D. 50–150), because he believed Philo's pagan views were an unwitting argument for the Christian view of God and the world. The first excerpt, a cosmogony (though Eusebius calls its latter part a "zoogony"), has the world coming into being *without* a creator god. The immediately following section, a *History of Culture,* tells how the human race discovered civilization without the help of the gods. The third, a *History of Kronos,* makes clear at the outset that the gods were really only human beings; Kronos' father is pointedly called *epigeios autochthōn* ("native inhabitant of the earth"). Eusebius was no great stylist, preferring to incorporate unchanged or abbreviated long passages from other writers. Few scholars, therefore, doubt the basic accuracy of Eusebius' excerpts from *The Phoenician History.* They question rather the accuracy of Philo: did he faithfully reproduce the sources he names—the ancient Phoenician sage Sakkunyaton and, further back, his Egyptian sources (under the name of Thot)—or did he merely give

---

²⁶ Whether Baal Shamem is to be identified with Baal Hadad is disputed. I follow M. L. Barré, *The God-List in the Treaty between Hannibal and Philip V of Macedonia: A Study in Light of the Ancient Near Eastern Treaty Tradition* (Baltimore: Johns Hopkins University, 1983) 40–57.

²⁷ The assembly is sometimes addressed as a distinct entity, as in *KAI* 4.4–5; 10.10, 16.

his own first-century synthesis of Phoenician religion, citing nonexistent ancient sources merely for verisimilitude?

Philo's fidelity has been judged differently over the past century and a half. Before the discovery of the Ugaritic texts in 1929, most scholars dismissed him as an innovator and thus an unreliable guide to late-first or early-second-millennium Phoenician religion. But when the Ugaritic texts (and the Hittite Kumarbi myth published in 1936) turned out to have affinities with *The Phoenician History,* Philo's reputation was rehabilitated. Skepticism returned, however, in the 1970s, chiefly because of heightened awareness of his pervasive euhemerism, which was a view prevalent in the hellenistic era that the stories of gods were actually stories of human heroes glorified after their death.[28]

The question of Philo's authenticity, which has dominated recent scholarship,[29] is not the main concern of this chapter. Our inquiry is rather twofold: What traditions and genres did he use, and what is the meaning of his *Cosmogony* and *History of Culture? The Cosmogony (Praeparatio evangelica* 1.9.30–10.5):

> 10.1 The beginning of everything he [Philo/Sakkunyaton] posits as a dark and windy air (*aēr*), or a blast of dark air, and turbid, dark chaos. These were limitless and for a long time without boundaries. He [Philo/Sakkunyaton] says, "When the wind lusted after its own beginnings and a mixing took place, that entwining was called desire. And that was the beginning of all things. But it [the wind] did not know its creation, and from the same entwining of the wind Mot came into being. 2 Some say this is mud, others the putrefaction of the watery mixture. And from this came every seed of creation and origin of all things.
>
> There were some living creatures without sense perception; from them arose creatures with sense perception, and they are called Zophasemim, that is, watchers of heaven. They were formed in the shape of an egg, and Mot shone forth, with sun and moon and stars and the great

---

[28] Euhemerus (311–298 B.C.) wrote a novel about his imaginary travels to an island in the Indian Ocean where he learned that Uranus, Kronos, and Zeus had been great kings in their day and were worshiped after their death by a grateful people. This view was compatible both with the practice of hellenistic rulers receiving worship from their subjects and with the old Greek epic, which blurred the distinction between man and god.

[29] See the review of opinions in H. W. Attridge and R. A. Oden, *Philo of Byblos: The Phoenician History: Introduction, Critical Text, Translation, Notes* (CBQMS 9; Washington: Catholic Biblical Association, 1981). Attridge and Oden are somewhat skeptical about Philo's value for the reconstruction of ancient Canaanite religion.

constellations." [Eusebius] ³Such was their cosmogony, which openly introduces atheism. Let us next see how he says the zoogony took place. He [Philo/Sakkunyaton] says:

⁴And as the air became luminous, because of the heating of the sea and the land, there arose winds and clouds and from the celestial waters came great downpours and floods. And when [the waters] were separated from each other and were removed from their proper place by the heating of the sun, and everything kept bumping into each other in the air and ran into each other, there were thunders and lightnings. At the crash of thunder the intelligent creatures already mentioned woke up, startled by the noise, and began to move on land and sea, male and female.

⁵Such is their zoogony.³⁰ Next the same author adds: "These are the things that are found written in the cosmogony of Taautos and in his writings both from conjectures and evidence that his mind saw, discovered, and clarified for us."

Among Philo's sources are Egyptian cosmogonies, especially those of Heliopolis and Hermopolis, which form part of the Egyptian legacy of Phoenicia.³¹ At Heliopolis, Atum generates from himself the first divine couple, Shu the god of air and Tefnut the god of moisture, from whom are born Geb (earth) and Nut (sky). At Hermopolis, Ptah emerges from Nun, the primeval ocean, and embodies himself in darkness. Though Egyptian cosmogonies often reflect natural activity such as creation taking place on a tiny hillock teeming with life after the inundation of the Nile, Philo's antitheological bias exceeds Egyptian naturalism. It resembles Greek (Ionian) science, which attests a similar conflict between traditional beliefs and scientific meteorology in the sixth century B.C.³²

---

³⁰ Though Eusebius in section 3 distinguishes the zoogony from the cosmogony, Philo must have told the two as one story, since section 4 directly continues section 2.

³¹ A point noted by many scholars, most recently A. I. Baumgarten, *The Phoenician History of Philo of Byblos: A Commentary* (Études préliminaires aux religions orientales dans l'Empire Romain; Leiden: Brill, 1981) 108, 110, and J. Ebach, *Weltentstehung und Kulturentwicklung bei Philo von Byblos: Ein Beitrag zur Überlieferung der biblischen Urgeschichte im Rahmen des altorientalischen und antiken Schöpfungsglauben* (BWANT 108; Stuttgart: Kohlhammer, 1979) 35–37.

³² Baumgarten, *The Phoenician History,* 121–24. In mainland Greece during the late fifth century, myths came under criticism for their approach to reality. The mysteries were also attacked. See W. Burkert, *Greek Religion* (Cambridge, MA: Harvard University, 1985) chapter 7.

If the book's antitheological perspective derives from Greek skepticism, it cannot antedate the sixth century B.C. (though the some of the myths may be older). Philo must also have drawn on native Phoenician lore. There is little Phoenician material extant to verify that presupposition, it is true, but the *Cosmogony* displays pervasive parallelism, evidence of Phoenician style. Baumgarten points out nine convincing examples, e.g., "dark and windy air // a blast of dark air," "at the crash of thunder . . . they awoke" // "they were startled by the noise."[33] In summary, Philo or Sakkunyaton combined native Egyptian and Phoenician traditions and transmitted them through a perspective derived from Greek science (building perhaps on the naturalism of Egyptian cosmogonies).

What does Philo's eclectic *Cosmogony* say? The universe originated when wind came into contact with moist and formless stuff. Initial movement is explained on the analogy of sexual desire, which leads to entwining; all personality is expressly denied to the wind ("it did not know its own creation"). From the contact of wind with muddy and dark chaos comes Mot (etymology unknown), which Philo acknowledges is a controverted term; it is either mud or moist rotting material. Non-sensing creatures arise in this seedbed, and from them another order of living beings, those with sense faculties. Their name *Zophasemin* (Hebrew ṣōpê šāmayim, "watchers of heavens"), to judge from the context, defines them as earthly observers of the heavens. In 1 Enoch 1:5 and 12:14 they are angelic figures, and it may be that the text is demythologizing here. Mot, previously dark, becomes light with the appearance of sun. The sun also brings heat, causing rains and displacement of the heavenly waters. The resultant thunder and lightning wake up the sensing (hearing) creatures, which then begin to move.

All the dynamism is immanent and modeled on human behavior such as sexual desire that moves toward union or noise that awakens animate beings. The sole agent is wind. Its arousal ("lusted") is explained by wind's ordinary movement. To J. Ebach, both Genesis 1 and Philo's *Cosmogony* demythologize their traditions but in different ways. In Genesis 1, the usual movers in cosmogonies such as the chaos dragon, sea, stars, and wind, become instruments or products of the one God who alone creates. In Philo's work, the creator god is eliminated; physical and intelligent

---

[33] Baumgarten, *The Phoenician History,* 98–99.

life arises through the dynamism of wind, the inherent fertility of moist environments, and the violence of thunder and lightning.[34]

Philo's *Cosmogony* suggests that between the sixth century B.C. and the first century A.D. there were eclectic cosmogonies in Phoenicia that derived their traditions, perspectives, and rhetorical techniques from Egypt, Greece, and Phoenicia. Philo's *Cosmogony* is presumably representative, since Eusebius chose it to indict Phoenician culture generally. Other instances of the same phenomenon are the cosmogonies of Eudemos, Moschos, and Genesis 1. Those cosmogonies deal with the origin of the world and the *Urstoff,* the principle of initial movement, and of the living beings populating the universe. They also demythologize primordial elements such as water and wind.

The *History of Culture* (*Praeparatio evangelica* 1.10.6–14) seems immediately to follow the *Cosmogony,* according to Eusebius ("thereafter" sec. 6). The great wind of the cosmogony is divided into smaller winds, which are given names. From a particular wind, "Kolpia and his wife Baau[35] (which means night), Aion and Protogonos, were born, mortal men, so named." Philo again eliminates all gods and insists that the initial principle was wind interacting with moist darkness. One of the winds couples with "his wife," expressly interpreted as "night," thus repeating the "turbid, dark chaos" (10) of the first cosmogony but on a smaller scale. Then appear pairs of culture heroes or discoverers of what is essential for civilization, e.g., arboriculture, worship, fire, giants lending their names to mountains, architecture, and the settlement of Tyre (apparently the first city, from the perspective of the work). It is important to note that the story of civilization continues the cosmogony directly, an instance of the close connection between creation and culture known in Mesopotamia and Egypt. The list of culture heroes here depends on Babylonian traditions of the *apkallu*s (the seven antediluvian men who discovered and transmitted culture) and *ummānu*s (the postdiluvian sages), figures that show up vestigially in the Levant.[36] Philo, in fact, links Sakkunyaton

[34] J. Ebach, *Weltentstehung,* 75. Eusebius remarked that Philo "openly introduces atheism" in *Praeparatio evangelica,* 10.3.

[35] "Kolpia" has been claimed as a Semitic and a Greek word, but no etymology has won general acceptance. *Baau* may well derive from Hebrew (or a Phoenician cognate) *bōhû* (see Gen 1:2).

[36] For recent discussion, see C. Wilcke, "Göttliche und menschliche Weisheit im Alten Orient: Magie und Wissenschaft, Mythos und Geschichte," *Weisheit: Archäologie der*

himself to the old sages: "But he [in contrast to his contemporaries], having access to what was found in the innermost part of sanctuaries, secret writings written in the script of the *ummānu,* which were obviously not known to all, devoted himself to learning all of them." Behind the Greek crux *ammounaion,* in Philo's preface (*Praeparatio evangelica* 9.26), H. Ewald, W. F. Albright, and Jonas Greenfield have read *ummānu:* Sakkunyaton took the writings of the ancient culture heroes and transmitted them in a unified fashion with the biases noted above.

Conclusions

Unfortunately for comparative purposes, the Canaanite religious evidence is far more random than that of Egypt and Mesopotamia and it has been too often made a foil for the alleged superiority of the Bible. The undoubted creator gods are El and his wife Asherah. One of the modes of creating is sexual generation, which is conveyed by the Ugaritic verbs *banaya* ("to beget, build") and *qanaya* ("to beget, create; own"). Baal's victory over Sea and Death and the political and social order resulting from it (symbolized by his temple and feast) cannot, on the basis of the present evidence, be called a cosmogony.

The object of El's creative activity is the earth in the inscriptional epithet "creator of the earth," and gods and human beings in the Ugaritic epithet "father of gods and man." With regard to the begetting of the gods, El's wife Asherah shares El's role, for she is several times called "creator of the gods."

Except for proper names, e.g., Abner (=" [My] father is a lamp"), the Bible seldom calls God "father."[37] Apart from references to God's paternal love, e.g., Ps 103:13 and Prov 3:12, only a few texts use "father" of God's creating. Deut 32:6, 18 are perhaps the strongest statements: "Is not he your father who created you (*qānekā*), who made you (*'āśekā*) and established you (*wayĕkōnĕnekā*)?" and "You neglected the Rock who bore you, you forgot the God who gave you birth."

As already noted, the battles between the storm god Baal (sometimes assisted by his consort Anat) and Sea and Death have certainly influenced

---

literarischen Kommunikation III (ed. A. Assman; Munich: Gink, 1991) 259–70; J. C. Greenfield, "The Seven Pillars of Wisdom (Prov. 9:1) — A Mistranslation," *JQR* 76 (1985) 13–20.

[37] H. Ringgren, "'*ābh,*" in *TDOT* 1. 17–18.

biblical cosmogonies in which Yahweh creates by defeating the sea. John Day has ably studied the biblical instances of *Chaoskampf* (Psalms 74:12–17; 89:10–15; 104:1–9; 65:7–8; 93, and some passages from Job) and properly pointed to Canaanite (as opposed to Babylonian) influence on the biblical passages. One might assume that, if the biblical battles with chaos are cosmogonic, then the Ugaritic battle would also be. Our present understanding of the Ugaritic sources does not allow us to draw that conclusion, however. Day suggests that Ugaritic religion regarded El as the creator and attributed all creation to him. The Bible, however, drawing on portraits of both El and Baal for its portrait of Yahweh, interpreted Yahweh's victories as cosmogonic.[38] Or it may be that Baal's victories are genuine cosmogonies but we do not sufficiently understand them.

It is not widely recognized that the Baal-Mot conflict has left its traces on the Bible though less frequently than the Baal-Yam conflict. The biblical wilderness occasionally depicted as a death-dealing environment, analogous to the underworld of the Ugaritic texts. Second Isaiah speaks of the return to Zion as a new exodus-conquest through the tamed desert, on the model of the first exodus-conquest through the tamed sea. Isa 43:16–21 juxtaposes the two hostile environments. Deuteronomy 32 sees the origin of Israel as an act of rescue from a baneful power and a movement toward "order," security, and abundance in Yahweh's precincts. The people's passage from danger, or "chaos," to secured existence resembles Exod 15:1–8; Pss 78:42–55; 114; 135; and 136. Deuteronomy 32 does not simply describe Israel in the desert before it was corrupted by false worship in Canaan, as do Hos 2:16–17 and Jer 2:1–3. The poem prefaces the rescue of Israel in the desert with a scene at the heavenly assembly in which the Most High assigns to each nation a land and a heavenly patron. There follows an account of how Israel came to be Yahweh's people in his land — by being rescued from the annihilating power of infertility. The verses are no less a true cosmogony than the victory over sea. Israel comes into existence as Yahweh's people when they are led away from the destructive force that keeps them out of his land. Thus has the Canaanite Baal-Mot conflict been transposed.

[38] Day, *God's Conflict*, 17–18.

PART TWO

Creation Accounts in the Bible

CHAPTER 6

Genesis 1–11

Genesis 1–11 are surely the best known biblical creation texts, supplying imagery and concepts to countless readers and hearers for over two and a half millennia. Not surprisingly, these chapters have been subjected to minute analysis from almost every conceivable standpoint. My purpose here will not be to rehearse those interpretations[1] but rather to make some comments on the text, most of them prompted by comparison with other cosmogonic traditions. But first a few general observations must be made.

According to the literary analysis done over the past century and a half, Genesis 1–11 is composed of a venerable basic story of some length (conventionally "the Yahwist"; German *Jahwist*=J), which has been introduced and supplemented by a later writer, the Priest (=P) of the sixth-century B.C. exile or a bit later. P is often regarded as the final redactor of the entire Pentateuch, though some scholars postulate a distinct redactor (=R) who brought the J and P traditions together.[2] The P-material in Genesis 1–11 is generally reckoned as follows: 1:1–2:3, 4a; 5:1–28, 30–32; 6:9–22; 7:6, 11, 13–16a, 18–21, 24; 8:1, 2a, 3b–5, 7, 13a, 14–19; 9:1–17, 28–29; 10:1–7, 20, 22–23, 24, 31–32; 11:20–27, 31–32. P or a redactor edited and supplemented the J tradition, which must have been sufficiently revered to be worth "resetting." P's editorial hand is most obvious in the fivefold

[1] For review of opinions, see the three-volume commentary of C. Westermann, *Genesis 1–11: A Commentary* (Minneapolis: Augsburg, 1985–1986).

[2] For persuasive arguments that P was a redactor and supplementer rather than an independent tradition on the analogy of J and E, see Cross, *CMHE,* chapter 11.

formula 'ēlleh tôlĕdôt or its variations ("these are the generations"), recurring in 2:4a, 5:1, 6:9, 10:1, and 11:10.[3] Elsewhere in Genesis the formula is introductory, suggesting that its very first occurrence in 2:4a introduces Gen 2:4b–4:26 rather than summarizes chapter 1.[4] That chapter 1 itself is introductory is an important clue to its function.

I. Genesis 1:1–2:3

Genesis 1 is obviously a cosmogony, though (as will be seen) its dependence on other ancient cosmogonies cannot be specified with any exactness. The function of the present text, however, is reasonably clear. The cosmogony is P's preface to the J-story of the creating and populating of the world, providing an interpretive lens for Israelites reading Genesis 2–11 in the exilic situation. Words and concepts from Genesis 1 echo through the chapters immediately following it. The most obvious example is the blessing over the man and woman in 1:26–30, which is repeated verbatim in 9:1–7. Other words and concepts correlate the flood in chapters 6–9 with the creation in chapter 1: in the P-sections of chapters 6–8, the flood waters are the same as those that were confined in chapter 1 to the upper and lower spheres; the P-formula of chapter 1 ("God saw that it was good") is reversed in 6:12 ("God saw that the earth was corrupt"); and the phrase "the face of the deep" in 1:2 is repeated in 6:18. P makes the flood story into a grand chiasm,[5] culminating in the sentence

---

[3] A fivefold set of formulas appears in the second major section of Genesis (11:27; 25:12; 25:19; 36:1 [=36:9]; 37:2), suggesting that the second part of Genesis, 11:27–50:26, consciously parallels the first. Thematically, the two parts reflect the familiar biblical polarity of the nations (Genesis 1–11) and Israel (Genesis 11–50).

[4] Cross, *CMHE,* 301.

[5] B. W. Anderson, "From Analysis to Synthesis: The Interpretation of Genesis 1–11," *JBL* 97 (1978) 23–29. The verb "remember" may well evoke P's emphatic use of the word in Exod 2:23–25 , where God remembers the oppressed Hebrews in Egypt.
Transitional introduction (6:9–10)
  1. Violence in God's creation (6:11–12)
    2. 1st divine address: destroy! (6:13–22)
      3. 2nd divine address: enter! (7:1–10)
        4. Beginning of flood (7:11–16)
          5. Rising of flood waters (7:17–23)
            GOD REMEMBERS NOAH (7:24–8:1)
        6. Receding of flood waters (8:2–8:5)
      7. Drying of earth 8:6–14)

at 7:24–8:1: "When the waters had swelled over the earth one hundred and fifty days, then God remembered Noah and all the wild and domestic animals with him in the ark, and he made the wind pass over the earth, and the waters subsided" (*NJV*). This long sentence reprises "the wind of God sweeping over the water" of 1:2.

The most pervasive influence of the preface on subsequent chapters is also the most subtle—its introduction of the key themes of progeny and land. The twofold divine imperative in 1:26–28 ("Be fruitful and multiply" and "take the land and subdue it"), together with the command to exercise dominion over the animals of sea, sky, and earth, defines the human task before God. It is like the assigning of one's destiny on the day of creation in Mesopotamian cosmogonies. According to the Genesis divine decree the human race is to sustain itself, receive God's bounty symbolized by the land, and rule over the universe. The twin themes of progeny and land dominate the primordial history. Progeny is implied in the "generations" (especially J's seven-member genealogy in chapter 4 and P's two genealogies of ten and nine members in, respectively, chapters 5 and 11). Land is prominent in chapters 10–11.[6] The prefatory function of Genesis 1 extends even beyond chapters 2–11 to chapters 12–50 (where the patriarchs' *lack* of land and progeny is precisely the problem) and indeed to the Pentateuch itself, which was written for an exiled community worried about losing its ancestral land and concerned about whether it would continue as a people.

Mesopotamian cosmogonies often functioned as prefaces. In disputations and incantations they set the scene and introduce the chief actors. The disputation, a common genre in Sumerian and Akkadian literature, usually begins with a cosmogony describing the creation of the world of the two disputants. *Palm and Tamarisk* (see Akkadian cosmogony 7b) portrays the gods founding the world, making cities, canals, and mountains, and bestowing kingship to the human race. It is in the king's courtyard that the two plants argue about which of them confers the most

8. 3rd divine address: leave the ark! (8:15–19)

9. God's resolve to preserve order (8:20–22)

10. 4th divine address: covenant blessing and peace (9:1–17) Transitional conclusion (9:18–19).

[6] Chapters 10 and 11 are linked as the assignment of land and the taking of it. U. Cassuto has shown their unity in *A Commentary on the Book of Genesis* (trans. I. Abrahams; Jerusalem: Magnes, 1964) 2. 142–47.

benefits. In incantations (see Akkadian cosmogonies 1abc) the creation of the elements of the world shows the original function of the element in question. Gen 1:1–2:3 introduces human society destined to exist through procreation and possession of land. These themes answer pressing exilic questions about national existence and possession of land.

Though its prefatory function is paralleled in Mesopotamia, attempts to show that Genesis 1 is directly dependent on *Enūma elish* cannot be judged successful. E. A. Speiser, who translated *Enūma elish* for *ANET* and also wrote a commentary on Genesis, simply adopted A. Heidel's chart of the sequence of acts in *Enūma elish* and Genesis 1, assuming that it proved borrowing.[7]

Enūma elish	Genesis
Divine spirit and cosmic matter are coexistent and coeternal.	Divine spirit creates cosmic matter and exists independently of it.
Primeval chaos: Tiamat enveloped in darkness.	The earth is a desolate waste, with darkness covering the deep (*tĕhôm*).
Light emanating from the gods.	Light is created.

Unfortunately, the similarities are misleading. In *Enūma elish,* Apsu and Tiamat have no dingir sign before their names (the determinative of divinity in Akkadian texts) and thus are not deities; the opening lines do not predicate darkness of the primordial state; light emanating from the gods is not even mentioned in the creation texts and, in any case, is a different phenomenon from the light in Genesis 1. Heidel's further parallels (not shown above) are technically correct but do not take into account the different structures of the two works. The sequence of events in the two works are not truly parallel.

Two other links between Genesis 1 and *Enūma elish* are sometimes proposed: that between Hebrew *tĕhôm* (Gen 1:2) ("the deep") and the Akkadian sea monster Tiamat, and that between Yahweh's rest on the seventh day and the gods' rest at the beginning of *Enūma elish*. Though

---

[7] Heidel, *The Babylonian Genesis* (2d ed.; Chicago: University of Chicago, 1951) 129, and Speiser, *Genesis* (AB 1; Garden City, NY: Doubleday, 1964) 9–10. Heidel is more cautious than Speiser, concluding that "the whole question must still be left open" (p. 139).

tĕhôm is etymologically related to Tiamat, it does not derive from the latter, since the Hebrew word is grammatically masculine and quite common in the Bible.[8] The parallel of divine rest after the work of creation has some validity, but divine rest in Genesis is closely related to Sabbath observance, which is unparalleled.[9] The worlds of the two texts are altogether different, in fact. *Enūma elish* begins with a watery mass, personified as two beings, in which two pairs of gods are born, and from them Anu and Ea. Genesis begins with a dark and watery mass swept by a massive wind, after which God speaks, creates, separates, and molds.

Genesis 1 does show, however, intriguing parallels to other oriental texts. The *Chaldean Cosmogony* (see Akkadian cosmogony 6) begins with undifferentiated sea. Other texts have a seven-fold creation process, e.g., an Akkadian incantation (see Akkadian cosmogony 2c) and the *Dunnu Theogony* (see Akkadian Cosmogony C). Egyptian influence on Genesis 1 has been argued by some scholars, who point to the Memphite cosmogonic traditions in which a watery mass is progressively given shape and light plays an important role.[10] Given our present knowledge, however, it is difficult to prove that any single work is the source of Genesis 1. The text may well be eclectic like the one extant Phoenician cosmogony, that of Philo of Byblos, which seems to be a mixture of Egyptian, Phoenician, and Greek conceptions.[11] A Phoenician prototype would be clearest for v. 2, which is parenthetical within the "when . . . then" construction of vv. 1 and 3.[12]

---

[8] For a similar view, see D. T. Tsumura, *The Earth and the Waters in Genesis 1 and 2: A Linguistic Investigation* (JSOTSup 83; Sheffield: JSOT, 1989).

[9] W. G. Lambert, who is generally skeptical of dependence Genesis on *Enūma elish*, concedes "very probable" borrowing here; see "A New Look at the Babylonian Background of Genesis," *JTS* 16 (1965) 298.

[10] See K. Koch, "Wort und Einheit des Schöpfergottes in Memphis und Jerusalem," *ZTK* 62 (1965) 251–93; and J. Ebach, *Weltentstehung und Kulturentwicklung bei Philo von Byblos* (BWANT 108; Stuttgart: Kohlhammer, 1979). J. D. Levenson argues that the *Hymn to the Aten* of the mid-fourteenth century B.C. has influenced Psalm 104, which resembles Genesis 1 (*Creation and the Persistence of Evil: The Jewish Drama of Divine Omnipotence* [San Francisco: Harper & Row, 1988], 59–65).

[11] See "Creation in Canaanite Texts," above.

[12] The construction is analogous to the parenthesis between 2:4b (*bĕyôm 'ăśôt*) and v. 7 (*wayyîṣer YHWH*): "when . . . then . . ."

The earth was (*hāyĕtâ*) formless and void (*tōhû wābōhû*).
And darkness was on the face of the deep (*tĕhôm*),
And the wind of God was sweeping over the face of the waters.

There are two polarities here: darkness and wind, and the deep and the waters.[13]

Philo of Byblos begins with the same polarities but refers to a different source of motion:

> . . . a dark and windy air or a blast of dark air, and turbid, dark chaos. These were limitless and for a long time without boundaries. He [Philo/Sakkunyaton] says, "When the wind lusted after its own beginnings and a mixing took place, that entwining was called desire. And that was the beginning of all things. But it [the wind] did not know its creation, and from the same entwining of the wind Mot came into being. Some say this is mud, others the putrefaction of the watery mixture. And from this came every seed of creation and origin of all things."

Genesis, like Philo, shows an interest in the cause of initial movement. In Genesis the divine word initiates all; "God said" occurs eight times. God makes, creates, forms, and separates. This variety of verbs is probably meant to underline divine activity. It is not necessarily a sign of different sources.[14] The plurality of verbs is paralleled in Akkadian cosmogonies, e.g., the *Chaldean Cosmogony,* which uses *banû* ("to build"), *epēšu* ("to make"), and *patāqu* ("to form"). Repetition of the divine name is unusual and emphasizes divine mastery.

[13] The phrase *tōhû wābōhû* is contrasted with the deep/the waters. *tōhû,* the first word of the formula, occurs twenty times; it means without shape or form, so as to be humanly uninhabitable and metaphorically groundless or unreal. The second word, *bōhû,* occurs three times, composing an assonant hendiadys with *tōhû.* Tsumura reaches similar conclusions (*The Earth and the Waters,* 43).

[14] B. W. Anderson, "A Stylistic Study of the Priestly Creation Story," in *Canon and Authority* (ed. G. W. Coats and B. O. Long; Philadelphia: Fortress, 1977) 148, has shown that the account forms a coherent pattern, obviating the need to explain the alleged disorder of the text. The week can be outlined as follows:

"began": chaos

1 light (day)/darkness (night)	= 4 sun/moon
2 dome between waters	= 5 fish, birds from waters
3 a) dry land	= 6 a) animals
b) vegetation	b) man: male/female

Day 7: "finished" fulfills "began" of v. 1.

If comparison with other cosmogonies does not prove dependence, it does reveal the emphases in Genesis. Genesis depicts the first man in royal terms, using the nouns "image" and "likeness" (which are found in Mesopotamian royal inscriptions) and the verbs "rule" and "subdue."[15] In Mesopotamian cosmogonies human beings are invariably slaves created to maintain the universe for the gods, who are idle by vocation. When Mesopotamian accounts include a king, he is created separately in order to oversee the human race's service of the gods, as in the Akkadian *Palm and Tamarisk* and the Mayer text (see Akkadian cosmogonies 7b, 9). Genesis 1 portrays the man (who with the woman stands for the race) as a king, and the human task as far broader than temple maintenance. The God of Genesis does not require human servants in the manner of other gods; the human race consequently has a different relation to work and to the world.

The universe that arises in Genesis 1 is a *system,* a network in which the elements are arranged hierarchically and assigned value. All ancient cosmogonies were systems, at least implicitly. Sometimes the system was articulated by describing the pre-creation period as the negative mirror image of the created world, e.g., "a holy house . . . had *not* been made; a reed had *not* come forth, a tree had *not* been created";[16] but more often it was implied by the actual sequence of divine actions, e.g., the gods make a plan, tame the sea or channel the cosmic waters, create the marshes to supply mud bricks and reeds for the temple, form the human race as slaves and animals as potential sacrifices, bestow cultural implements such as work tools. In comparison with Mesopotamian systems, the universe of Genesis 1 stands out in its complexity and coherence, and in not being completely oriented toward the care and feeding of Elohim, God. The seven-day sequence of actions (see n. 14) shows some of the interconnections: days 1–3 correspond to days 4–6, and the climactic day 7 (God's rest) lies outside the series. Though penultimate in relation to the whole week, the man and woman on day 6 are the center of a web stretching backward and forward through all seven days. The fifth-day

[15] Phyllis Bird, "'Male and Female He Created Them': Gen 1:27b in the Context of the Priestly Account of Creation," *HTR* 74 (1981) 140–44.

[16] Line 1 of the *Chaldean Cosmogony,* Akkadian cosmogony no. 6. The elaborate pre-creation tableau in *Enki and Ninhursag* (=The *Dilmun Myth*) also illustrates the pre-creation period as a social system. Gen 2:4–6 and Prov 8:22–26 similarly negatively mirror the created order.

blessing of the birds and fishes (1:22) is repeated in expanded form to the human couple (1:28). The phrase for the reproduction of each species, "plants yielding seed, and fruit trees bearing fruit in which is their seed, each according to its kind" (1:11, 21, 24) is transposed for the human race into "male and female he created them." Sexuality, "male and female," is created as the human version of the reproductive capacity inherent in all life forms.[17] Further, the human race is linked to each tier of the world by its dominion over sea, heaven, and earth (1:26). The human race rules (*rādâ*, 1:26) the life of each of the three domains as the sun and moon govern (*māšal*) day and night. And only the human race, by virtue of its climactic sixth-day position and its freedom to respond to the divine word, directly encounters God.[18]

In the Genesis system the human race is the center of a harmonious universe, spanning and uniting it and bringing it before God. Because God is not needy like the gods of comparable cosmogonies, the Genesis system is designed less immediately to provide essential services for the divine world. God does not make things primarily for the divine world (e.g., marshes as sources of the bricks and reeds for the temple, animals for its sacrifices, and human beings to build it), but rather to enable the human race to play its role in the world. In the course of the week, the world is made increasingly fit for *human* habitation by God's control over darkness and the waters and God's arrangement of the universe.

In summary, Genesis 1 develops the introductory function of cosmogonies in prefacing the venerable Yahwist story. Betraying the influence of different traditions, it is eclectic and concerned with divine speech as the animating principle of creation activity.

II. Genesis 2–11

Christian tradition has tended to concentrate its attention on Genesis 1–3 and to read those chapters as two independent creation accounts. But Genesis 1 is distinct and prefatory to what follows, as we have seen; Genesis 2–3, the story of Adam and Eve, is the opening chapter in a story that

[17] Bird, "'Male and Female'" 146–47.

[18] Sir 16:24–17:14, which is based upon Genesis 1–3, affirms the connection with the earth common to both the human (17:1–4) and nonhuman (16:26–30) worlds. At the same time, it contrasts the regularity and unfailing obedience of nature with the freedom and responsibility of the human race.

continues up to 11:26.[19] There are several reasons for believing that chapters 2–11 make up a single, long story: (1) the five occurrences of the *tôlēdôt* formula ("these are the generations of X") in 2:4b–11:10 match the five in 11:27–50:26,[20] suggesting that chapters 2–11 (on the nations) constitute a complete story parallel to the story of chapters 11–50 (on Israel in the person of its ancestors);[21] (2) the plot of chapters 2–11 (creation, offence, flood, re-creation) is the typical plot of the creation-flood genre; (3) the dual themes of progeny and land run persistently through chapters 2–11; (4) most important, there is a single dramatic movement. Genealogies and foreshadowing unify the story before the flood; the postflood restoration recapitulates Genesis 1 and then tells of the repopulating of the earth. Like the Akkadian anthological cosmogonies *Atrahasis* or *Enūma elish*, Genesis 2–11 is long and complex.

A useful approach to Genesis 2–11 is to view it in relation to its genre. The genre of chapters 2–11 is a creation-flood story, directly and indirectly attested in Mesopotamian literature, e.g., the *Sumerian Flood Story*, *Atrahasis*, *Gilgamesh* XI, and Berossus, and echoed in some versions of the *Sumerian King List* and the flood story from Ras Shamra. Typically, a preflood period (expressed or implied) is ended by a flood, the god of wisdom helps his client (named variously Ziusudra, Utnapishtim, Atrahasis, or Noah) to ride out the storm in a boat, and after the flood there is a new beginning for the human race.

The process by which a second-millennium Mesopotamian genre found realization in the tenth-century Yahwist epic is, David Damrosch suggests, the result of literary development in the late-second and early-first millennium. Ancient Mesopotamian belles lettres fell into two broad categories—poetic epics such as *Gilgamesh* and prose chronicles such as royal inscriptions. Though the epics had gods and heroes as characters, they dealt with quite human and existential themes, for example, the limits of culture and mortality. Conversely, prose chronicles, though

[19] C. Westermann (*Creation* [Philadelphia: Fortress, 1974]) gives an excellent critique of the narrowing of creation in the Christian tradition to Genesis 1–3. One reason for concern only with chapters 2–3 was Paul's New Adam Christology (clearest in Rom 5:12–21 and 1 Cor 15:21–22): just as through the disobedience of one man, Adam, death came to the whole human race, so through the obedience of one man, Jesus, life came to the race.

[20] The first five are 2:4a; 5:1; 6:9; 10:1; 11:10; and the second five are 11:27; 25:12; 25:19; 36:1 [=36:9]; 37:2.

[21] The contrast between Israel and the nations constitutes one of the fundamental polarities of the Bible.

concerned with human and especially royal history, generally dealt with divine purpose and decisions. Late second-millennium Mesopotamia already saw some merging of the two categories: existential themes began to appear in prose chronicles and historical perspectives in epics. The merger came to completion in the Yahwist tradition of the Bible; Genesis 2–11 explores existential and cultural issues, but in prose and with historical awareness.[22]

Enough is now known of the genre to shed some light on Genesis 2–11. We should not forget that a genre is not an ideal form enabling one to reconstruct and predict, but a cluster of conventions around language, plot, and character. Further, ancient writers were not precise about the genres they used.[23] To identify its genre is only a preliminary step toward appreciating a particular text. Yet ancient composers, much more than modern authors, worked within conventions, following or subverting them. Although the Yahwist worked within the conventions of the creation-flood genre, like similar composers he exercised great freedom and originality. Knowing the genre helps us to understand the special contribution of Genesis 2–11.

A persistent feature of creation and flood epics was the flood itself, which provides a good point of departure for studying the genre. In Mesopotamian examples the flood is the dividing line between the primordial world and the world of contemporary experience. In the *Sumerian King List,* for example, kings lived much longer before the flood than after it, a sign of greater vitality in the preflood world. In *Atrahasis* and the Standard Babylonian *Gilgamesh* XI the major difference between the two worlds is mortality: human beings were immortal before the flood and mortal after it. In *Gilgamesh* X.vi, Utnapishtim tells Gilgamesh that his quest for immortality is futile since death is inevitable. "Suddenly there is nothing. / The prisoner and the dead are alike, / Death itself

---

[22] Damrosch, *The Narrative Covenant: Transformations of Genre in the Growth of Biblical Literature* (San Francisco: Harper and Row, 1987) chapters 2 and 3.

[23] The difficulties of determining genre in ancient Near Eastern literature are considerable. "A classification ('native categories') of ancient Oriental literature using ancient Mesopotamian concepts is not possible, for such concepts are not available to us nor able to be re-conceived, except in a preliminary way" (D. O. Edzard, "Literatur," in *RLA* 7:34). See also H. Vanstiphout, "Some Thoughts on Genre in Mesopotamian Literature," *Keilschriftliche Literatur* (32d Rencontre assyriologique internationale; ed. K. Hecker and W. Sommerfeld; Berliner Beiträge zum Vorderen Orient 6; Berlin: Reimer, 1986) 1–11.

cannot be depicted, / But Lullû — man — is incarcerated."[24] Why is death inevitable for Gilgamesh but not for the preflood Utnapishtim? Utnapishtim explains: "After they had pronounced the blessing on me, / The Anunnaku, the great gods, were assembled, / And Mammitum, creatress of destiny, / Decreed destinies with them. / They established life and death. / Death they fixed to have no ending."[25] *Atrahasis* III.vi, which tells of the measures taken by the gods to limit human population in the postflood order, is more explicit regarding the context of post-flood mortality. As plausibly restored by Lambert, the text reads: [*at-ti sa-a*]*s-sú-ru ba-ni-a-at ši-ma-ti* / [*mu-ta šu-uk-ni*] *a-na ni-ši* "[You], birth-goddess, creatress of destinies, / [Assign death] to the peoples."[26] Utnapishtim is immortal simply because he belongs to the preflood human race and Gilgamesh is mortal simply because he belongs to the redesigned postflood human race. Human beings, of course, could die in the antediluvian order but only from external causes such as flood or murder, not from any inherent mortality. In the postflood world, human beings are truly mortal.

Were Adam and Eve created immortal only to lose it in the sentence imposed on them in 2:17, "on the day you eat [the fruit] you shall die"? The question is difficult to answer. For one thing, Genesis 2–11 drew on more traditions than *Atrahasis and Gilgamesh.* The ten preflood ancestors of Noah seem derived from the ten kings found in some versions of the *Sumerian King List;* in that tradition pre-flood human beings lived long but were not immortal. The antediluvian kings ruled anywhere from 18,000 to 43,000 years, whereas the postflood kings ruled in the hundreds of years (though a few ruled up to 1,500 years). Of the biblical preflood figures, Methuselah lived the longest — 969 years (Gen 5:26). For the postflood generation, God revised the span of human beings downward to 120 years (Gen 6:3). The question of Adam's mortality must ultimately, of course, be decided from Genesis and not its sources. Genesis 2-3, however, has apparently conflicting data: (1) to eat from the tree of the knowledge of good and evil, which is semantically parallel to the tree of life (and derived from the plant conferring immortality in *Gilgamesh* XI), is forbidden to the couple with the threat "on the day

[24] X.vi.24–27. Edition and translation of W. G. Lambert, "The Theology of Death," *Death in Mesopotamia* (Mesopotamia 8; 26th Rencontre assyriologique internationale; ed. B. Alster; Copenhagen: Akademisk, 1980) 54–55.

[25] X.vi.28–32. Ibid., 55.

[26] Ibid., 58.

you eat of it you shall die"; (2) the "death" that Adam and Eve actually undergo in the story is not biological death but expulsion from the garden of God and alienation from the soil and from bodily ease. Hence questions about life and death in Genesis are not simply about immortality. *Gilgamesh* and *Atrahasis* suggest that immortality in Genesis simply means being without inherent mortality; immortality ought to be dissociated from the Greek notion of the immortal spiritual soul. Though preflood human beings could die by plague or flood they did not have a life span; they lived without limit of time. Genesis 2–3 transposes the traditional pre- and postflood difference regarding human mortality to the very first scene of the creation-flood story.[27] Further, in neither Genesis 2–3 nor Gilgamesh is life merely a biological reality. The life sought by the hero in both works is the opposite of ordinary human life and is linked to other qualities — association with the gods, wisdom, and renown. In Genesis the couple appear to enjoy from the start some of these qualities linked to life; they live in the garden of God in peaceful relationships — that between God and the couple, between the man and the woman, between the couple and their defining tasks or functions (gardening and childbearing).

Unlike the plots of *Atrahasis* and *Gilgamesh* XI, human life in Genesis undergoes a radical change virtually in the first scene instead of after the flood. The J-storyteller takes the *Gilgamesh* motif of the snake's theft of the plant of life from the hero (a postflood occurrence in *Gilgamesh* XI) and places it *before* the flood (Genesis 3). As in *Gilgamesh,* Adam is naked when the loss takes place, the snake deceitfully steals the fruit supposed to transform life, and a tree or plant of life is involved. Such kaleidoscopic reuse of traditional details may seem strange to modern readers, but ancient authors evidently liked to put familiar objects in new contexts. *Enūma elish,* for example, took the Ninurta tradition about the scattered feathers of the defeated bird Anzu that announced victory, and transposed it into the scattered blood of Tiamat announcing victory.[28] Another example comes from *Gilgamesh* I: the naked and animal-

---

[27] Lambert also believes that in the case of both Utnapishtim and Adam "man was first created without any limit being fixed on his life-span. As a result of misdemeanor death was laid upon him" ("The Theology of Death," 58).

[28] Lambert, "Ninurta Mythology in the Babylonian Epic of Creation," in *Keilschriftliche Literaturen: Ausgewählte Vorträge der XXXII. Rencontre assyriologique internationale*

like Enkidu acquires wisdom from his seven-day dalliance with a prostitute. Afterward she clothes him and leads him to the city of Uruk and its king Gilgamesh. Genesis rearranges the same traditions to describe the institution of marriage!

Even though the flood in Genesis does not function as the great divide between immortal and mortal life, it nonetheless represents an important stage. Before the flood in Genesis, the human race is not identified ethnically or nationally; "man," individual or corporate, acts. Only after the flood is it said that the peoples of the earth are descended from the sons of Noah (9:19). Only after the flood does the real-life diversity of nations and cultures (including the crucial contrast between Israel and the nations) begin as well as the real-life custom of eating meat (9:3).

Genesis 2–11 moves in a different direction than the creation-flood genre of Mesopotamian literature. In *Atrahasis* the emphasis is on the gods; only they are rendered in socially and psychologically interesting detail. Human beings, even Atrahasis, remain abstractions. In Genesis humans are portrayed with bold strokes, to be sure, but in vivid detail. *Atrahasis* is a critique of the gods; their assembly is bumbling and fragmented; their leader is the bullying and cowardly Enlil. This unflattering picture is relieved only by the introduction of the wise and compassionate Enlil and Nintu. Fault lies with the gods rather than with human beings. The gods' miscalculations lead to the annihilation of the race, and their needs to its restoration. In Genesis, God does it right the first time and after the flood re-blesses the human race with his original words. The only adjustment to the antediluvian order—permission to eat meat—is occasioned by human, not divine, fault. Both *Atrahasis* and Genesis were written with a sense of confidence. *Atrahasis* shows confidence in the human race; people are necessary because the gods are generally lazy, shortsighted, and impetuous. Confidence in Genesis is founded on God's justice and mercy, and the reliability of the created world.

Finally, it is important to note that Genesis 2–11 begins with creation and ends with historical narrative. It is anthological not only in collecting a multitude of traditions, but also in developing a sense of history. Jacobsen has suggested that the author of the "Eridu Genesis" was aware

(ed. K. Hecker and W. Sommerfeld; Berliner Beiträge zum Vorderen Orient 6; Berlin: Reimer, 1986) 55–60.

of historical cause and effect in depicting the movement from nature to urban civilization and the link between a stable food supply and population growth: he proposes a new and separate genre of mythohistorical account.[29] Genesis 2–11 seems also to unite a sense of historical cause and effect with a traditional respect for the privileged moment of creation.

[29] Jacobsen, "The Eridu Genesis," *JBL* 100 (1981) 528.

CHAPTER 7

Creation in the Psalms

The theological meaning of creation in the psalms has captured the interest of many scholars only in recent years.[1] This chapter looks at creation in only two genres of the Psalter: the communal lament and the hymn. Not every instance of these genres is examined; for example, Psalms 8 and 104, both hymns, are omitted on the grounds that they have already been well studied. The focus on genre is deliberate. Even a cursory glance at ancient Near Eastern literature shows that creation accounts function differently according to the genre in which they occur. A cosmogony in an incantation, for example, performs differently than a cosmogony in an astrological text or an epic. The biblical psalms, convention-bound and stereotyped like most liturgical literature, must be read with an eye to their genre. Singling out two of the many genres in the Psalter has the further advantage of limiting a large topic.

The topic and focus of this chapter coincide to a remarkable degree with those of a 1974 monograph by Rainer Albertz, *Weltschöpfung und Menschenschöpfung: Untersucht bei Deutero-jesaja, Hiob und in den Psalmen,* a slightly revised doctoral dissertation done under Claus Westermann. Albertz concluded that for the Psalms, as for Second Isaiah, there

---

[1] In his 1974 survey of research, R. Albertz noted how little had been done, apart from the "Catholic works" of G. Lambert, E. Beaucamp, L. Legrand, and B. Rigaux (*Weltschöpfung*) 176, n. 1. Since then, studies on creation in the psalms include H.-J. Kraus, *Theology of the Psalms* (Minneapolis: Augsburg, 1986) 59–67; and T. E. Fretheim, "Nature's Praise of God in the Psalms," *Ex auditu* 3 (1988) 16–30.

were two distinct creation traditions — creation of the world (*Weltschöp-fung*) and creation of human beings (*Menschenschöpfung*). The former tradition is found in the genre of hymn, where it serves to emphasize Yahweh's majesty. The latter occurs in the genre of lament, where it forms the basis for appeals to Yahweh's mercy, something like "Do not abandon the person you have created!" Not until the postexilic period did the two traditions come together and then only rarely (e.g., Neh 9:6 and Zech 12:1), though Second Isaiah had opened the door to linking the two. Albertz's sharp distinction between the two creation traditions derives from his analysis of Second Isaiah as well as Sumero-Babylonian, Egyptian, and primitive prayers.[2]

This essay comes to conclusions quite different from Albertz's. His distinction between two creation traditions is not substantiated in comparable oriental literatures nor does it work for the communal lament and the hymn. Our differences on how cosmogonies function in the two genres will become evident in the analyses of individual psalms below. Before dealing with specific psalms, however, the alleged distinction between creation of the world and creation of human beings must be briefly examined.

The differences between ancient and modern conceptions of creation have already been detailed in the first chapter, so only a few points need emphasizing here. Ancient Near Eastern cosmogonies are concerned with the origin of the world people daily experience — the here-and-now world of the gods and of human society and how the two realms relate to each another. The perspective of most texts is theocentric or templocentric. Human beings were created to serve the gods, which meant building and maintaining their palaces (frequently under the direction of the king). The perspective at the same time is often implicitly ethnocentric; the society in question is not always the human race as such but a particular people or nation, e.g, Babylon or Israel.

These remarks about ancient Near Eastern conceptions bear directly on cosmogonies in the Psalter. Since ancient cosmogonies are usually stories about the gods making the world of temples and human beings for their own use and comfort, one expects the Psalms' cosmogonies to

---

[2] Albertz, *Weltschöpfung*. He owes the distinction to his teacher C. Westermann, who makes use of it in his *Isaiah 40–66* (OTL; Philadelphia: Westminster, 1969) 24–26, and *Genesis 1–11: A Commentary* (Minneapolis: Augsburg, 1984) 19–25.

be not only about the physical universe but also a *peopled* universe. And the human community is imagined concretely with kingship, land, language, god, and laws. It is well known that many psalms contain historical accounts of Israel's origins, preeminently the exodus from Egypt and taking of Canaan (sometimes only by allusion), e.g., Pss 44:2–9; 66:5–9; 74:1–2; 77:16; 78:42–55; 80:9–12; 105; 135; 136; 149. It is not always noticed, however, that several of the little histories in these psalms mix historical and cosmogonic language, e.g., Pss 77:17–21; 89:6–38. Some psalms use predominantly cosmogonic language, e.g., Pss 74:12–17, 93 and, one can plausibly argue, Pss 96–99. The language of cosmogony in these instances is incorporated into the stories. The cosmogonies *function* like the story of the exodus and conquest. Hence both the narratives of the exodus-conquest and the cosmogonies deserve to be called a "national story," since both tell how a nation or people arose.

Although the purpose of both historical recital and cosmogony in these psalms is the same (to narrate how this people came into existence), the two are not completely identical. What are the differences between them? There are two major differences: language and perspective. In psalm cosmogonies God or the gods are the actors, and the language is mythic. As in comparable Ugaritic texts, the actors are gods rather than flesh-and-blood inhabitants of the earth.

To express the relationship between the two levels of activity, I suggest a change in the customary terminology. The term "myth" labors under too many disadvantages to be useful; it connotes "untruth" in English and usually implies a dichotomy with history. I propose as new terms "suprahistoric" and "historic" and limit these terms to language and perspective, for the difference between them is mainly one of perspective and language. The key issue is the viewpoint from which the story is told—is it that of heaven or earth? Does the narrative focus on the human world or on the divine world, on God and the gods or on superhuman actors? My argument is that the national story can be told according to two ideal versions: one historic, in which the emphasis falls on human characters and motivations, and the other suprahistoric, in which the emphasis falls on heavenly beings. The types are ideal; usually there is mixing between the two perspectives.

It is time to test these general observations in the two genres of communal lament and hymn.

I. Communal Laments

A regular feature of the communal lament is a recital of the glorious past (e.g., Pss 44:2–9; 74:12–17; 77:12–21; 80:9–12; 83:10–13; 89:2–38). Such recitals have generally been regarded as attempts to highlight the tragedy of the present by contrasting it with the glorious past.[3] But mere contrast between past and present is not an adequate explanation. It explains neither the length nor the varied details of the narratives. The recital in Ps 44:2–9 describes Israel entering Canaan as a victorious army led by Yahweh and constitutes a third of the poem. Ps 77:12–21 (including the invocation) amounts to one half of the psalm; it tells of God's redeeming arm, a cosmic battle between Sea and Yahweh the God of storm, Israel's passage through that Sea, and the appointment of Moses and Aaron as leaders. Ps 89:2–38 describes Yahweh's victory over Sea and his arrangement of the universe, which climaxes in the installation of the Davidic king; it comprises two-thirds of the lament. Psalm 74 devotes six of its twenty-three verses (vv 12–17) to Yahweh's slaying of Leviathan and his orderly arrangement of the world. Ps 80:9–12, on the transplanting of the vine Israel from Egypt to Canaan, makes up a fifth of that psalm. If the psalmists wanted to contrast past glory with present misery they could have done so directly and economically by a simple allusion to the glorious events of the past.

The answer to the question why the psalmists put such artistry into the historical recital can only be that they tailored the recital to the specific lament. The selection of details from the "days of old" differs in each lament according to what is being lamented. Psalm 89, lamenting the defeat of the Davidic king by his enemies, recites Yahweh's sharing of the fruits of his cosmogonic victory with David in the past and his naming David *'elyôn* ("Most High") among the kings of the earth by an unconditional oath.[4] This recital poses a specific question to God: if you unconditionally promised worldwide sovereignty to the Davidic line when

---

[3] See H. Gunkel, *Einleitung in den Psalmen* (3d ed.; Göttingen: Vandenhoeck & Ruprecht, 1977) 129–30; S. Mowinckel, *The Psalms* (New York: Abingdon, 1967) 1. 196–97, 205; and C. Westermann, *The Praise of God in the Psalms* (Richmond: John Knox, 1965) 55–57. These authors argue that the old saving events are used as motives to persuade God to act now in like manner, but none explains in detail how the particulars of that history are related to the prayer.

[4] For the unity of this psalm, see R. J. Clifford, "Psalm 89: A Lament over the Davidic Ruler's Continued Failure," *HTR* 73 (1980) 35–47.

you created the world, why does your king now suffer defeat? Psalm 74 retells Yahweh's ordering of the paired elements of the universe (springs and torrents, lands and waters, day and night, moon and sun). These elements are now threatened by the destruction of the Temple, which commemorates that creation. The question: will you let your enemies destroy the symbol of your creation? Psalm 77, sung by a cantor for a community doubting the ancient promises (vv 8–11), recites the story of Yahweh's superiority over gods and nations, as it was once demonstrated by his bringing his people through the hostile waters to their land and appointing their leaders. It poses the question: will you let another power annul that founding event? Psalm 44 tells of Yahweh's conquest of the land in order to ask why Israel's enemies now rove at will through Canaan.

The recitals of the past in the laments describe not just any period in the past but the moment of Israel's origin: the creation of Israel as Yahweh's people in his land (or shrine) living under his law and leaders.[5] An objection to this proposal must be answered here: if all these psalms speak of one and the same divine act, why has that fact gone generally unrecognized by scholars? Because that act is narrated in a variety of ways and on different linguistic levels. One and the same act can be depicted as the military conquest of Palestine (Psalm 44), as the transplanting of a vine (Psalm 80), as the defeat of Sea and the appointment of David (Psalm 89), as the defeat of Sea and pairing of cosmic elements (Psalm 74), or as a march and a cosmic battle (Psalm 77). The language ranges from historic to suprahistoric. Ps 44:2–4 uses ordinary military language to tell how Israel's army conquered Canaan:

> 2O God, we have heard with our own ears;
>   our ancestors have told us
> the deeds you did in their days,
>   with your own hand in days of old:
> 3you rooted out nations to plant them,
>   crushed peoples to make room for them.

---

[5] "What is 're-presented' are not isolated incidents in history but rather something that had happened which was on-going and all-inclusive, viz., the deliverance at the beginning, as for example in the Credo of Deut. 26 where it is told as a unified story. It is a history which takes place between God and the people. It is to this on-going event that the 're-presentation' of historical events in the Psalms refers, even if only a single event is named" (C. Westermann, "The 'Re-presentation' of History in the Psalms," in *Praise and Lament in the Psalms* [Atlanta: Knox, 1981] 246).

[4]Not with their own swords did they take the land,
    nor did their own arms bring victory;
it was your right hand, your own arm,
    the light of your face, for you favored them.

The metaphor of (up)rooting in Ps 44:3a is developed in Ps 80:9–17, where Yahweh transplants his vine from Egypt to Canaan. Ps 89:6–38, on the other hand, describes "in the beginning" as a battle between Sea (personified in Rahab and other enemies), followed by a procession of victorious warriors from whom David is chosen and given dominion over the earth. The psalm regards the founding of the house of David as part of the foundation of the world, just as several Mesopotamian cosmogonies list the king and the temple as things created at the creation. Ps 74:12–17 similarly takes a suprahistoric perspective. Psalm 77 mixes both perspectives; Moses and Aaron are mentioned (v 21), but so is the cosmic battle between Yahweh as storm God and Sea. Sea is identified with the particular body of water through which Israel passed on route from Egypt to Canaan. Like Exodus 15, the suprahistoric perspective on the defeat of Sea (which had barred the people from their land) is blended with the historic perspective of predominantly human actors: Moses, Aaron, the people, Pharaoh, the Egyptians. The recitals are all concerned with the emergence of a peopled universe. They are cosmogonies.

Albertz denies that the primordial conflict depicted in Psalms 74 and 89 represents creation of the world on the grounds that the Baal-Mot and Baal-Yam conflicts in the Ugaritic myths (the source for the psalmic imagery) are not cosmogonies.[6] Though it is certainly true on the present evidence that the Baal conflicts in the Ugaritic Baal cycle cannot be proved to be cosmogonies, one cannot argue from that evidence that Yahweh's victories over Sea are not cosmogonies. The reason is that the Canaanite imagery of El (who is a creator) and Baal have been combined in the biblical portrait of Yahweh.[7] Moreover, one must argue from a text rather than its source.[8] In both Psalms 77 and 89, Yahweh's battle with Sea creates the world of which Israel is a part.

---

[6] Albertz, *Weltschöpfung*, 111–18.

[7] See chapter 5, section B, for evaluation of this argument.

[8] Albertz's dismissal of the cosmogonic combat of Marduk and Tiamat in *Enūma elish* as late and derivative (pp. 112–13) is an instance of the genetic fallacy, i.e., explaining a phenomenon by its origins. As is increasingly recognized, Marduk's combat is not derived

Psalm 77 tells of "the wonders of old," the victory of the storm God over cosmic waters that brought Israel as a people into being.

> 16With your arm you redeemed your people,
>   the descendants of Jacob and Joseph.
> 17The waters saw you, O God,
>   the waters saw you, they were convulsed.
>   Yea, the deep quaked.
> 18The clouds poured forth water,
>   the clouds thundered forth.
>   Yea, the lightning bolts shot to and fro.
> 19The crash of your thunder was in the whirlwind,
>   your lightning lit up the world.
>   The earth quaked and trembled.
> 20In the sea was your way,
>   your path through the mighty waters,
>   your tracks could not be seen.
> 21You led your people like a flock
>   by the hand of Moses and Aaron.

Yahweh uses weapons of thunder and lightning to destroy Sea, who has blocked the people from their land. The seemingly abrupt end of the psalm is not really so. By v 21 all the elements constituting a people are in place—god, land, and leaders—and so the psalm can end.

In Psalm 89 the defeat of Sea is also cosmogonic; it is part of the founding event that includes establishment of the Davidic king.[9]

> 2Your merciful deeds, Yahweh, forever will I sing,
>   Unto all generations my mouth will make known your fidelity.
> 3For you have said, "Forever is (my) steadfast love built,
>   (Like) the heavens is my fidelity established.
> 4I have made a covenant with my chosen one,
>   I have sworn to David my servant.
> 5Forever I will establish your line,
>   I will build unto all generations your throne.

Verses 2–38 constitute a single event. The defeat of Sea and the ordering

---

from the west Semitic Baal-Yam combat via the Amorites; it is a native adaptation of the Anzu myth. See chapter 3, under *Enūma elish*.

   9 For further details, see n. 4.

of the world (vv 6–15) are followed by a victory procession (vv 16–19) in which one of the warriors, David, is raised up and made "the highest of the kings of the earth." The customary translation of 'āz in v 20 as "once" or "of old" is tendentious and contrary to the usual meaning of 'āz as "next" or "then" in old poetry.[10] The psalm is mainly concerned with the promise to David in vv 20–38, since that promise is the foil to the lament in vv 39–52.

Communal laments remember the founding event, the act by which Israel came into existence. The act can be told (ideally) in either a historic or a suprahistoric version. The suprahistoric version is by definition a cosmogony.

II. Hymns

The genre of hymn invites the community to praise Yahweh for his deeds on its behalf.[11] The typical hymn structure consists of invitatory, description of the divine action for which praise is to be given (introduced by "for," Hebrew *kî*), and repetition of the invitatory. The divine "deeds" or "work(s)" mentioned in several psalms (e.g., in Psalms 66:5–7; 105; 111; 114; 135; 136; and 149) are the events that brought Israel into existence, preeminently the exodus and land taking. As in communal laments, the events can be described in language that is predominantly cosmogonic (see Psalms 93, 96, and 114).[12] The cosmogonies in these psalms function like the national story; in other words, they are the founding action for which Israel is invited to give praise.

Psalm 136 is a good starting point from which to examine the hymn genre (a few scholars class it as a thanksgiving). It praises God for essentially one act—the emergence of Israel as a people in their land. Its version of the founding event incorporates into a single story the making of heaven and earth, the sun, the moon, and the stars (vv 4–9) and the

[10] As, for example, in Exod 15:15; Judg 5:8, 11, 13, 19, 22; Pss 2:5; 40:8; 96:12. God selects David through a dream. Promises made to a king in a vision are common; see 2 Sam 7:4, 17; and 1 Kgs 3:5, 15.

[11] A hymn is "the song which extols the glory and greatness of Yahweh as it is revealed in nature and history, and particularly in Israel's history," O. Eissfeldt, *The Old Testament: An Introduction* (New York: Harper and Row, 1965) 105–6.

[12] The list is minimal. One could include several psalms that are sometimes classed as hymns, e.g., Psalms 68, 78, 97, 98, 99, and 100. The so called creation hymns, Psalms 8, 19, and 104, treat creation differently, i.e., not as related to the national story.

exodus-conquest (from the smiting of the Egyptian firstborn to the arrival in the land, vv 10–22). Though many commentators divide the psalm into "creation" and "redemption,"[13] the Hebrew syntax supports no such division. To the psalmist, the origin of the people Israel includes the making of the physical environment and the bringing of Israel into the land.

> [1]Praise Yahweh for he is good,
>
> . . . .
> [4]who alone did great wonders,
> [5]who made the heavens through understanding,
> who spread the earth upon the waters,
> who made the great lights,
> the sun to rule the day,
> the moon and the stars to rule the night,
> [10]who smote Egypt through their first-born,
> [11]who brought out Israel from their midst,
>
> . . . .
> [21]and gave their land as a heritage,
> [22]a heritage to Israel his servant.

Since cosmogonies are usually concerned with the origins of a people it is not surprising that the creation of heaven and earth, and that of the sun, moon, and stars, are chapters in the story of the rescue of the people from Egypt, their journey through the Red Sea, and their taking of the land. The same logic appears in Psalm 135: verse 7 ("who raises the clouds from the ends of the earth, // makes lightnings for the rain, // brings wind from his storehouses") continues without interruption into verse 8 ("who smote the first-born of Egypt . . ."). The two psalms tell the story of Israel's emergence as a people; the story is told from both a suprahistoric and historic perspective.

A much more concise example of a single cosmogonic act occurs in

---

[13] G. von Rad is not untypical of the tendency: "Verses 5–9 deal with the creation of the world, and at verse ten the psalm *abruptly changes its course* in order to recount the mighty deeds of Yahweh in history. In this psalm, therefore, the doctrine of creation and the doctrine of redemption stand side by side, yet wholly unrelated the one to the other. Because of the rigid form of the litany, nothing of particular interest emerges from this psalm with regard to the two doctrines which it embraces" ("The Theological Problem of Creation," in *The Problem of the Hexateuch and Other Essays* [New York: McGraw-Hill, 1966] 133; [italics mine]). See H.-J. Kraus, *Psalms 60–150: A Commentary* (Minneapolis: Augsburg, 1989) 498. *NAB* and *NRSV* separate vv 4–9 from vv 10–22 in their stanza divisions, whereas *NJV, REB,* and *NIV* rightly make no such division.

Psalm 114. In its dramatically foreshortened perspective, Sea is parallel to the Jordan River;[14] Israel goes directly from Egypt to Canaan. The poem is abrupt: there is no invitatory, the third-person suffix in v 2 has no antecedent, and the divine name is not even mentioned until v 7. Unmistakable, however, are the allusions to the crossing of the Red Sea and entry into Canaan and to the battle between the God of storm and Sea. The latter is derived from the Ugaritic Baal myth. In *KTU* I.4.7.38–39, Baal's thunder puts his enemies to flight, taunting them, "O enemies of Baal, why do you flee? Why do you flee, O attackers of the Valiant One?" This is the mockery of a heroic-age warrior. Sea had attempted to prevent Yahweh's people from entering the land, and now flees in defeat. A similar taunt is found in the psalm.

In the hymns examined so far, and also in the communal laments, the key event is not the exodus alone but equally the taking of the land of Canaan. The point needs emphasizing because tradition criticism of the Pentateuch has tended to regard the exodus from Egypt and the land taking as separately transmitted traditions that were later woven into a single story. Martin Noth, for example, distinguished five themes in the Pentateuch: guidance out of Egypt, guidance into the arable land, the promise to the patriarchs, guidance in the wilderness, and the revelation at Sinai.[15] His distinction is not valid for these psalms. One must speak here of an exodus *and* taking of the land. Israel's story begins with freedom from Pharaoh's dominion in Egypt and ends with service of Yahweh in Canaan, the territory of Yahweh.[16]

Other hymns make the exodus-land taking the basis for praise, for example, Psalm 66.

> [5]Come and see the works of God,
>   awesome in the deeds done for us.
> [6]He changed the sea to dry land,
>   through the river they passed on foot.

[14] Parallelism of "sea" and "river" is frequent in both Ugaritic literature and the Bible. See M. Dahood, *Ras Shamra Parallels* (ed. L. R. Fisher; AnOr 49; Rome: Biblical Institute, 1972) 1. 203, and Cross, *CMHE,* 138–39.

[15] M. Noth, *A History of Pentateuchal Traditions* (trans. and ed. B. W. Anderson; Englewood Cliffs, NJ: Prentice-Hall, 1972).

[16] A similar point is made by J. Levenson, in "Liberation Theology and the Exodus," *Midstream* 35 (1989) 30–36, reprinted in *The Hebrew Bible, the Old Testament, and Historical Criticism: Jews and Christians in Biblical Studies* (Louisville: Westminster/Knox, 1993) 140–51.

Psalm 111 defines "the works of the Lord" (v 2) as giving "food to the those who fear you" (v 5) and "giving [Israel] the lands of the nations" (v 6). Psalm 149 makes a clear allusion to the exodus. In all these psalms, the story ends when Israel arrives safely in its land.

In the so-called enthronement psalms, which acclaim Yahweh as universal king, the explicitly reason for giving praise is Yahweh's cosmogony. Universal kingship is based on Yahweh's sole creation of the world. In Psalm 93, the basis for kingship is the victory over Sea that established the world:

> ¹Yahweh reigns, with splendor is he clothed,
>   Yahweh is clothed, is girded with might.
> The world is founded, it shall never be shaken.
> ²Your throne is established from of old,
>   From of old you are.
> ³The Floods lifted up, O Yahweh,
>   The Floods lifted up their roar,
>   The Floods lifted up their pounding waves.
> ⁴Mightier than the roar of the Mighty Waters,
>   Mightier than the breakers of Sea,
>   Mighty in heaven is Yahweh!
> ⁵Your decrees are firmly set,
>   Holiness is fitting to your house,
>   For length of days, O Yahweh!

Yahweh's universal dominion results from his defeat of Flood or Mighty Waters, which would otherwise cover the earth. Once the floods are tamed, Yahweh issues his authoritative decrees (analogous to the assigning of destinies in Mesopotamian cosmogonies) and builds his house. The real interest of the psalm is divine kingship. The cosmogonic victory shows why that kingship is absolute and universal. Other enthronement psalms, one can argue, allude to the same event, e.g., Pss 47:4–5; 93:3–4; 96:5, 10; 97:2–6; 98:1.

Psalm 33 deals with the theme of creation from another angle. For Albertz, v 5 exemplifies the polarity between divine majesty, shown chiefly in praise of the Lord of creation, and divine mercy, shown chiefly in praise of the Lord of history:

> Yahweh loves justice and right
>   and fills the earth with goodness.

"[Yahweh] loves justice" expresses majesty, and "of Yahweh's grace is the earth full" expresses mercy.[17] Albertz's polarity between majesty and mercy, creation and history, is a modern distinction, however; the psalm verses are semantically parallel. For Albertz, vv 6–11 develop the first polarity, divine majesty, and vv 13–19 develop the second polarity, divine mercy.[18] A better interpretation is that vv 6–8 describe God's creation of the biblical three-tiered universe of the heavens, the waters, and the earth. With vv 8–9 the psalmist turns to the third tier, the earth and the human race in order to state the appropriate human response to God as creator: the human race ought to fear the creator God who foils the plots of the nations in order to favor Israel (vv 10–15). Before God's gaze, all human actions except faith and hope effect nothing (vv 16–19). Any distinction between creation and history, majesty and mercy, is artificial from the perspective of the psalm.

The hymns just reviewed show that the divine act celebrated in the liturgy is the moment of Israel's origin. It can be described either as the exodus-conquest or as a cosmogony. As in the communal laments, the act is presented from either a historic or suprahistoric perspective, or from both perspectives simultaneously. The mixed perspective invests human history with cosmic significance, and God's action with a here-and-now earthly dimension.

In summary, the dichotomy suggested by "myth" and "history" does not hold at least for the story of Israel's origins in several communal laments and hymns. That privileged moment can be narrated from a suprahistoric or historic viewpoint or from a blending of both. The reason that a cosmogony can function as the national story is that ancient cosmogonies customarily included society in the origin of the universe.

If the viewpoint expressed in the foregoing pages has any merit, creation is a much more important theological theme in the psalms than has previously been allowed. It is perhaps possible to show that even more psalms than are mentioned here recite the national story. One might even ask whether the same national story is also the unifying theme of the Pentateuch, and thereby establish a link between the Psalter and other parts of the Bible.

[17] Albertz, *Weltschöpfung*, 91–93.
[18] Ibid., 91–93.

CHAPTER 8

Creation in Isaiah 40–55

Given the many verbs of creating in Second Isaiah (*bārā'* [16 times], *yāṣar* [15 times], *'āśâ* [24 times], *pā'al* [5 times], *nāṭâ šāmayim* [6 times], *kûn* and *yāsad* [1 each]), it is remarkable that explicit scholarly discussion of the topic began only in the 1930s. Recent years have made up for previous neglect; there now exist over a dozen articles, three books, and numerous treatments within commentaries and monographs on creation in Second Isaiah. The first part of this chapter reviews critically some of the scholarly contributions, for several questionable assumptions have crept into the consensus, viz., that the "problematic" is the relation between originally distinct concepts of redemption and creation; that the concept of creation is subordinated to redemption; and that a distinction between creation of the whole and of the individual is operative in Second Isaian hymns and individual laments. After the review, I will analyze two representative texts and make some proposals about the function of creation in Second Isaiah.

I. Review of Scholarship[1]

Ancient commentators, and even modern scholars before the wide availability of comparative evidence, made surprisingly little of creation in Second Isaiah. For Jerome, creation in Isa 44:24–28 was simply a proof

---

[1] The survey is selective. For a more complete review, see A. Richter, "Hauptlinien der Deuterojesaja-Forschung von 1964–1979," in C. Westermann, *Sprache und Struktur der Prophetie Deuterojesaja* (rev. ed.; Stuttgart: Calwer, 1981) 89–123.

that the God who created the world could redeem Israel; his real concern was to show that Christ is the creator.[2] Even the twelfth-century commentator Ibn Ezra, who questioned First Isaian authorship of chapters 40–66, took creation either as proof (under Isa 40:12) or as coded prediction; thus he interpreted "the one who makes a path in the sea" (43:16) as predicting that an enemy fleet would defeat Babylon, and the "new thing" a few verses later as signifying the Israelite escape from Babylon.[3] In the late nineteenth century F. Delitzsch[4] and B. Duhm did not interpret creation within Second Isaiah's system of thought and have little to say about it in any case. For Duhm, the key clause "who says of the deep, 'Be dry!'" (44:27) refers to Babylon and is a probable echo of the Red Sea crossing (cf. 43:16–21). Creation, in short, is the primordial deed proving that nothing can stand against God today.[5]

The modern posing of the historical-critical problem appeared in G. von Rad's 1936 essay, entitled "The Theological Problem of the Old Testament Doctrine of Creation." The article characterized the doctrine of creation in the Bible as a late import that originally had nothing to do with redemption. Second Isaiah was the first to combine the two themes and give creation a redemptive significance: "What appear theologically to be two distinct acts [creation and redemption] are in fact one and the same act of the universal redemptive purpose of God."[6] Von Rad nevertheless retained his main thesis: "Because of the exclusive commitment of Israel's faith to historical salvation, the doctrine of creation was never able to attain to independent existence in its own right. Either it remained a cosmic foil against which soteriological pronouncements stood out the more effectively, or it was wholly incorporated into the complex of

---

[2] S. Hieronymi Presbyteri Commentariorum in Esaiam Libri I–XVIII (Turnhold: Brepols, 1963).

[3] The Commentary of Ibn Ezra on Isaiah (ed. and trans. M. Friedlander; New York: Feldheim, 1873).

[4] F. Delitzsch, Biblical Commentaries on the Prophecies of Isaiah (trans. from the 4th ed., vol. 2; Edinburgh: T. &. T. Clark, 1890).

[5] B. Duhm, Das Buch Jesaia (5th ed.; Göttingen: Vandenhoeck & Ruprecht, 1968). Later commentators, namely C. C. Torrey, P.-E. Bonnard, and E. J. Kissane, do not regard creation as part of a system of thought.

[6] G. von Rad, "The Theological Problem of the Old Testament Doctrine of Creation," in The Problem of the Hexateuch and Other Essays (New York: McGraw-Hill, 1966) 136. Von Rad's negative evaluation of creation was directed against Nazi master-race ideology rooted in "natural" superiority, according to Albertz (Weltschöpfung, 174).

soteriological thought."[7] Von Rad's characterization of "creation" as a foreign body, empty of real significance except when joined to "history" (as in Second Isaiah), determined the agenda for subsequent scholarship. Even though it is now widely recognized that creation is neither a late import into biblical thought (since it is found in early poetry) nor devoid of redemptive significance, scholars still begin with von Rad's "problematic" of relating what continue to be seen as two distinct doctrines.

R. Rendtorff in 1954 accepted von Rad's judgment that creation and redemption had been separate prior to Second Isaiah, advancing the discussion by the observation that creation appears only in the genres of disputation and oracle of salvation. In the disputations it becomes part of the prophet's contemporary proclamation and is no longer simply a past event. Second Isaiah changed the oracle of salvation (a genre original to the psalms) so that creation was transformed from creation of the world to creation of Israel, and addressed the people in the second-person. Second Isaiah united the two originally separate traditions: introductions to the oracles of salvation put "choose" and "create" in parallel (see 42:6; 43:1; 44:1). As Rendtorff concluded: "Creation, call, commission fully include one another. 'I have created you' and 'I have called you' are only different expressions for the same event." Likewise: "The creation of Israel took place in its election."[8]

C. Westermann's widely used commentary, *Isaiah 40-66*, consciously stepped back from Rendtorff's bold conclusions: "God's work in creation and his work in redemption are here looked on as very closely connected: however, this must never be taken as meaning that, in whole or in part, the two merge, for that would be a misconception of what the prophet had in mind."[9] One reason for Westermann's rejection of Rendtorff's thesis was his conviction that cosmogonies existed in two separate traditions—creation of the world and creation of the individual: "The creation of humans is originally an event completely different from the creation of the world and is told in a different way."[10] This distinction

---

[7] Ibid., 142.

[8] R. Rendtorff, "Die theologische Stellung des Schöpfungsglaubens bei Deuterojesaja," *ZTK* 51 (1954) 12.

[9] C. Westermann, *Isaiah 40–66* (OTL; Philadelphia: Westminster, 1969) 25. Rendtorff had written of 44:2–5: "A more complete blending of creation faith and salvation faith cannot be imagined" ("Die theologische Stellung," 10).

[10] C. Westermann, *Genesis 1–11* (Minneapolis: Augsburg, 1984) 24.

is important in Westermann's form-critical work. In Psalms and Second Isaiah he finds creation of the world in the genre of hymn where it forms the basis of praise. Creation of human beings appears in the genre of individual lament including oracles of salvation; divine compassion is based on God's having created the psalmist. Second Isaiah brought the two traditions into relationship. Creation he associated with God's majesty, and redemption with God's compassionate action. This polarity shows that "God's saving action upon his chosen people as proclaimed by himself was, as it were, an island within the mighty universe of God's work as creator."[11]

In his 1974 book, *Weltschöpfung und Menschenschöpfung*,[12] R. Albertz sought to refine the work of both Westermann and Rendtorff and to advance their thought. He argued that Westermann's hymn polarity did not really influence his exegesis of individual creation passages, and that Rendtorff's observation that all creation statements in Second Isaiah are in disputations or oracles of salvation was valuable but inconsistently Rendtorff derived all creation statements exclusively from the hymn. Albertz's solution to these and other difficulties was to emphasize even more Westermann's distinction between creation of the world and creation of human beings and their separate tradition histories. And the distinction remains central in K. Eberlein's explicitly theological Erlangen-Nurnberg dissertation written under E. Kutsch in 1986.[13]

Albertz's contribution was not a step forward. Rendtorff's correct insight about the similar function of creation and redemption statements was put aside, analysis of the text gave way to analysis of abstract genres and, worst of all, the questionable distinction between creation of the world and creation of individual human beings became an operating assumption.

---

[11] Westermann, *Isaiah 40–66*, 25. Westermann's analysis of the hymn, developed at length in his *Praise and Lament in the Psalms* (Atlanta: Knox, 1981), book 1, part 3, is not without its critics. See Erhard Gerstenberger, "Psalms," in *Old Testament Form Criticism* (ed. J. H. Hayes; San Antonio, TX: Trinity University, 1974) 202.

[12] Albertz, *Weltschöpfung*. The distinction between the two types of creation is actually Westermann's. Albertz in his preface expresses his gratitude to Rendtorff, whose concept of creation he is careful to respect.

[13] K. Eberlein, *Gott der Schöpfer — Israels Gott: Eine exegetisch-hermeneutische Studie zur theologischen Funktion alttestamentlicher Schöpfungaussagen* (Frankfurt: Peter Lang, 1986). The distinction is also accepted by Ernst Haag, in "Gott als Schöpfer und Erlöser in der Prophetie des Deuterojesaja," *TTZ* 85 (1976) 193–213.

C. Stuhlmueller's valuable 1970 Biblical Institute dissertation is comprehensive and synthetic. He places creation within the development of the prophet's thought: beginning with Israel's traditional faith in Yahweh as redeemer, Second Isaiah recognized that same redemption on a cosmic scale and proceeded to announce not only the cosmic redemption of Israel but also cosmic first creation by Yahweh.[14] Stuhlmueller's valuable conclusions would be strengthened if he had begun with a definition of creation more precise than "God makes someone or something" [p. 3]). Further he so emphasizes the mutuality of creation and redemption ("creative redemption") that their precise relationship becomes difficult to understand.

M. Fishbane's contribution stands somewhat outside the discussion just described. He reads chapters 40–55 as "aggadic exegesis" of Genesis 1, a type of exegesis that had parallels in the ancient Near East. For example, Marduk absorbs Ea and Enlil traditions in *Enūma elish,* and the *Memphite Theology* reinterprets Atum's creation with "his semen and his fingers" by Ptah's creation with "teeth and lips in his mouth, which pronounced the name of everything." Thus Isa 45:7, "He forms light and creates darkness," interprets Gen 1:2, answering doubts that God did not create *tōhû wābōhû* and *ḥōšek;* Isaiah's question "Who is like (*dĕmût*) God?" (40:18, 25) qualifies Gen 1:26, "Let us make man in our image (*kidmûtēnû*); and the Isaian insistence that God is not weary or tired (40:28) comments on the divine rest on the seventh day of creation.[15] Second Isaiah's cosmological event is "the prototype or warrant for a historical redemption to come."[16] The process of primordial beginnings (in Second Isaiah the destruction of the monsters of chaos) is a fundamental expression of divine power and can be reexpressed in historical forms, e.g., the exodus: "Perceiving the past in typological terms, he is able to perceive in the present the conditions for an extension of the typology; indeed, it is the prophet's *exegetical correlation* between a

---

[14] C. Stuhlmueller, *Creative Redemption in Deutero-Isaiah* (AnBib 43; Rome: Biblical Institute, 1970). The work contains a thorough bibliography. Stuhlmueller gives his own summary: "From the new redemption of Israel, to the creation of the entire world of Israel; from the creation of the entire world of Israel, to the creation of the entire world *simpliciter;* from the creation of the entire world, to the redemption of this world" (p. 237).

[15] M. Fishbane, *Biblical Interpretation in Ancient Israel* (Oxford: Clarendon, 1985) 322–26.

[16] Ibid., 354.

primordial theomachy and the exodus that is returned to YHWH in prayer and request [in 51:9–11]."[17] The correlation of primordial and historical events has old roots; Isa 11:15–16 speaks of the redemption "a second time" of the northern tribes and of the cleaving of the sea (reading *bāqaʿ yam* for *bāʿyam*), and psalms such as 74:12–14; 78:13; 89:11 provide other examples.

Fishbane's theory of aggadic exegesis is helpful for Second Isaiah. There is indeed an exegetical correlation between primordial cosmogony and the exodus. I would add that cosmogony and exodus-conquest (the latter interpreted as a unified act) both issue in a new community and for this reason are placed in parallel.

Recently J. Vermeylen has proposed that creation is prominent in all three of his proposed stages of composition for chapters 40–55. In the first stage, Second Isaiah's own "oracles make the Persian sovereign the instrument Yahweh uses to impose on society his creation order" (40:12, 21a, 22–23, 26; 41:2–4; 42:5–6a; 44:24, 24*, 26*, 28, etc.); Cyrus is the legitimate king around whom the Judeans are to rally ("my shepherd," 44:28; "his anointed," 45:1). In the second stage, an editor in the mid-fifth century envisioned the community of Israel being molded (*yāṣar*) like man in Gen 2:7 (40:21b, 27–28a; 42:6bα; 43:1–7*, etc.). Representations of the cosmic order were transposed onto the human plane. The third stage of redaction took place around Ezra's time (ca. 400 B.C.) and interpreted creation as victory over evil; creation was the establishment of cosmic order over the forces of chaos (41:17–20; 44:27; 45:7, 8; 51:9–11).[18]

Quite apart from the validity of his redactional theory, Vermeylen's analysis of creation in Second Isaiah is faulty because he uses as criteria for distinct redactions what ancient Near Eastern cosmogonies routinely united: the involvement of the king, emergence of a people, and establishment of a moral order. Consequently, his criteria for distinguishing stages are actually arguments for the coherence of the prophet's ideas of creation.

To sum up the recent scholarship on creation in Second Isaiah, von Rad correctly pointed to the redemptive function of creation in Second Isaiah but unfortunately formulated it as a relation between primary and secondary concepts. He overlooked the meaning of creation in early poetry such as Exodus 15 and Psalms 77, 78, and 89, where the people Israel

---

[17] Ibid., 355 (italics his).
[18] J. Vermeylen, "Le motif de la création dans le Deutéro-Isaïe," in *La création*, 183–240.

are created as well as redeemed. Rendtorff's correct observation about the close connection between the two concepts of creation and redemption was resisted by Westermann on the basis of his invalid distinction between creation of the whole and of individuals. That distinction was, unfortunately, developed by Albertz and Eberlein. Some of the discussion has been carried on in an excessively form-critical atmosphere, as analyses of reconstructed genres rather than of actual speeches and without sufficient comparison of extra-biblical cosmogonies.

II. Representative Texts on Creation in Second Isaiah

The review given above has shown the importance of creation in Second Isaiah as well as the lack of consensus regarding its meaning. I will now seek to show how Deutero-Isaiah remains close to ancient Near Eastern usage of cosmogonic traditions as he persuades the exiles to return to Zion.

Second Isaiah uses traditional cosmogonies in original and rhetorically effective ways. A good example is the disputation in 40:12–31, which invites the audience to look at the world in order to recognize that Yahweh, who created the three tiers of the universe (waters, heavens, earth), also created their inhabitants who now dishearten Israel — the nations (in the person of kings and princes) and their heavenly patrons (vv 25 26). Israel has nothing to fear, for Yahweh is master over all, as is shown by his effortless weighing of the world and its inhabitants on a scale. Isa 40:12–16 makes this especially clear.[19]

Weighing of the world (v 12)	*Weighing of the nations* (vv 15–16)
waters	drop of water
heavens	cloud
earth	dust of earth
mountains and hills	Mount Lebanon

The entire exhortation assumes that the world is a system in which the inhabitants of each tier (kings and princes on earth, heavenly beings in the heavens) are under God. The people, therefore, need not fear from the inhabitants of heaven and earth; all stand under the power of Yahweh.

Already in 40:12–31 the distinctive features of the Deutero-Isaian use of cosmogony are visible: Yahweh as storm God employing wind as a

---

[19] I owe this observation to Prof. Paul Mosca.

weapon, his victory over desert or sea that results in a populated world, the emergence of Israel (or Zion, the temple-city)[20] as the term of the act of creation, and (often) the complementary placement of cosmogony and exodus-conquest. The uses of cosmogony in chapters 40–55 fall into two broad categories—those that emphasize its complementarity with the exodus-land taking, and those mainly concerned with cosmogony as the building of the temple or temple-city. A maximally inclusive list of the first group includes 41:17–20; 42:13–17; 43:1–7; 43:16–21; 49:8–12; 51:9–11. A maximally inclusive list of the second group includes 44:24–45:13; and 45:14–25, and to a lesser extent chapters 54 and 55, which are about the rebuilding of Zion. Chapters 60–62, 65, and 66, are also relevant but lie beyond the scope of this chapter.

The first use, cosmogony as a complement to the exodus-conquest (the founding event of Israel), was already traditional by the time of Second Isaiah in the second half of the sixth century. The ancient poem Exod 15:1–18 uses cosmogonic language in hymning the God who defeated Pharaoh and brought the people to his holy mountain: "The floods covered them, they went down into the depths like a stone" (Exod 15:6). The goal of the journey from Egypt was the holy land: "You brought them in and planted them on your own mountain, the site where you made your dwelling, the sanctuary, Yahweh, your hands founded" (Exod 15:17). Ps 77:12–21 speaks similarly: "You redeemed with (your) arm your people, the children of Jacob and Joseph. When the waters saw you, O God, when the waters saw you, they were afraid, yea the deeps trembled" (vv 16–17). Psalm 89 likewise unites the conquest of the sea (vv 10–13) with the emergence of Israel (vv 20–38), and so do Psalms 93 and 114.

Why did Second Isaiah wish to make cosmogony and exodus parallel? For the same reason as the tradition that he inherited did: to give cosmic breadth to the historical event. As an incursion into the domain of Pharaoh the king of Egypt the exodus had worldwide effects! Those effects were underscored by associating the victory over Pharaoh with the primordial victory that brought the world into being. Both acts resulted in the emergence of a new people. From Second Isaiah's rhetorical perspective, Israel in Babylon found itself in a position like that of the Hebrews in

---

[20] Temple and temple-city are ultimately the same. See M. Weinfeld, "Zion and Jerusalem as Religious and Political Capital: Ideology and Utopia," in *The Poet and the Historian: Essays in Literary and Historical Biblical Criticism* (ed. R. E. Friedman; HSS 26; Chico, CA: Scholars Press, 1983) 75–115.

Egypt. Away from its rightful, divinely given land, the people had ceased in any true sense to be Yahweh's people. To become fully alive again, they needed to embark on a new exodus-land taking, a new cosmogony.[21]

Second Isaiah's originality was less in speaking of a *new* exodus-land taking than in developing the contrast of new and old cosmogony. To him, the return of the exiles from Babylon to Zion would be a veritable conquest of the desert, and that conquest of the desert would renew the conquest of the sea in the time of Moses. Both sea and desert had interposed themselves between the people and their land. The barrier must be overcome by cutting a pathway through the sea or desert.

A good example of the complementarity of new and old occurs Isa in 43:16–21. This passage puts into parallel new and old cosmogony and new and old exodus and land taking with almost mathematical precision. The prophet fuses historic and suprahistoric language in drawing the analogy:

> [16]Thus says Yahweh,
> the one who makes a way in the Sea,
>   a path in the Mighty Waters,
> [17]the one who musters chariot and horse,
>   all the mighty army;
> they lie prostrate, no more to rise,
>   they are extinguished, quenched like a wick:
> [18]"Recall no more the former things,
>   the ancient events bring no longer to mind.
> [19]I am now doing something new,
>   now it springs forth, do you not recognize it?
> I am making a way in the wilderness,
>   paths[22] in the desert.
> [20]The wild beasts will honor me,
>   jackals and ostriches.
> For I have placed waters in the wilderness,
>   rivers in the desert,
> to give drink to my chosen people,
> [21]the people whom I have formed for myself,
>   to narrate my praiseworthy deeds.

---

[21] For a fuller development of these ideas, see R. J. Clifford, *Fair Spoken and Persuading: An Interpretation of Second Isaiah* (New York: Paulist, 1984) chapter 2.

[22] Reading *ntybt* with 1QIs[a]. *Nĕhārôt* has been attracted from v 20d.

Yahweh, identified by the participles *hannôtēn* ("who makes") in v 16b and *hammôṣî'* ("who musters") in v 17a (continued by the prefix form in v 17cd), is conqueror of Sea and of Pharaoh's troops. Verses 18–21 tell Israel to replace the traditional recital with a recital of the action being experienced today. The new event repeats the old act: way in the Sea (v 16) // way in the Wilderness (v 20); path in the Mighty Waters (v 16) // paths in the Desert (v 20d). Instead of the sea, the impassable desert stands between land and people and must have a highway driven through it. The desert as Yahweh's enemy that is ultimately defeated may ultimately reflect the Baal-Mot conflict in the Ugaritic texts.[23] More immediately, it seems to reflect Yahweh's mastery of the desert in the Mosaic period, when manna, quail, and water nourished the people on their journey.[24] Desert's sterility is overcome so thoroughly that even its exotic animals offer worship and water becomes abundant for the "people you have formed for yourself" (v 21). The new, always under suspicion in the ancient Near East, is validated by the old. The power of the old event appears in the new event that resembles it.[25]

Isa 51:9–16, apparently a communal lament set within a prophetic speech, likewise makes Yahweh's defeat of Sea (vv 9–10) parallel to the exodus-conquest (v 10d), and then aligns that primordial act with the contemporary return to Zion (v 11).

The second major classification of cosmogony texts in Second Isaiah is concerned with building the temple or temple-city in 44:24–45:13 and 45:14–25. Isa 44:24–45:7 gives the clearest illustration in Second Isaiah of standard oriental creation: the building of the temple and temple-city, the king as builder of the temple and as agent of the god, and the promulgation of justice and peace.

> 24Thus says Yahweh who redeemed you,
> who fashioned you from the womb,

---

[23] For the argument, see R. J. Clifford, "Cosmogonies in the Ugaritic Texts and in the Bible," *Or* 53 (1984) 183–201.

[24] I owe this observation to Prof. Theodore Hiebert.

[25] Ernst Haag is not accurate in saying that "Yahweh had gone back on the saving act of the exodus from Egypt. The people saw itself as it were banished to an area devoid of saving history, which must have called into question not only Israel as the people of God but also Yahweh himself" ("Gott als Schöpfer und Erlöser in der Prophetie des Deuterojesaja," *TTZ* 85 [1976] 210). Second Isaiah presumes here the validity of the old events, and states that the power of the old is in the new.

"It is I, Yahweh, maker of all things,
   who alone stretches out the heavens,
   flattens out the earth—who was with me?—
25who nullifies the signs of diviners,
   makes fools of augurs,
thwarts the wise,
   turns their lore into nonsense;
26who establishes the word of his servant,
   fulfills the statements of his messengers;
who says of Jerusalem, 'Be inhabited!'
   of the cities of Judah, 'Be built!
   I will rebuild your ruins!'
27who says to the Deep, 'Be dry!
   I will dry up your Rivers!'
28who says to Cyrus, 'My Shepherd!
   he will do my pleasure';
(Cyrus) will say of Jerusalem, 'Let it be built!
   Let the temple be founded!'
45:1Thus says Yahweh to Cyrus his anointed,
   whose right hand he has grasped,
subduing nations before him,
   ungirding the loins of kings,
opening doors before him,
   no gate will remain shut.
2I will march at your head,
   mountains I will level,
doors of bronze I will break down,
   bars of iron I will slice through.
3I will give you treasures lying in darkness,
   hoards in secret places,
so that you may recognize that I am Yahweh,
   the one who calls you by your name,
   the God of Israel.
4For the benefit of my servant Jacob,
   Israel my chosen,
I call you by your name;
   I confer your title, though you know me not.
5I am Yahweh; there is no other,
   beside me there is no god.
I gird you with authority though you know me not,

⁶that people may recognize from the rising of the sun to its setting
   that there is none but me.
I am Yahweh and there is no other,
⁷ the maker of light and creator of darkness,
   the maker of peace and creator of evil.
It is I, Yahweh, maker of all things.

Yahweh's authority to speak comes from redeeming and creating his people (the suffix "your" in v 24ab) and from creating "everything" alone (v 24cde). This means that all the words of other gods (delivered through their spokespersons) are ineffective (v 25); only Yahweh's word (through his spokespersons) is effective (v 26ab). Emphasis on the divine word continues with the thrice repeated participle *'ōmēr* and the infinitive *lē'mōr* in vv 26–28. God commands that the temple and temple-city be rebuilt (v 26cde), that the deep be controlled (v 27), and that the king as his agent execute his command (v 28).²⁶ Worldwide dominion is promised to the king in 45:1–7. "Shower down, O heavens" (45:8) probably reprises 44:23, "Sing, O Heavens." 45:9–13 completes the poem by refuting those who will not believe that Cyrus is Yahweh's anointed.

A glance at Akkadian cosmogonies²⁷ shows how traditionally Near Eastern the Isaian account is: divine control of cosmic waters, building of a temple-city or temple, creation of a king and human beings to build and tend the temple, and creation of necessities for the care and feeding of the gods — trees, rushes and clay for bricks, animals for sacrifices. The appointment of a king during creation in 45:1–7 also has biblical parallels: "You are my son; today I have begotten you. Ask of me, and I will make the nations your heritage, and the ends of earth your possession" (Ps 2:7–8); "I place his hand on the Sea, on the Rivers [same word as here] his right hand . . . Yes, I make him my firstborn, the highest of the kings of the earth" (Ps 89:25, 27).

To Second Isaiah, the building of Jerusalem and the temple and the appointment of a king are part of the act of creation. His cosmogonic language is traditional except for one thing — the king is a Persian rather than an Israelite! In 45:9–13, which uses the vocabulary of Isa 10:5–19,

---

²⁶ The syntax of Isa 44:24–28 (*'āmar* [finite verb]+participles+*lĕ*+infinitive) occurs also in 49:5. In both cases the syntax suggests that the action of the human agent expressed by the infinitive, which is dependent on the finite verb of speaking, is done at the behest of Yahweh. See also the similar syntax in 42:6–7 and 49:5, 8.

²⁷ "Creation Accounts in Mesopotamia: Akkadian Texts," nos. 3–6, 9.

the prophet vehemently defends the divine choice of the Assyrian king as the rod of God's anger. His point: Cyrus, the instrument of restoration, is the negative mirror image of First Isaiah's Assyrian king, the instrument of destruction (10:5–19). The historical event has a cosmic meaning. The prophet stays within the conventions of ancient cosmogonies; cosmogony results in a world made for the gods—with temples, cities, king, people, raw materials for temple worship, and heavenly bodies to determine proper times for worship. Second Isaiah's perspective is predominantly ethnocentric; he is concerned primarily with the creation of Israel. Israel could not exist authentically in Babylon the city of false gods; now it is coming back into existence, however, as Cyrus builds the temple-city and lets the people return. Creation apparently could be repeated (a departure from modern notions), as it was repeated in the ancient Near East with the return of the agricultural year and dedication of the temple (even if only a brick was removed from the temple and replaced).

In summary, the first category of cosmogonic texts juxtaposes suprahistoric language (cosmogony as the conquest of the sterility of the desert) and historic language (cosmogony as the journey from Babylon to Zion across the desert). Further, it applies an "old-new" polarity both to the cosmogony (old: sea=new: desert) and to the historical event (old: the crossing of the Red Sea=new: the crossing of the desert).

I would like to end this chapter with a speculative scenario suggesting how Second Isaiah might have come to the conviction that God was acting through the events of his time. These speculations at least have the merit of developing further what cosmogony meant to the prophet. From his observation of Cyrus's defeat of Babylon, rebuilding of native temples, and return of displaced peoples, Second Isaiah may well have concluded that God was engaged in an act of creation. Such royal actions were traditional in ancient oriental cosmogonies. To the Israelite prophet, these acts could only have been done by Yahweh, the sole God. Hence Cyrus must be Yahweh's choice as king. Did the prophet's observations lead him perhaps to reexamine the old poetry about Israel's origins and discover that exodus-conquest and cosmogony were alternative expressions of one and the same event—the founding of Israel? Cyrus's rebuilding of the temple had to have as its complement a new exodus. From the spectacular success of Cyrus and from First Isaian traditions, the prophet could have concluded that Cyrus was the antithesis of the Assyrian king (see 10:5–19), restoring where the Assyrian had destroyed. Land defined domain. Only in Zion could Israel really exist, for only there could Yahweh be truly accessible and powerful in human affairs. The prophet's task was therefore to persuade the people to leave Babylon and return to Zion. The divine act of creation with exodus-conquest contained an ethical imperative: leave Babylon, cross the desert, and live in Zion. Thus Israel once upon a time had come into existence, and thus would Israel now come back into existence. Though these remarks are hypothetical, they do put into a specific historical context the creation traditions of Second Isaiah.

CHAPTER 9

Creation in
the Wisdom Literature

The surge of scholarly interest in the Wisdom Literature of the Bible[1] has had, as one of its results, a deepened appreciation of the theological importance of creation. Biblical theologians of the past were inclined to find the God of Israel chiefly in the historical books, in the free interaction between God and the people of Israel. The Wisdom books, similar to Mesopotamian and Egyptian literature in their pragmatic outlook, seemed less revelatory of Yahweh, the God of Israel. But biblicists are increasingly coming to appreciate the honest probing, sustained irony, and undeniable Yahwism of the wisdom books. One scholar whose writings typify the changed outlook was the great Heidelberg biblical theologian Gerhard von Rad. Though his 1936 essay saw creation as theologically significant only when joined and subordinated to the (historical) concept of redemption, his book *Wisdom in Israel* (1972) assigned to creation much greater significance.[2]

Despite increasing scholarly interest in "creation theology," L. Perdue correctly notes that "few have attempted to describe in comprehensive fashion the salient features of the sapiential understanding of creation."[3]

---

[1] The Wisdom books of the Hebrew Bible are commonly reckoned as Proverbs, Job, and Qoheleth. Sirach and Wisdom of Solomon, as apocryphal or Deuterocanonical literature, lie beyond the scope of this book.

[2] Von Rad's essay in English is "The Theological Problem of the Old Testament Doctrine of Creation," in *The Problem of the Hexateuch and Other Essays* (New York: McGraw-Hill, 1966). His book in English is *Wisdom in Israel* (Nashville: Abingdon, 1972).

[3] L. G. Perdue, "Job's Assault on Creation," *HAR* 10 (1986) 295. Perdue himself attempts

The present chapter deals with cosmogonies or references to them in
Proverbs and Job, not with all references to creation in Wisdom Literature. Cosmogonies are found in Proverbs 3:19–20 and 8:22–31. Relevant
cosmogonic passages in Job include an incantation in chapter 3; doxologies
to the creator in chapter 5, 9, 10, and 12; a hymn in 25:2–6+26:5–14;
and God's speeches from the whirlwind in chapters 38–42.

I. Creation in the Book of Proverbs

Chapters 1–9 of Proverbs, which contain several long poems and instructions, comprise a kind of preface to the collections of sayings (usually
of two or three lines) in chapters 10–31. Chapters 1–9 personify wisdom
as an attractive woman who urges the young man (the typical recipient
of ancient Near Eastern instruction) to follow her way of life (Prov 1:20–33;
8; 9:1–11). These chapters openly use the language of love, e.g., urging
the young man to address Wisdom with the intimate term "my sister,"
to wait at her door, to keep away from other women, to share her life.[4]
The contrasting female figure of Folly addresses the youth in similar
language, but her offer will bring death (Prov 2:16–19; 5:3–6; 7; 9:13–18).
    The two cosmogonies in Proverbs 1–9 occur within longer poems—
3:13–26 and 8:1–36.[5] The creation accounts establish the authority of

---

such a comprehensive description in *Wisdom in Revolt: Metaphorical Theology in the
Book of Job* (Bible and Literature 29; Sheffield: Almond, 1991). His survey of recent scholarship on pp. 13–22 lists four ideas that have been used to organize recent study of creation
in Wisdom Literature: anthropology (W. Zimmerli and W. Brueggemann), theodicy (J.
Crenshaw), cosmology or world order (H. Gese, H.-J. Hermisson), and cosmology-
anthropology (G. von Rad).

    [4] The commonly used titles "Dame" and "Lady" for Wisdom and Folly wrongly sug-
gest a matronly figure. Wisdom's appeal is erotic and envisions a personal relationship,
perhaps even marriage. See R. Murphy, "Wisdom and Eros in Proverbs 1–9," *CBQ* 50
(1988) 600–3, and W. McKane, *Proverbs: A New Approach* (OTL; Philadelphia: Westminster, 1970) 94.

    [5] The three references to God the creator (and protector) of the poor person in Prov
14:31; 17:5; 22:2, and the more general references to God the maker in Prov 16:4; 20:12;
29:14 will not be studied here in according with our interest in cosmogonies rather than
in every reference to creation. For these passages, see P. Doll, *Menschenschöpfung und
Weltschöpfung in der alttestamentlichen Weisheit* (SBS 117; Stuttgart: Katholisches Bibelwerk, 1985) 15–39. According to Doll all references to creation of the individual human
being occur in chapters 10–29, the first of the three stages of composition that he postulates

Woman Wisdom, especially over against Woman Folly. Prov 3:19–20 affirms that the world was created in wisdom and that wisdom is within the grasped of the insistent seeker. Prov 8:22–31 develops the same thought by personifying Wisdom and giving her a lengthy speech: intimately associated with Yahweh before creation, she can mediate a like intimacy to the human beings who court her (8:22–31).

A. Proverbs 3:16–26

Many commentators do not regard vv 13–26 as a complete poem,[6] yet formal indicators suggest unity: six bicola precede God's creation in vv 19–20 and six bicola follow, thus making the two verses on creation central; the seven substantives for wisdom in the poem occur only in the centerpiece (vv 19–20) and in the first line of each section (vv 13, 21b). All the verses are necessary to make the statement: vv 13–18 declare the finder of wisdom blessed ($\sqrt{}$ '*šr* in vv 13a and 18b) with life, wealth, honor, favor, and peace, without explaining why. The explanation is only given in vv 19–20: Yahweh built the world "by wisdom," and those who live "by wisdom" will enjoy the good things of that world. The second set of six bicola (vv 21–26) exhorts "my son" (the conventional addressee in such instructions) to seek those same gifts of life, favor, and blessing, and to live without fear. These gifts accrue to the very body of the recipient—eyes, throat, gullet (*NRSV* "soul"), loins, and feet. Thus the youth must not let shrewdness and foresight, synonyms for wisdom, depart from his eyes (v 21, see also Deut 6:8).

> 13Happy the person who finds wisdom,
>   the one who gets understanding.

---

for the book. All references to creation of the world occur in his third and final stage, the wisdom poems of chapters 1–9 (see pp. 41–58). Doll's sharp distinction between traditions of creation of the (individual) person and the world is not valid for these traditions.

6 Scholars favoring unity include W. Zimmerli, in *Sprüche, Prediger* (ATD 16/1; Göttingen: Vandenhoeck & Ruprecht, 1962) 21–22; and Doll, *Menschenschöpfung und Weltschöpfung*, 49. R. B. Y. Scott posits three separate sections: vv 13–18, 19–20, and 21–26 (*Proverbs, Ecclesiastes* [AB 18; Garden City, NY: Doubleday, 1965] 45–48). W. McKane reads vv 13–20 as a single poem (*Proverbs: A New Approach* [OTL; Philadelphia: Westminster, 1970] 289–90, 294–99). R. Murphy takes vv 13–24 as an instruction introduced by a hymn (vv 13–18) in his *Wisdom Literature* (FOTL 13; Grand Rapids: Eerdmans, 1981) 57–58.

14For her value in trade is better than silver,
  Better than gold is her yield.
15She is more precious than jewels;
  No treasure can compare with her.
16Length of days is in her right hand,
  In her left are riches and honor.
17Her ways are pleasant,
  All her paths are peace.
18A tree of life is she to those who embrace her,
  Those who hold her fast are declared happy.
19Yahweh by wisdom founded the earth,
  Established the heavens by understanding.
20By his knowledge the deeps broke open;[7]
  The clouds dropped down dew.
21My son, do not let them escape from your eyes;
  Guard shrewdness and foresight,
22So that there will be life in your throat,
  Favor in your gullet.
23Then you will go your way with confidence;
  Your feet will not stumble.
24When you lie down, you will not be afraid;
  When you sleep, your slumber will be sweet.
25You will not be afraid of sudden terror,
  The disaster that comes upon the wicked.
26For Yahweh will be your trust (lit., "in your loins");
  He will keep your feet from being caught.

The little cosmogony in vv 19–20 resembles traditions associating wisdom with creation, which are attested elsewhere in Mesopotamia and in the Bible. In the Sumerian Eridu tradition, Enki, god of water and wisdom, creates by bringing up water from the underworld to fertilize the earth through rivers and canals. In the literature of both Sumer (*Enki and Ninmah*) and Akkad (*Atrahasis* and the Mayer text), the wise Enki creates human beings to resolve a particular problem. The Bible also associates wisdom with creation, as in the hymnic statement "[Yahweh] made the earth by his power, established the world by his wisdom, and by his understanding stretched out the heavens" (Jer 10:12=51:15; see also Ps 104:24).

---

[7] The cosmic waters surrounding the earth fertilize it through springs and clouds.

The manner of creation in Proverbs 3 is similar to that in Prov 8:22–31. Earth, mentioned before heaven (v 19b, contrary to the order of the usual hendiadys "heaven and earth"), is established; it rests upon gigantic pillars sunk into the all-encompassing sea (see 8:24–25). Heaven is similarly established, i.e., raised up over the earth. In 3:20a, the waters are "broken," or tapped, to provide water for the earth (see 8:27b–28). The themes of wisdom and of cosmic water fertilizing the earth are found in the Eridu cosmogonic tradition, though that tradition is concerned with canals and rivers rather than with rain water (3:20b).

Although the Bible associates creation with the divine attribute of power as well as wisdom (Jer 10:12=51:15; 32:17; Ps 65:7), Proverbs prefers the association with divine wisdom in order to provide a rationale for the human quest for it. The very wisdom by which Yahweh created the world is available to all who seek it. Wisdom thus mediates between the all-wise Yahweh and the human seeker.

The general purpose of 3:19–20 does not differ from many ancient Near Eastern cosmogonies: to ground or explain an element of "culture." In this instance the reality is not a temple or a king, but a way of life — the pursuit of wisdom. Whoever finds wisdom will experience every good known to human beings — long life, wealth, honor, beauty, shalom. This is what Yahweh intended for Israel and the human race, according to the confident outlook of the Book of Proverbs.[8]

B. Proverbs 8

Proverbs 8 is part of a literary section, chapters 7–9. The section is shaped by a chiasm:

a	7:1–27	Wanton woman
b	8:1–36	Woman Wisdom
b′	9:1–12	Woman Wisdom
a′	9:13–18	Wanton woman

---

[8] Doll regards the main point of 3:19–20 as the praise of Yahweh's wisdom in creation analogous to that in several hymns, and cites Ps 104:24, "How many are your works, O Yahweh. In wisdom you have made them all" (*Menschenschöpfung und Weltschöpfung*, 50–51). But the poem is an explanation of why wisdom enriches the person who seeks her; it is not a hymn.

There are other indications that chapters 7–9 form a distinct section. A similar exhortation ends both chapter 7 and chapter 8. Section *a′* (9:13–18) is connected to section *a* (chapter 7) by several verbal links: *hōmîyâ* in 7:11 and 9:13; "house" six times in chapter 7 and twice in chapter 9; "passing by" (*'ōbēr*) in 7:8 and 9:15; "way" in 7:8, 25, and 9:15; "lacking sense" in 7:7 and 9:16; and "Sheol" in 7:27 and 9:18. Wisdom in chapter 8 speaks the truth to crowds in broad daylight, whereas the wanton woman in chapter 7 speaks lies in the night to the lone young man. Finally, the opening *hălō'* in 8:1 ("surely" or "doesn't . . . ?") perhaps implies a deliberate contrast with what has preceded.

Chapter 8 can be divided into seven stanzas: vv 1–5 (Wisdom's broad appeal), vv 6–11 (her truthfulness), vv 12–16 (her rule through kings), vv 17–21 (her gifts to her lovers), vv 22–26 (her preeminent creation), vv 27–31 (her privileged and affectionate place with Yahweh), vv 32–36 (her appeal to the young to listen to her and wait at her gates).[9]

The cosmogony in vv 22–31 grounds the extraordinary claims of Wisdom in chapter 8, just as 3:19–20 grounds the claims of 3:13–18.

> 22Yahweh begot me at the beginning of his work,
>   The first of his deeds of long ago.
> 23From of old I was established,
>   At the beginning, before the origin of the earth.
> 24When there was no deep I was brought forth,
>   When there were no springs abounding in water.
> 25Before the mountains were sunk,
>   Before the hills, I was brought forth,
> 26When he had not made the earth and fields,
>   The first of the soil of the earth.
> 27When he established the heavens, I was there,
>   When he drew the circle on the face of the deep,
> 28When he put in place the cloud above,
>   When he installed the springs of the deep,
> 29When he made for the sea its boundary
>   So the waters would not transgress his command,

[9] For the structure, see M. Gilbert, "Le discours de la Sagesse en Proverbes 8," in *La Sagesse de l'Ancien Testament* (ed. M. Gilbert; BETL 51; Paris: Duculot, 1979) 209–14; P. W. Skehan, "Structure in Poems on Wisdom," *CBQ* 41 (1979) 367–73; Doll, *Menschenschöpfung und Weltschöpfung*, 53–54; and B. Lang, *Wisdom and the Book of Proverbs: A Hebrew Goddess Redefined* (New York: Pilgrim, 1986) 77–78. Lang asks colleagues (p. x) to cite this book rather than the original German work *Frau Weisheit*.

When he fixed the foundations of earth,
   30I was at his side, a sage.[10]
I was a source of delight daily,
   Playing before him at all times,
   31Playing in his inhabited world,
   My delight is to be with the human race.

The structure of vv 22–31 is chiastic:

  a vv 22–23 Yahweh creates Wisdom in honored first place;
  b vv 24–26 Creation "negatively" described;[11]
  b' vv 27–30a Creation "positively" described;
  a' vv 30b–31 Wisdom's intimacy with Yahweh.

Vv 22–23 and 30b–31 (two bicola each) both concern Wisdom's relationship with Yahweh, unlike vv 24–30a, which narrate Wisdom's honored first place. The chiasm shows that "I was at his side" (v 30a) matches "I was there" (v 27a).[12]

Vv 24–26 portray precreation chaos or nothingness concretely, i.e., by listing specific cosmic elements not in existence rather than through the abstract concept of nothingness. In the primordial sea God sank massive pillars (probably the mountains on the horizon) and piled loam upon the earth. "Earth" (*'ereṣ*) is mentioned twice in vv 22–26, but the other noun in the common hendiadys for "world"—heaven—occurs only in the positive picture (v 27a). Vv 27–30a put the divine acts in an order slightly different from that of 3:19–30: God made firm the heavens, drew the circle of the horizon upon the deep (v 27), took from it water suitable for the human race by arranging rain and springs (vv 28), set boundaries for the sea (29ab), and fixed the foundations of the earth (v 29c). The final

---

[10] The translation of this word is disputed; "artisan" and "nursling" have also been suggested. For a recent survey of the question, see H. P. Rüger, "'Amôn: Pflegekind zur Auslegungsgeschichte von Prov. 8:30a," in *Übersetzung und Deutung: Studien zu dem AT and seiner Umwelt A. R. Hulst gewidmet von Freunden und Kollegen* (Nijkerk: Callenbach, 1977) 154–63. For the proposal that Hebrew *'amôn* is related to Akkadian *ummānu* "(postdiluvian) sage," see J. C. Greenfield, "The Seven Pillars of Wisdom (Prov. 9:1)—A Mistranslation," *JQR* 76 (1985) 13–20.

[11] I.e., "when there were *no* . . ."

[12] So also G. Yee, "The Theology of Creation in Proverbs 8:22–31," in *Creation in the Biblical Traditions* (ed. R. J. Clifford and J. J. Collins; CBQMS 24; Washington, D.C.: Catholic Biblical Association, 1992), 85–96.

act in chapter 8 is the first in 3:19–20; chapter 8 reverses it for the sake of the chiasm.

Particularly important for understanding the speech are the final two bicola (vv 30b–31), describing the intimate relations between Woman Wisdom and Yahweh:

wā'ehyeh ša'ăšu'îm yôm yôm   měśaḥeqet lěpānāyw běkōl-'ēt
měśaḥeqet bětēbēl 'arṣô   wěša'ăšu'ay 'et běnê 'ādām

The chiastic placement of Hebrew ša'ăšu'îm ("delight") and śāḥaq ("play") binds the two lines together, emphasizing the parity of Wisdom delighting in Yahweh and wisdom delighting in the human race. As Wisdom is Yahweh's delight "every day" in v 30b, so the youth is to wait at her doors "every day" in v 34. The affectionate relationship between Woman Wisdom and human beings on earth is portrayed in vv 32–34, reflecting the affectionate relationship between Woman Wisdom and Yahweh in heaven. One might perhaps expect Wisdom to ground her authority on the fact that she has seen Yahweh create and hence can communicate to her clients the secrets of how the world works. Yet she bases her authority solely on her intimacy with Yahweh; she has been with him from the beginning. The chiasm of the phrases "I was there" and "I was with him" in vv 27a and 30a underscores the affective intimate association. Yahweh's creating of Wisdom first was primarily a mark of esteem and affection. Wisdom is the subject of only three verbs in the section and they are all passive: "I was formed" and "I was born (twice)."[13]

The cosmogonies in Proverbs 3 and 8 display a similar literary structure:

1. wisdom's value and benefits   3:13–18 // 8:1–21
2. cosmogony grounding Wisdom's appeal   3:19–20 // 8:22–31
3. exhortation to live with Wisdom   3:21–26 // 8:32–36

Proverbs 8 goes a step beyond chapter 3 firstly by personifying wisdom, a quality traditionally associated with the divine act of creation and of cosmic order, and secondly by contrasting Wisdom with Folly or the wanton woman. Personification and contrast make chapter 8 an effective speech on how the search for wisdom brings with it every blessing. The search for wisdom in Proverbs is more than performing or avoiding

---

[13] There may be an allusion to the marital bond between Israel or Zion and Yahweh, a metaphor found in Hosea and Jeremiah.

certain actions, which was the common understanding of a life of wisdom. One is to seek Wisdom herself. To court her is to touch a quality of Yahweh the creator, and to marry her is to come into the fullness of divine blessings.[14]

II. Creation in Job

Even the casual reader cannot miss the importance of creation in the Book of Job. Job's first extended speech in chapter 3 curses the day of his creation; the book contains many hymns to God the creator, e.g., 9:4–13; 10:8–13; 12:13–25; 25:1–6+26:5–14; 36:24–37:24; God answers Job with two lengthy speeches about creation (38:1–40:5 and 40:6–42:6). Creation has been the subject of several articles and monographs.[15]

The present chapter is limited to observations about how traditional cosmogonies or hymns of creation are given a new twist by the author. The Book of Job subverts the ordinary purpose of cosmogonies. To Job, creation of the universe is so closely linked to his own creation that God's randomness and injustice toward him is simply one more instance of God's randomness and injustice toward the world.

The tone of the creation accounts differs according to who is speaking. Job sees God's creation as a violent and careless manipulation of things and living beings (9:5–13; 10:8–13; 12:13–25). The pious Bildad sees only order and majesty in God's work (25:1–6+26:5–24), and Elihu sees in the workings of nature a basis for unquestioning awe (36:24–37:24).

[14] For the view that the final chapter of Proverbs depicts the blessings of a person who has married Wisdom, see T. P. McCreesh, "Wisdom as Wife: Proverbs 31:10–31," *RB* 92 (1985) 25–46.

[15] Albertz, *Weltschöpfung;* and Perdue, *Wisdom in Revolt* (n. 3). Perdue argues that two patterns of creation have shaped the book: the cosmological pattern (found in *Enūma elish* and the Ugaritic Baal cycle) with its sequence of battle, victory, kingship, judgment, and re-creation; and the anthropological pattern (found in *Atrahasis*) with its sequence of judgment (slavery), slavery and toil, revolt, fall, and judgment culminating in redemption. In addition, see N. Habel, "He Who Stretches Out the Heavens," *CBQ* 34 (1972) 417–30 and n. 18.

[16] The Masoretic Text attributes 25:1–6 to Bildad and chap. 26 to Job. Possibly "Bildad's speech is short and sounds like what Job says in reply precisely because Job cuts him off and finishes the speech for him," as P. Skehan suggests in "Strophic Patterns in the Book of Job," *CBQ* 23 (1961) 141 (cited in M. Greenberg, "Job," in *The Literary Guide to the Bible* [ed. R. Alter and F. Kermode; Cambridge, MA: Harvard University, 1987] 293); but the majority of commentators correct the text by joining 26:6–14 immediately to 25:6.

God's defense of the wisdom and justice of his own creation (38:1–40:5; 40:6–42:6) diverges from the perspective of all the human speakers.

Because Job is so thoroughly a narrative, as correctly noted by Norman Habel,[17] analysis must reckon with the interaction between Job and his friends. Bildad in chapters 25–26 as well as Elihu in chapters 36–37 responds to Job's speeches on creation; God in chapters 38–41 reacts to both.

A. Job's Speeches on Creation

Job's first speech curses the day of his creation: "Perish the day I was born, the night on which they said 'a male is conceived'" (3:3). In vv 4–5 he utters six incantations summoning darkness and oblivion upon that day, and in vv 6–9, nine more incantations summoning chaos.[18] Job's reversal of creation shocks his friends into vehement reaction, and his curses become a foil to God's speech ending the dialogues. Job's solution to his overwhelming sufferings is to wish creation away and invite chaos. God's response is simply to describe the created world, unapologetically affirming that chaos (darkness, unbounded waters, Behemoth and Leviathan) is part of the warp and woof of the cosmic fabric.

By chapter 9 Job is convinced that it is impossible to win a suit against God. His speech in 9:4–15 parodies creation hymnody by its use of hymnic participles ("you who do such and such").

> 4Wise in heart and mighty in power—
>   who has challenged you and emerged unscathed?—
> 5The one who moves mountains without their knowing it,
>   Who overturns them in his anger;
> 6Who shakes the earth from its place,
>   so that its pillars totter;
> 7Who says to the sun, "Do not rise!"
>   He shuts up the stars;
> 8Who stretches out the heavens all by himself,
>   Who treads on the back of Sea;
> 9Who makes the Bear and Orion,

---

[17] N. Habel, *The Book of Job* (OTL; Philadelphia: Westminster, 1985).

[18] Besides the commentaries, see M. Fishbane, "Jeremiah iv 23–26 and Job iii 3–13: A Recovered Use of the Creation Pattern," *VT* 21 (1971) 151–67; and L. G. Perdue, "Job's Assault on Creation," *HAR* 10 (1986) 295–315.

The Pleiades and the Chambers of the south wind;
10Who does great deeds beyond searching,
   wondrous deeds beyond counting.
11He goes by me and I do not see him,
   he passes me and I do not know it.
12When he seizes, who can make him return it?
   Who says to him, "What are you doing?"
13God does not restrain his anger,
   under him the allies of Rahab bow low.
14How then can I answer him,
   choose my words with him?
15Though I am innocent, I will not respond,
   From my adversary-at-law I must beg for mercy.

Job wants to meet God in a court of law but acknowledges its impossibility. He mocks the God who masters the elements of the world—mountains, earth, earth's pillars (vv 5–6), luminaries (v 7), sea and heavens (vv 8–9)—with such power that no one can assess him (v 10). God is untouchable and unreachable (v 11). How can Job expect answers from such a creator!

The next few verses (9:16–24) attack the traditional ancient Near Eastern belief that justice is a constituent part of the created world. For example, the creation hymn Ps 104:35 prays that sinners be removed from the beautiful world just constructed, and Genesis 2–11 narrates how sinners are punished and the righteous (Noah) protected in the newly created world. But Job asserts that the universe is in the hands of the unjust (9:16–24): "The earth has been handed over to the power of the wicked" (9:24).

In the same speech he speaks about his creation as a man. The vocabulary is traditional, indeed, may even parody Psalm 139 in which the psalmist delights in being transparent before the all-seeing Lord.[19] But to Job, God's attention is hostile.

10:3Is it good for you to oppress,
   To spurn the work of your hands,
   To favor the counsel of the wicked?

---

[19] Ps 139:13–15: "For you created my inward parts, / you knit me in my mother's womb. / I will praise you for you do wondrous deeds, / wonderful are your works, / my being is most aware. / My frame was not concealed from you, / when I was shaped in a hidden place, / intricately wrought in the depths of the earth."

4Do you have eyes of flesh,
  Do you see as mere mortals see?
5Are your days like the days of a mortal,
  Are your years like the years of a human being,
6That you have to search out my iniquity,
  Have to look for my sin?
7You know I am not guilty,
  There is no one to rescue from my hand.
8Your hands have fashioned and made me,
  Then turned around and destroyed me.
9Remember, you made me as clay,
  To dust you shall bring me back.
10Did you not pour me out like milk,
  Like curds curdle me?
11With skin and flesh you clothed me,
  With bones and sinews you knit me.
12Life and kindness you made for me,
  Your watchful care preserved my breath.
13But you hid these things in your heart,
  I know this is the case with you:
14To watch whether I would sin,
  And not clear me of my guilt.
15If I am guilty, woe is me!
  If I am innocent, I cannot lift my head,
  So sated am I with misery, so filled with shame.

Job says that God already knows him thoroughly from having formed him. So God's incessant scrutiny now can only arise from a hostile desire to record faults. Job's conduct, good or bad, has no effect.

Job's final extended statement on creation, made in 12:13–25, is a defense (based his own experience) against the friends who urge him to admit that he has sinned and is being punished for it. Claiming the same intelligence as they, Job has seen with his own eyes (12:2–3; 13:1–2) exactly how arbitrary and perverse God's governance of the world is.

12:13With him is wisdom and might,
  length of days, wisdom.
14What he tears down cannot be rebuilt,
  whom he imprisons cannot be freed.
15When he restrains the waters, they dry up,
  when he releases them, they tear up the land.

16With him is strength and cunning,
  from him, the deceiver and the deceived.
17He is the one who causes counsellors to walk about stripped,
  he makes judges into fools.
18He undoes the belt of kings,
  removes the girdle from their loins.
19He causes priests to go stripped,
  cultic officials he overthrows.
20He takes away speech from the trustworthy,
  he takes discernment from the elders.
21He pours contempt upon nobles,
  the girdles of the strong he looses,
22He reveals profound things from darkness,
  bringing darkness to light.
23He makes nations mighty and then destroys them,
  makes them great and then scatters them.
24He deprives of intelligence the people of the land,
  makes them wander in trackless chaos.
25They grope without light in the darkness,
  and stagger as if drunk.

Job concedes God's skill and power in creating the world (vv 13–15)
but maintains that these qualities (v 16a) are used arbitrarily to overturn
innocent people like himself. The world God made is without design since
it does not reward righteous human beings, and it is unjust since the
wicked are favored over the righteous. Job imitates hymnic style, alluding
ironically to God's wisdom and power.

B. Bildad's Traditional Speech

Bildad's speech in 25:1–6+26:5–14 responds to Job. God's creation awes
Bildad and makes him submissive (25:4–6; 26:14).

  25:2Dominion and dread are his;
    he makes peace in the heavens.
  3Can his troops be numbered?
    Upon whom does his light not shine?
  4Then how can a human being be in the right before God?
    How can one born of woman be cleared of guilt?
  5Even the moon is not bright,
    the stars are not cleared of guilt in his eyes.

26:5The rephaim writhe below,
　　the waters and their inhabitants.
6Naked is Sheol before him,
　　Abaddon has no cover.
7He stretches out heaven over chaos,
　　hangs earth on nothing.
8Cramming the waters into his clouds,
　　the clouds do not break beneath them.
9He who covers the face of his throne,
　　spreading his clouds upon it.[20]
10He drew a boundary on the face of the waters,
　　at the intersection of light and darkness.
11The pillars of heaven are rocked,
　　they are thrown into panic at your rebuke.
12By his power he stilled Sea,
　　and by his wisdom he slew Rahab.
13By his breath he stilled the heaven,
　　his hand pierced the wicked serpent.
14These are but the outer edges of his power,
　　a mere whisper that we perceived of him.
　　Who can comprehend the thunder of his deeds?

Not unexpectedly, Bildad follows a traditional sequence of divine acts, similar to that in Psalm 104: God *in se* (25:2; see Ps 104:1); the inhabitants of the world above the heavens and below the earth (25:3+26:5–6; see Ps 104:3b–4); the establishment of heaven and earth (v 7), the apportionment of water to the clouds (v 8) and the establishment of God's throne in hidden heights (v 9); assigning to primordial waters and night their place (v 10). In Ps 104:6–18, God chases the waters to their proper sphere, sea, where they can benefit the world of the living; and in vv 19–23, God makes darkness into something positive.

C. God's Speeches

In the course of the dialogues, Job comes to realize that his only hope of being cleared is through a direct meeting with God. Hence the goal of his final speeches is to summon God to court so as to obtain a bill

---

[20] So that Job cannot see him.

of particulars. Chapters 29–31 end in a lengthy oath designed to make God face Job, his accuser, in a court of law.[21]

The logic of the two divine speeches in chapters 38–41 has puzzled many scholars and provoked many rearrangements; none has won general assent. I follow in the main Norman Habel's analysis of them, which accepts the Hebrew text.[22] The divine speeches are not just an undifferentiated blast at Job; they also address his desire that God appear in person to respond to the charge of governing the world arbitrarily and unjustly. God handles the first complaint capricious governance—in his first speech (38:1–40:5), beginning, "Who is this who obscures design ('ēṣâ)?"[23] The second complaint—unjust governance (in the biblical sense of inability or failure to uphold the rights of the aggrieved innocent)—is answered in the second speech (40:6–41:26), beginning, "Will you impugn my justice?"

The two speeches form large-scale parallelism producing resonances for ancient hearers. The force of the speeches is better shown by Habel's outline than by extensive citation.

A Introductory formula with report of theophany event	38:1	A1 Introductory formula with report of theophany event	40:6
B Thematic challenge	38:2–3	B1 Thematic challenge	40:7–14
i Theme A "Who is this who clouds my design?"		*i* Theme B "Would you impugn my justice?"	

---

[21] In recent years scholars have come to realize the important role played by legal language and metaphor in the Book of Job. For the legal aspect, see M. Dick, "The Legal Metaphor in Job 31," *CBQ* 41 (1979) 37–50. Habel in *The Book of Job* argues that the controverted Elihu speeches in the narrative present Elihu as the human intermediary that Job has been seeking, a task for which the young and self-important Elihu is unsuited; God's speech in chapters 38–41 is, in fact, the encounter that Job has sought.

[22] *The Book of Job*, 517–74.

[23] Hebrew 'ēṣâ ("design") occurs in Job nine times. Apart from the speeches of God in chapters 38–41, six times it means "plan," usually the plan of the wicked that God seemingly allows to prosper (5:13; 10:3; 12:13; 18:7; 21:16; 22:18). God's first reply to Job picks up this word, which implies arbitrary and capricious rule.

ii Summons		*ii* Summons	
"Gird your loins"		"Gird your loins"	
C Elaboration of theme		C1 Elaboration of theme	
i in the physical world	38:4–38	*i* with Behemoth	40:15–24
ii in the animal kingdom	38:39–39:3	*ii* with Leviathan	40:25–41:26
D Challenge to Legal Adversary	40:1–2		
E Answer of Job	40:3–5	E1 Answer of Job	42:1–6

The first speech. Job has denied God's wisdom by emphasizing God's arbitrary and capricious positioning of the elements of the world—mountains, seas etc.—and his failure to care for his creatures, especially Job. God responds in the same legal idiom as that of Job's attack. The divine questions are legal in nature: "Who is this who obscures design?" (38:2); and later, "Where were you when I? . . . ," "Who placed? . . . ," "Where is? . . ." They equivalently ask who created the world, and resemble questions in the great trial scenes of Second Isaiah such as, "Who has measured the waters in the hollow of his hand?" (40:12); "Who has directed the spirit of Yahweh?" (40:13); "Who has stirred up one from the east?" (41:2); "Who declared it from the beginning that we might know?" (44:7) In Second Isaiah the trial scenes summon the nations and their gods (or the gods' images) to a great trial to determine who is God—Yahweh or the gods of the nations. What deity foretold the Persian king's (Cyrus's) remaking of the world by his military victories or more abstractly, empowering by mere word that instrument of the world's remaking, Cyrus? The gods (or their images) are mute; Yahweh is the only deity, because only Yahweh spoke the word empowering Cyrus. In the Book of Job the questions have the same intent: to remind Job that God, not Job, is God. Only a deity could answer them affirmatively. The legal context had been set by Job in chapters 29–31, who haled God into court.

As in Job's and Bildad's speeches, the outward structure of the universe in God's speeches is traditional: God's artisan-like building of the universe, hemming in of the sea, and placement of the heavenly luminaries. What is untraditional is the challenge these elements pose to Job. Throughout the book Job has been seeking a face-to-face encounter with God. In the encounter itself God treats Job as a rival claimant to deity, asking him questions only a deity would be able to answer affirmatively. Can Job play God, bring a universe into being, sustain it, and control it?

A general outline illustrates the point more clearly than any single verse. The first divine speech, chapters 38–39, can be schematized as follows:

Were you there? or, do you know about

A. the inanimate physical world (38:4–38)?
- the construction of the earth 38:4–7
- the hemming in of the sea 38:8–11
- dawn's role in ridding the earth of sinners 38:12–15
- God's dominion over the underworld of death 38:16–18
- the placement of light and darkness 38:19–21
- the storehouses of earth's weather 38:22–30
- the constellations controlling earth's destiny 38:31–33
- the thunderstorms fertilizing the earth 38:34–38, and
B. the animal and bird kingdoms (38:39–39:30)?
- the feeding of the lion 38:39–40
- the feeding of the raven 38:41
- the ibex and the hind 39:1–4
- the wild ass 39:5–8
- the wild ox 39:9–12
- the ostrich 39:13–18
- the horse 39:19–25
- the hawk and the eagle 39:26–30.

The speech is about "design" (38:2). Job had accused God in 9:5–6 of making a reckless and violent attack upon mountains and earth: "the one who moves mountains without their knowing it, who overturns them in his anger, who shakes the earth from its place, so that its pillars totter." God asks Job in 38:4–7 if he actually witnessed the foundation of the earth, and then reveals how, like a careful artisan, he built with measuring line, sockets, and cornerstone while a festive chorus sang as at a temple dedication. In 9:24 Job had claimed that God does not distinguish between the wicked and the righteous, that the earth has been handed over to the wicked. God responds that dawn exposes the deeds done by the wicked during the night, but that he does not necessarily punish them (38:12–15). Job's assumption that human beings are the center of the world is countered by God's question about the rain that falls where human beings do not live (38:26–27). Job had accused God of hunting him like a lion (10:16); God is rather the one who hunts *for* the lion (38:39–40). Even the ostrich, proverbial for its stupidity, is so by design (39:13–18), a reminder that God's design does not operate exclusively for human beings or rational purposes. It includes the useful, the bizarre, even the playful. God creates for his inscrutable purposes; even Behemoth and Leviathan are admirable in the divine sight. God creates for God, not for human beings, and need not answer the single-minded Job who assumes he is the center of the universe.

Just before Job's response to this catalogue, God again affirms the legal context: "Will the one with a suit against Shadday correct me? Will the one arraigning God answer me?" (40:2).[24] Job's answer is also legal: "See, I am small, what can I answer you? I put my hand on my mouth. I have spoken once, and will not reply, twice, I will not do so again" (40:4–5). The words are a promise not to speak, an acknowledgment that he is dropping his suit (not that he repents in a religious sense).

The Second Speech. The second speech, 40:6–41:26, is a defense of God's justice impugned by Job: "Would you impugn my justice?" (40:8). Justice here, as commonly in the Bible, is the ability to put down the unjust and uphold the just. From Job's perspective, God has allowed the wicked to prosper and the righteous, in particular Job, to suffer. God initially asks questions that only a deity could answer affirmatively: "Have you an arm like God, and can you thunder with a voice like his? . . . Look down upon every proud person and bring him low, and tread upon the wicked where they stand" (40:9, 12). Job falls silent because he cannot be just in this cosmic sense.

God's speech mainly describes two great animals (extending the descriptions of the animal kingdom of the first speech): Behemoth (40:15–24) and Leviathan (40:25–41:26). Behemoth has been identified by many modern commentators as the hippopotamus, i.e., simply a powerful and frightening animal, but this is unlikely. His mate, Leviathan, is undoubtedly a mythological beast, as is clear from the Ugaritic texts, in which he is allied with Sea, the enemy of Baal the storm god; the same usage is reflected in the Bible. In 1 Enoch 60:7–9, Leviathan and Behemoth are

---

[24] Hebrew *rōb* is a participle of *rîb* "to bring suit, complain." So Habel, *The Book of Job,* s.v. 40:2.

creatures, respectively, of the depths of the sea and the immense desert.[25] Behemoth is thus a creature symbolizing the sterile wilderness (in the Ugaritic texts, the milieu of the god Mot, Baal's enemy).

The first speech answered the design argument by demonstrating God's care for an intricate world that Job scarcely knows. The second speech answers Job's charge of injustice by showing that God has power over cosmic evil, represented by Behemoth and Leviathan. God does not say that he always controls evil for the sake of human beings. The question to Job is—can he contain these animals and so prove he is God?

The two beasts are proposed as examples of exulting power. The massive Behemoth (40:15–26) is made as Job was (v 15), i.e., he is a creature like him. For all Behemoth's strength, however, he can be taken by the face: "By his eyes he is captured, by hooks his nose is pierced" (40:24).[26] God can capture this beast (by the eyes or the face). One is tempted to see Job as the real subject of God's interest here: God takes him by the eyes and nose, i.e., refutes him by a mere word.[27]

The second portrait, of Leviathan, is much longer than the first. Leviathan is known from the Bible and from the Ugaritic texts as the great primordial monster who was killed or tamed by Baal or Yahweh. As with Behemoth, God controls him by the mouth (40:25–28).

> 41:2There is no one so fierce as to stir him up.
>   Who then can stand before *me*?
> 3Who will challenge me whom I will not requite,
>   For everything under heaven is mine.
> 4Did I not silence his boasting,
>   his mighty words and martial deeds?

[25] The Similitudes of Enoch are usually dated to the last half of the first century B.C. or the first three quarters of the first century A.D. but contain old mythology. For solid arguments against taking the creatures merely as natural animals, see M. Pope, *Job* (AB 15; 3d ed.; Garden City, NY: Doubleday, 1973) 320–23.

[26] The preceding Hebrew verse is overlong and v 24a is too short, leading many scholars to one of two emendations: to add *mî hû'* ("Who is there who") to the beginning of v 24a, or to attach the last two words of v 23b to v 24a. In the latter solution, they revocalize *'el pîhû* as *'ēl* ("God"). In any case, the Hebrew text correctly understands the subject to be God.

[27] For this interpretation, see J. Gammie, "Behemoth and Leviathan: On the Didactic and Theological Significance of Job 40:15–41:26," in *Israelite Wisdom: Theological and Literary Essays in Honor of Samuel Terrien* (Chico, CA: Scholars Press, 1978) 465–74.

Magnificent and laudatory poetry follows, describing Leviathan as built for no other purpose than to display untrammeled power and might.

What is the purpose of these two beasts in the book? In 40:12, God defined justice (which Job claimed is lacking in the universe) by the command, "Look down upon every proud one and bring him low, and tread upon the wicked where they stand." The two beasts exemplify fearsome power that is beyond human knowledge or control, yet they are allowed a place in God's universe. They fulfill no function; they cannot be domesticated and do not serve human beings. Though they are under divine control (40:15, 24; 41:2–4) God, for reasons not stated, allows them to exist despite their evil potential. Jon Levenson, properly taking issue with the common view that Behemoth and Leviathan are mere playthings in God's hand, notes that "whereas Job 40–41 explicitly states that Behemoth is a work of God, no such statement is made of Leviathan in the much longer section devoted to him. Instead, we hear only of God's heroic capture and conquest of the great sea beast."[28] In the literary structure of the book, the beasts echo the Satan of chapters 1 and 2, whom God allowed to "incite" him (2:3). Why should there be an enemy of the human race within the heavenly court itself? No answer is given to this particular problem of evil, beyond the assurance that the Adversary, like the beasts, is somehow under the control of God. God retains control over the beasts as over the Adversary: "All [Job] possesses is in your hand; only do not lay a hand on him" (1:12); "So be it. He is in your hand; only watch over his life" (2:6). There is no guarantee, however, that evil will not ravage human beings.

Thus creation in Job is an act that an utterly transcendent God does in wisdom and justice. It cannot be searched out (chapter 28) and summed up with traditional wisdom, as is shown by the three friends' inability to speak rightly for God (42:7–8). God creates for God; the divine purpose is inscrutable; human beings cannot assume that they are the center of the universe. Traditional cosmogonies often began with the gods vanquishing evil, often personified as a monster. But creation in the Book of Job *ends* with the monsters unvanquished, with God admiring them in splendid poetry! They are, to be sure, on God's leash, but move in ways that terrify the human race.

---

[28] J. D. Levenson, *Creation and the Persistence of Evil: The Jewish Drama of Divine Omnipotence* (San Francisco: Harper & Row, 1988), 49.

The anthropocentric perspective of the creation accounts of Genesis 1–11, the Psalms, and Second Isaiah does not extend to Job. "How different this survey of creation [chapters 38–41] is from that of Genesis 1 or the hymn to nature of Psalm 104. Here man is incidental—mainly an impotent foil to God. In Genesis 1 (and its echo, Psalm 8) teleology pervades a process of creation whose goal and crown is man. All is directed to his benefit; the earth and its creatures are his to rule. In Psalm 104 nature exhibits a providential harmony of which man is an integral part. But the God of Job celebrates each act and product of his creation for itself, an independent value attesting his power and grace. Job, representing mankind, stands outside the picture, displaced from its center to a remote perifery."[29] The book presents a deliberate counterargument that human society is not the center of creation and that the wonders of the world are an invitation to hymn the creator.

[29] Greenberg, "Job," in *The Literary Guide to the Bible,* 298.

CHAPTER 10

Conclusions

I. The Concept of Creation

The world of the ancient Near East is not the world of Greece and Rome, which became the basis of modern Western culture. Ancient oriental literature is alien and difficult to understand, though the many biblical phrases and ideas in our discourse may trick us into thinking otherwise. We find it relatively easy to appreciate Homer and Thucydides, Horace and Tacitus, but even specialists find difficult the Akkadian *Myth of Anzu* or the Egyptian *Pyramid Texts*. Particularly difficult are ancient cosmogonies. Major differences separate them from modern conceptions. As much as possible, one's definition of ancient Oriental cosmogony should be empirical, educed from the ancient texts mentioned in the preceding chapters. The task is obviously not finished, and questions remain. This book has attempted to lay a groundwork.

Even at this stage of investigation, however, it is clear that in the ancient world creation was a privileged moment. In that era, to know the origin of something was somehow to intuit its essence, for the imprint of the gods on the day of creation was fresh and still visible. The initial shaping of the world lasted into the present time of the community, motivating people to tell the old story again and again. Certain times were right for reciting cosmogonies—New Year's Day, for example, when the temple might be rededicated and the god's choice of the king reaffirmed. Ancient peoples' intuitions about creation and its reappearance in time and history are difficult for modern readers to grasp. One can doubt whether modern

198

theological notions, such as continuous creation, adequately express the ancient conception of the recurrence of the primordial act. How does the originating power remain latent in history? What is the meaning of "new" in new creation and new song? The material gathered here, I hope, will stimulate fresh thinking about these and related topics.

Perhaps the single most important feature of ancient Near Eastern cosmogonies is that they generally issued in a peopled universe, a world, a system. Even when focusing on a single item, as in the Sumerian *Praise of the Pickax,* they put that item in the context of the whole: how the pickax plays a role in the human race's service of the gods. Since the gods created the world for their own benefit, cosmogonies described (or presumed) the creation of human beings who managed the world in the gods' interest. The creation of the king fitted within the same framework: in the Mesopotamian examples where he is created separately from the human race, the king organizes its service of the gods (Sumerian *Bird and Fish, Sumerian Flood Story, Rulers of Lagash,* Akkadian cosmogonies nos. 4, 5, 7b, 9). Any dichotomous distinction between creation of the whole and creation of the individual is not warranted for the ancient Near East. The populated universe that emerged did not have to be the whole world; sometimes it was a particular nation, e.g., Babylon or Israel.

Modes of creation generally were modeled on human activity (planning, conquering, building, molding, begetting) or on natural phenomena such as teeming hillocks left by the receding Nile or vegetative life arising from a pool. In the Bible God creates in many ways but not through generation, presumably because procreation would imply a divine consort. The world that came into being was often conceived as a finite "box" of light, space, and order within an infinite expanse of dark, formless waters.

Many ancient cosmogonies are narratives and depend on plot and character for their movement; they must be read as drama rather than "objective" description. Perhaps because of their dramatic quality, ancient people apparently did not find it difficult to receive several versions of creation. Sumerian religion had two different systems of creation, and Egypt had as many systems as shrines. Genesis 1 and 2–11 present two different versions of creation, and Second Isaiah tells different stories about God overcoming chaos.

II. The Nonbiblical Cosmogonies

Egypt had a broad repertoire of cosmogonies, developed and preserved at the major shrines. On first reading, the texts are bewildering, since they mix objective and subjective perspectives ("philosophy" and "religion") and use nonabstract (often biological) imagery. When read with proper awareness, however, they turn out to be profound and sophisticated explorations of the world and the divine purpose. Though Egyptian wisdom literature directly influenced such biblical books as Proverbs, Egyptian cosmogonies evidently had no direct influence. Influence from the *Memphite Theology* on Genesis 1 has been argued by some scholars, but if there was influence it reached Genesis blended with Canaanite and other speculations. Egyptian creation thought nonetheless is a worthwhile study in and of itself—an important witness to the shrewd and imaginative philosophy and theology of a neighboring culture.

Mesopotamian cosmogonies are attested from the late-third to the late-first millennium. The Sumerian cosmogonies found in god lists are difficult to interpret, but generally seem to belong to either the Nippur or the Eridu systems. In the Nippur system, creation is seen as a cosmic marriage between Heaven (An) and Earth (Ki) in which Enki of Nippur plays a major role. Human beings emerge like plants from the soil loosened by a hoe (*emersio*). In the Eridu system, which is preserved in several long tales about Enki, god of wisdom and water, creation takes place when the god brings up the vast underground waters to fertilize the earth. The human race seems already to be in existence since cities along the river banks are mentioned. Occasionally, in response to a crisis, texts mention the creation of human beings from clay (*formatio*) by Enki with the help of the mother goddess.

Bottéro has collected most of the Akkadian minor cosmogonies. They are generally brief and tied to a function or operation such as an incantation, dedication of a temple, or introduction to a debate. Two compositions cannot be classed as minor—*Atrahasis* of the seventeenth century B.C. (1,245 lines in one edition) and *Enūma elish* of the late-first millennium (ca. 1,100 lines). In these works cosmogonies are no longer function-bound but incorporated into a larger work with a large philosophical or theological aim. Thus *Atrahasis* and *Enūma elish* are anthological, or compendious, because they incorporate venerable traditions, including cosmogonies, for purposes that are "philosophical" (*Atrahasis*) or theological and political (*Enūma elish*).

Direct influence of Mesopotamian cosmogonies on the Bible is demonstrable only for Genesis 2–11. The Mesopotamian genre of the creation-flood epic, best represented by *Atrahasis,* has left its mark on the plot and themes of Genesis 2–11. Some scholars have argued that *Enūma elish* directly influenced Genesis 1, but the claim is difficult to prove. Influence on Second Isaiah is also possible and, if the prophet actually lived in sixth-century Babylon, highly probable. Isa 44:24–45:13, for example, might well have been shaped by the traditions found in several minor cosmogonies and in *Enūma elish:* control of the waters, building of a temple, appointment of a king. On the other hand, these ideas could simply have come from the common stock of the ancient orient.

A common Canaanite culture existed in the eastern littoral of the Mediterranean in the second and first millennium B.C. The most valuable literary witnesses to the religion of Canaan for the period are the Ugaritic texts and the Hebrew Bible. Ugarit provides a northern sampling of Canaanite religious literature but unfortunately has not lived up to its potential of furnishing cosmogonies contemporary with the Bible. The two Ugaritic deities that influenced the portrait of Yahweh, the God of Israel, are the old patriarch El and the young storm god Baal. El has only a few creation epithets, though, and Baal is the subject of vividly described but inconclusive military victories over Sea and Death. El's epithets are "builder of what is built," "father of gods and human beings;" that of his wife, Asherah, is "creator of the gods." The epithet "father of gods" is dramatized in one text where El sires two giant gods, but its full import remains unclear; his other epithets go unillustrated. The lengthy narratives about Baal's victories over Sea and Death, construction of a temple, and celebration of kingship, do not use the term "creation." A minority of scholars argue that Baal is truly a creator in defeating the monsters, on the grounds that his victory brings peace and fertility to the earth and that his temple, like other Eastern temples, enshrines the act of creation. This argument may well be correct, but as long as the relation between El (who alone is addressed as creator) and Baal remains obscure, one cannot safely conclude that Baal was viewed as a creator at Ugarit. In the Bible Yahweh's victory over sea and desert is cosmogonic but that fact cannot be used as evidence with regard to the Ugaritic texts, for the Bible blends El (who was a creator) and Baal traditions to portray Yahweh. Few scholars question, however, that Canaanite traditions of Baal's victories over Sea or Death influenced the biblical picture of Yahweh the creator.

III. The Bible

In common with all ancient Near Eastern literature, the Bible shows a profound interest in creation. Creation was a moment of enormous significance, revealing much about the world and God. In the light of the universal ancient interest in creation, biblical scholars can no longer claim that creation came late to biblical consciousness, i.e., after Israel had discovered its God in history. Such a dichotomy between history (redemption) and myth (creation) is modern and does not do justice to ancient Near Eastern thinking.

Biblical cosmogonies employ literary genres current in Mesopotamia and Canaan. Mesopotamian genres and concepts entered Canaan through trade and diplomatic exchange. Such commercial crossroads as Emar illustrate the process of transmission. Because cosmogonies occur in a great variety of works (Genesis, Psalms, Isaiah, Proverbs, and Job), and in a great variety of genres (creation-flood epics, communal laments, hymns, prophetic disputations and announcements of restoration, wisdom instructions and speeches, parodies of hymns, divine speeches), it is difficult to formulate *one* biblical doctrine of creation. Biblical authors had diverse purposes in mind when they composed their creation accounts; their rhetorical strategies and aims must be determined before one can talk about their views of creation.

Genesis 1–11 establishes at the very beginning of the Pentateuch the polarity of Israel and the nations, which is a constant biblical theme. As the opening chapter of the Priestly project to revise the venerable Yahwist story for the exiles, Genesis 1 is eclectic. A cosmogony, to be sure, it is thoroughly informed by the rhetorical strategy of its author, i.e., to introduce an exilic work. Genesis 2–11 is a creation-flood epic in genre, sharing with Mesopotamian counterparts both plot (creation, disturbance of the gods, flood, and restoration) and thematic interest in culture and its limits. *Atrahasis* has proved to be a rich field for comparison with Genesis not only in its plot and motifs but also in its incorporation of a cosmogony into a story that continues in some sense into the present.

Cosmogonies in the Psalter are strongly determined by genre. In both communal laments and hymns, cosmogonies narrate the origin of the people Israel. In both, the community holds up to God in prayer the originating moment of Israel, employing the historic language of exodus-conquest and the suprahistoric language of Yahweh's victory over Sea. In the communal lament, the community appeals to God's honor: Will you let an enemy power destroy the people whom you have created and redeemed? In the hymn, the people praise God for gracious actions, principally the great deed of creating Israel.

Second Isaian usage resembles that of the hymns of the Psalter. For the prophet, Israel's moment of origin amounted to a cosmogony, which could be told with either a historic or a suprahistoric slant — as exodus or as victory over Sea/Wilderness. Since Second Isaiah believed that a new beginning was taking place in his lifetime, he spoke of a new cosmogony (=victory over the desert) and a new exodus (=journey across the wilderness). His understanding of cosmogony may have been influenced by Akkadian cosmogonies as much as by the old psalmic usage, for he mentions as part of creation the building of the temple-city and election of a king. These themes are more prominent in Babylonian than in biblical creation accounts.

Wisdom Literature contains several cosmogonies and related hymns and speeches. The two cosmogonies in the Book of Proverbs are intended to enhance the status of Woman Wisdom and her invitation to the young person. The world was created in wisdom so that anyone seeking wisdom will grasp the secrets of the world — life and prosperity. Woman Wisdom's intimate friendship with Yahweh guarantees that the youth's association with her will bring well-being and shalom. The subversive viewpoint of the Book of Job is reflected in its use of creation traditions. Job parodies hymns to the creator to show that God's power is directed arbitrarily against just persons. His friends, on the contrary, argue vigorously for an orderly universe. The opinions of Job and his friends are swept away authoritatively by God's magnificent description of creation: the human race is not at the center but at the periphery of the universe; God did not divest the chaos monsters of all power at creation but is pleased to let them roam free on a leash; Behemoth and Leviathan are as much a part of the world as the ordinary animals in the first divine speech. The traditional key to creation, wisdom, does not work in its usual sense. The world is not anthropocentric but theocentric; its secret lies hidden with God.

Select Bibliography

Albertz, R., *Weltschöpfung und Menschenschöpfung: Untersucht bei Deutero-jesaja, Hiob und in den Psalmen* (Calwer Theologische Monographien 3; Stuttgart: Calwer, 1974).

Allen, J. P., *Genesis in Egypt: The Philosophy of Ancient Egyptian Creation Accounts* (Yale Egyptological Studies 2; New Haven, CT: Yale University, 1988).

Anderson, B. W., ed., *Creation in the Old Testament* (Issues in Religion and Theology 6; Philadelphia: Fortress, 1984).

——. *Creation Versus Chaos* (Philadelphia: Fortress, 1987).

Angerstorfer, A. *Der Schöpfergott des Alten Testaments: Herkunft und Bedeutungsentwicklung des hebräischen Terminus BR' (bara) "Schaffen"* (Frankfurt: Lang, 1979).

Attridge, H. W. and Oden, R. A., *Philo of Byblos: The Phoenician History: Introduction, Critical Text, Translation, Notes* (CBQMS 9; Washington, DC: Catholic Biblical Association, 1981).

Batto, B. F., *Slaying the Dragon: Mythmaking in the Biblical Tradition* (Louisville: Westminster/Knox, 1992).

Baumgarten, A. I., *The Phoenician History of Philo of Byblos: A Commentary* (Études préliminaires aux religions orientales dans l'Empire Romain 89; Leiden: Brill, 1981).

Bellenger, W. H., "Maker of Heaven and Earth: The Old Testament and Creation Theology," *Swedish Journal of Theology* 32 (1990) 27–35.

Beaucamp, Paul, *Création et séparation: Étude exégetique du chapitre premier de la Genèse* (Paris: Declée, 1969).

Bottéro, J., and Kramer, S. N., *Lorsque les dieux faisaient l'homme: Mythologie mésopotamienne* (Paris: Gallimard, 1989).

Brandon, G. F., *Creation Legends of the Ancient Near East* (London: Hodder & Stoughton, 1963).

Clifford, R. J., "The Hebrew Scriptures and the Theology of Creation," *TS* 46 (1985) 507–23.

——, "Cosmogonies in the Ugaritic Texts," *Or* 53 (1984) 183–201.

—— and J. J. Collins, eds., *Creation in the Biblical Tradition* (CBQMS 24; Washington, DC: Catholic Biblical Association, 1992).

Collins, J. J., "Cosmos and Salvation: Jewish Wisdom and Apocalyptic in the Hellenistic Age," *History of Religions* 17 (1977–1978) 121–42.

La création dans l'Orient Ancien (LD 27; Congrès de l'ACFEB, Lille [1985]; ed. F. Blanquart; Paris: Cerf, 1987).

Crenshaw, J. L., "Prolegomenon," in *Studies in Ancient Israelite Wisdom* (ed. J. L. Crenshaw; New York: Ktav, 1976) 1–45.

Cross, F. M., "The Song of the Sea and Canaanite Myth," in *Canaanite Myth and Hebrew Epic* (Cambridge, MA: Harvard University, 1973).

Dalley, S., *Myths from Mesopotamia: Creation, the Flood, Gilgamesh and Others* (New York: Oxford University, 1989).

Day, J., *God's Conflict with the Dragon and the Sea: Echoes of a Canaanite Myth in the Old Testament* (Cambridge: Cambridge University, 1985).

Doll, P., *Menschenschöpfung und Weltschöpfung in der alttestamentlichen Weisheit* (SBS 117; Stuttgart: Katholisches Bibelwerk, 1985).

Ebach, J., *Weltentstehung und Kulturentwicklung bei Philo von Byblos: Ein Beitrag zur Überlieferung der biblischen Urgeschichte im Rahmen des altorientalischen und antiken Schöpfungsglauben* (BWANT 108; Stuttgart: Kohlhammer, 1979).

Eberlein, K., *Gott der Schöpfer—Israels Gott. Eine exegetisch-hermeneutische Studie zur theologischen Funktion alttestamentlicher Schöpfungsaussagen* (Frankfurt: Lang, 1986).

H. A. Frankfort *et al.*, *Before Philosophy: The Intellectual Adventure of Ancient Man* (Hammondsworth: Penguin, 1949).

Gibert, P., *Bible, mythes et récits de commencement* (Parole de Dieu; Paris: Seuil, 1986).

Haag, E., "Gott als Schöpfer und Erlöser in der Prophetie des Deuterojesaja," *TTZ* 85 (1976) 193–213.

Habel, N., "Yahweh, Maker of Heaven and Earth," *JBL* 91 (1972) 31–37.

Hardie, P. R., *Virgil's Aeneid: Cosmos and Imperium* (Oxford: Clarendon, 1986).

Harner, P. B., "Creation Faith in Deutero-Isaiah," *VT* 17 (1967) 298–300.

Heidel, A., *The Babylonian Genesis: The Story of Creation* (2d ed.; Chicago: University of Chicago, 1951).

In the Beginning: Creation Myths from Ancient Mesopotamia, Israel and Greece (ed. J. O'Brien and W. Major; American Academy of Religion Aids for the Study of Religion 11; Chico, CA: Scholars Press, 1982).

Jacobsen, T., "The Eridu Genesis," *JBL* 100 (1981) 513–29.

———, *The Treasures of Darkness* (New Haven, CT: Yale University, 1976).

———, *The Harps that Once . . . : Sumerian Poetry in Translation* (New Haven, CT: Yale University, 1987).

Knierim, R., "Cosmos and History in Israel's Theology," *Horizons in Biblical Theology* 3 (1981) 59–123.

Knight, D. A., "Cosmogony and Order in the Hebrew Tradition," *Cosmogony and Ethical Order* (ed. R. Lovin and F. E. Reynolds; Chicago: University of Chicago, 1985) 133–57.

Kramer, S. N., and Maier, J., *Myths of Enki, the Crafty God* (New York: Oxford University, 1989).

Lambert, W. G., and Millard, A. R., *Atra-hasis: The Babylonian Story of the Flood* (Oxford: Clarendon, 1969).

Lambert, W. G., "The Cosmology of Sumer and Babylon," *Ancient Cosmogonies* (ed. C. Blacker and M. Loewe; London: Allen & Unwin, 1975) 42–65.

Levenson, J., *Creation and the Persistence of Evil* (San Francisco: Harper & Row, 1986).

Lohfink, N., "The Priestly Document and the Limits of Growth," and "Biblical Witness to the Idea of a Stable World," in *Great Themes from the Old Testament* (Edinburgh: T. & T. Clark, 1982) 167–82, 183–201.

McCurley, F., *Ancient Myths and Biblical Faith: Biblical Transformations* (Philadelphia: Fortress, 1983).

Miller, P. D., "Eridu, Dunnu, and Babel: A Study in Comparative Mythology," *HAR* 9 (1985) 227–51.

Murray, R., *The Cosmic Covenant: Biblical Themes of Justice, Peace and the Integrity of Creation* (Heythrop Monographs; London: Sheed & Ward, 1992).

Niditch, S., *Chaos to Cosmos: Studies in Biblical Patterns of Creation* (Chico, CA: Scholars Press, 1985).

Oden, R. A., "Cosmogony, Cosmology," in *The Anchor Bible Dictionary* (Garden City, NY: Doubleday, 1992) 1. 1162–71.

Perdue, L. G., "Cosmology and the Social Order in the Wisdom Literature," in *The Sage in Israel and the Ancient Near East* (ed. J. G. Gammie and L. G. Perdue; Winona Lake, IN: Eisenbrauns, 1990) 457–78.

———, "Job's Assault on Creation," *HAR* 10 (1986) 295–315.

———, *Wisdom in Revolt: Metaphorical Theology in the Book of Job* (Bible and Literature Series 29; Sheffield: Almond, 1991).

Pettinato, G., *Das altorientalische Menschenbild und die sumerischen und akkadischen Schöpfungsmythen* (Heidelberg: Winter, 1971).

Rendtorff, R., "Die theologische Stellung der Schöpfungsglaubens bei Deutero-jesaja," *ZTK* 51 (1954) 3–13.

Reventlow, H. Graf, "The World Horizons of Old Testament Theology," in *Problems of Old Testament Theology in the Twentieth Century* (Philadelphia: Fortress, 1985) 134–86.

Robert, P. de, "Perception de la nature et confession de la Création selon la Bible hebraïque," *Études théologiques et religieuses* 65 (1990) 49–57.

Römer, T., "La redécouverte d'un myth dans l'Ancien Testament: La création comme combat," *Études théologiques et religieuses* 64 (1989) 561–73.

Schöpfung und Neuschöpfung (Jahrbuch für Biblische Theologie 5; Neukirchen-Vluyn: Neukirchener Verlag, 1990).

Ska, J. L., *Le passage de la mer* (AnBib 109; Rome: Pontifical Biblical Institute, 1986).

Sproul, B., *Primal Myths: Creation Myths Around the World* (San Francisco: Harper, 1991).

Stadelmann, L. I. J., *The Hebrew Conception of the World: A Philological and Literary Study* (AnBib 39; Rome: Pontifical Biblical Institute, 1970).

Stuhlmueller, C., *Creative Redemption in Deutero-Isaiah* (AnBib 43; Rome: Biblical Institute, 1970).

Van Dijk, J., "Le motif cosmique dans la pensée sumérienne," *Acta Orientalia* 28 (1964) 1–59.

Von Rad, G., "The Theological Problem of the Old Testament Doctrine of Creation," in *The Problem of the Hexateuch and Other Essays* (New York: McGraw-Hill, 1966) 131–43.

——, *Wisdom in Israel* (Nashville: Abingdon, 1972).

Westermann, C., *Creation* (Philadelphia: Fortress, 1974).

——, *Genesis 1–11: A Commentary* (trans. J. J. Scullion; Minneapolis: Augsburg, 1984).

Index

of Ancient Works

Index

of Authors

Index

of Subjects

The Catholic Biblical Quarterly
Monograph Series (CBQMS)

1. Patrick W. Skehan, *Studies in Israelite Poetry and Wisdom* (CBQMS 1) $9.00 ($7.20 for CBA members) ISBN 0-915170-00-0 (LC 77-153511)

2. Aloysius M. Ambrozic, *The Hidden Kingdom: A Redactional-Critical Study of the References to the Kingdom of God in Mark's Gospel* (CBQMS 2) $9.00 ($7.20 for CBA members) ISBN 0-915170-01-9 (LC 72-89100)

3. Joseph Jensen, O.S.B., *The Use of tôrâ by Isaiah: His Debate with the Wisdom Tradition* (CBQMS 3) $3.00 ($2.40 for CBA members) ISBN 0-915170-02-7 (LC 73-83134)

4. George W. Coats, *From Canaan to Egypt: Structural and Theological Context for the Joseph Story* (CBQMS 4) $4.00 ($3.20 for CBA members) ISBN 0-915170-03-5 (LC 75-11382)

5. O. Lamar Cope, *Matthew: A Scribe Trained for the Kingdom of Heaven* (CBQMS 5) $4.50 ($3.60 for CBA members) ISBN 0-915170-04-3 (LC 75-36778)

6. Madeleine Boucher, *The Mysterious Parable: A Literary Study* (CBQMS 6) $2.50 ($2.00 for CBA members) ISBN 0-915170-05-1 (LC 76-51260)

7. Jay Braverman, *Jerome's Commentary on Daniel: A Study of Comparative Jewish and Christian Interpretations of the Hebrew Bible* (CBQMS 7) $4.00 ($3.20 for CBA members) ISBN 0-915170-06-X (LC 78-55726)

8. Maurya P. Horgan, *Pesharim: Qumran Interpretations of Biblical Books* (CBQMS 8) $6.00 ($4.80 for CBA members) ISBN 0-915170-07-8 (LC 78-12910)

9. Harold W. Attridge and Robert A. Oden, Jr., *Philo of Byblos, The Phoenician History* (CBQMS 9) $3.50 ($2.80 for CBA members) ISBN 0-915170-08-6 (LC 80-25781)

10. Paul J. Kobelski, *Melchizedek and Melchireša'* (CBQMS 10) $4.50 ($3.60 for CBA members) ISBN 0-915170-09-4 (LC 80-28379)

11. Homer Heater, *A Septuagint Translation Technique in the Book of Job* (CBQMS 11) $4.00 ($3.20 for CBA members) ISBN 0-915170-10-8 (LC 81-10085)

12. Robert Doran, *Temple Propaganda: The Purpose and Character of 2 Maccabees* (CBQMS 12) $4.50 ($3.60 for CBA members) ISBN 0-915170-11-6 (LC 81-10084)

13. James Thompson, *The Beginnings of Christian Philosophy: The Epistle to the Hebrews* (CBQMS 13) $5.50 ($4.50 for CBA members) ISBN 0-915170-12-4 (LC 81-12295)

14. Thomas H. Tobin, S.J., *The Creation of Man: Philo and the History of Interpretation* (CBQMS 14) $6.00 ($4.80 for CBA members) ISBN 0-915170-13-2 (LC 82-19891)

15. Carolyn Osiek, *Rich and Poor in the Shepherd of Hermes* (CBQMS 15) $6.00 ($4.80 for CBA members) ISBN 0-915170-14-0 (LC 83-7385)

16. James C. VanderKam, *Enoch and the Growth of an Apocalyptic Tradition* (CBQMS 16) $6.50 ($5.20 for CBA members) ISBN 0-915170-15-9 (LC 83-10134)

17. Antony F. Campbell, S.J., *Of Prophets and Kings: A Late Ninth-Century Document (1 Samuel 1–2 Kings 10)* (CBQMS 17) $7.50 ($6.00 for CBA members) ISBN 0-915170-16-7 (LC 85-12791)

18. John C. Endres, S.J., *Biblical Interpretation in the Book of Jubilees* (CBQMS 18) $8.50 ($6.80 for CBA members) ISBN 0-915170-17-5 (LC 86-6845)

19. Sharon Pace Jeansonne, *The Old Greek Translation of Daniel 7–12* (CBQMS 19) $5.00 ($4.00 for CBA members) ISBN 0-915170-18-3 (LC 87-15865)

20. Lloyd M. Barré, *The Rhetoric of Political Persuasion: The Narrative Artistry and Political Intentions of 2 Kings 9–11* (CBQMS 20) $5.00 ($4.00 for CBA members) ISBN 0-915170-19-1 (LC 87-15878)

21. John J. Clabeaux, *A Lost Edition of the Letters of Paul: A Reassessment of the Text of the Pauline Corpus Attested by Marcion* (CBQMS 21) $8.50 ($6.80 for CBA members) ISBN 0-915170-20-5 (LC 88-28511)

22. Craig Koester, *The Dwelling of God: The Tabernacle in the Old Testament, Intertestamental Jewish Literature, and the New Testament* (CBQMS 22) $9.00 ($7.20 for CBA members) ISBN 0-915170-21-3 (LC 89-9853)

23. William Michael Soll, *Psalm 119: Matrix, Form, and Setting* (CBQMS 23) $9.00 ($7.20 for CBA members) ISBN 0-915170-22-1 (LC 90-27610)

24. Richard J. Clifford and John J. Collins (eds.), *Creation in the Biblical Traditions* (CBQMS 24) $7.00 ($5.60 for CBA members) ISBN 0-915170-23-X (LC 92-20268)

25. John E. Course, *Speech and Response: A Rhetorical Analysis of the Introductions to the Speeches of the Book of Job, Chaps. 4–24* (CBQMS 25) ISBN 0-915170-24-8 (LC 94-26566)

26. Richard J. Clifford, *Creation Accounts in the Ancient Near East and in the Bible* (CBQMS 26) ISBN 0-915170-25-6 (LC 94-26565)

Order from:

The Catholic Biblical Association of America
The Catholic University of America
Washington, D.C. 20064